CHANGE HERE NOW

PERMACULTURE SOLUTIONS FOR PERSONAL
AND COMMUNITY TRANSFORMATION

Adam Brock

**with illustrations by
Holly White**

North Atlantic Books
Berkeley, California

Published by
North Atlantic Books
Berkeley, California

Cover design by Jasmine Hromjak
Book design by Happenstance Type-O-Rama
Printed in the United States of America

Change Here Now: Permaculture Solutions for Personal and Community Transformation is sponsored and published by the Society for the Study of Native Arts and Sciences (dba North Atlantic Books), an educational nonprofit based in Berkeley, California, that collaborates with partners to develop cross-cultural perspectives, nurture holistic views of art, science, the humanities, and healing, and seed personal and global transformation by publishing work on the relationship of body, spirit, and nature.

North Atlantic Books' publications are available through most bookstores. For further information, visit our website at www.northatlanticbooks.com or call 800-733-3000.

Library of Congress Cataloging-in-Publication Data

Names: Brock, Adam, 1986– author.
Title: Change here now : permaculture solutions for personal and community
  transformation / Adam Brock ; with illustrations by Holly White.
Description: Berkeley, California : North Atlantic Books, [2017]
Identifiers: LCCN 2016047448 | ISBN 9781623170646 (trade pbk.)
Subjects: LCSH: Community life. | Community development. | Social change. |
  Social ecology. | Permaculture--Social aspects.
Classification: LCC HM761 .B76 2017 | DDC 303.4--dc23
LC record available at https://lccn.loc.gov/201604744

1 2 3 4 5 6 7 8 9 Sheridan 22 21 20 19 18 17

North Atlantic Books is committed to the protection of
our environment. We partner with FSC-certified printers using soy-based inks
and print on recycled paper whenever possible.

CHANGE
HERE NOW

THIS BOOK IS DEDICATED
TO MY ANCESTORS,
WHO STRUGGLED SO THAT
I COULD THRIVE.

CONTENTS

PREFACE xi

ACKNOWLEDGMENTS xv

INTRODUCTION: PERMACULTURE AND PATTERN LITERACY xvii

HOW TO USE THIS BOOK xxv

PART 1: VISION FOR A PERMANENT CULTURE 1

1. The Long Game 5

2. Biophilia 8

3. Interdependent Communities 11

4. Commoning 15

5. The Right Size 23

6. Relationship Zones 27

7. Subsidiarity 35

8. Dethroning the Antimarkets 39

9. Zones of Autonomy 43

10. Going Home 47

11. The Edge of Change 50

12. Multitudes of Knowing 53

13. Fear Burns Bright, Hope Burns Long 57

14. Design Tool: Creative Process 60

15. Design Tool: Sector and Zone Analyses 68

16. Design Tool: Network Analysis 73

PART 2: PATTERNS OF JUSTICE AND RESISTANCE 77

17. Decolonization. 81

18. Telling the Story. 85

19. Sankofa 90

20. Ritual and Ceremony .93

21. Stewardship 98

22. Humanizing the Other 101

23. Slow Cities. 104

24. Citizen Governance 107

25. Infrastructure Commons 113

26. Creative Destruction. 116

27. Nonviolent Struggle 121

28. Solidarity. 125

29. Arts of Resistance 130

30. Disrobing the Emperor 133

31. Coordinated Noncompliance. 136

32. Truth and Reconciliation 140

33. Breaking Bread 143

34. Letting Loose 145

35. Rites of Passage. 148

36. Gadugi 151

37. Intimacy through Adversity 157

38. Practicing Grief. 159

39. Design Tool: Power Analysis. 163

PART 3: ORGANIZATIONS THAT LIVE 167

40. Nurtured Networks 171

41. Consensual Hierarchies. 174

42. Human Polycultures. 177

43. Nemawashi. 189

44. Streams of Engagement. 193

45. The Right Way to Decide 201

46. Converge and Disperse 207

47. Leadership from Within 211

48. Regenerative Management. 216

49. Naming Norms 219

50. Skilled Facilitation 224

51. Circle Dialogue 229

52. The Caucus. 234

53. Calling Out, Calling In. 236

54. Restorative Justice. 240

55. Document the Process. 243

56. Measuring Success. 245

57. Design Tool: Team Analysis 249

PART 4: ENVISIONING THE ECOMMONY 251

58. The Gift. 255

59. Heirloom Currencies. 258

60. Financial Ram Pumps 265

61. Debt Forgiveness 268

62. Household Economies. 272

63. Small Business 276

64. Import Substitution 279

65. Regenerative Enterprise .284

66. Xeric Enterprise 288

67. Community-Supported Enterprise 293

68. Employee Ownership 296

69. Dynamic Pricing 299

70. Design Tool: Capital Analysis 303

71. Design Tool: Business Model Canvas. 305

PART 5: TRAINING THE SACRED WARRIOR. 313

72. Sacred Activism. 317

73. Right Livelihood. 321

74. Spirals of Abundance 326

75. Know Your Community 329

76. Actions, Not Intentions 333

77. iSites. 336

78. Unplugging 341

79. Commitment Pruning 344

80. Reduce the Need to Earn 347

81. Personal Mythology 352

82. Design Tool: Personal Vision 354

NOTES. 356

INDEX. 367

ABOUT THE AUTHOR 374

PREFACE

In the year 2000, when I was in eighth grade, my teacher handed me a copy of Daniel Quinn's *Ishmael* and, with a straight face, gave me the assignment of writing a paper on what human society would look like in a million years. Needless to say, the assignment left me a little bewildered. Science and technology was progressing faster than ever. How was I supposed to predict where we'd be in even a century, let alone a million years?

The book didn't seem to help much either. I was expecting a sci-fi novel set a million years in the future, but instead found a kind of Socratic dialogue between an everyman narrator and a wise telepathic gorilla. What's more, *Ishmael* appeared to be focused squarely in the distant past, with the whole thing amounting to a critique of agriculture and the civilization that sprang from it. The agricultural revolution, claimed the gorilla, was the beginning of a spiral of rising population and exploitation of cultures and ecosystems that continues to this day—and which was now bringing us to the brink of societal collapse.

All of which was kind of interesting to think about, but a little too much for my pubescent brain to handle. I wound up turning in a paper that hemmed and hawed about uncertainty and space travel for several pages, and then I promptly went back to obsessing about muscle cars and grunge music.

Still, my teacher had planted a seed. What if our society of limitless abundance really *was* a dead end? As the cornucopian 1990s segued into the paranoia of 9/11 and the war in Iraq, that possibility seemed to become more real. During my undergraduate education at New York University, my professors seemed hell-bent on blaming society's ills on the evils of modern-day capitalism—a critique that became harder and harder to refute. As scientists began giving ever-more dire warnings about climate change and the economy was brought to its knees by the robber barons of Wall Street, the narrative of a culture spiraling out of control began to feel a lot more realistic than one of limitless progress.

Looking for some kind of solution to all this doom and gloom, I stumbled upon permaculture design—and all of the sudden, everything came into focus.

Tying together indigenous wisdom and modern science, permaculture seemed to offer a common-sense, coherent framework for digging ourselves out of our destructive feedback loops. After spending my college years wringing my hands over ecological apocalypse, hearing my permaculture teachers claim that humans *weren't* an inherent scourge on the landscape felt like coming up for air after a long, deep dive. I learned that with a combination of love, patience, and intelligent design, we could actually *improve* the natural and human communities around us. Here, finally, seemed to be the radical solution to *Ishmael's* radical challenge.

And the examples I learned about sparkled with promise. Gorgeous homes made of clay and straw that could somehow heat and cool themselves using the energy of the sun. Desert gardens that produced bushels of unique and delicious crops with nothing but the rain that fell from the sky. Outdoor showers that kept their water warm by burying pipe in a large pile of wood chips.

It was all the more frustrating, then, once I started to realize that few of these examples were actually being used in the real world. It wasn't that the technology was wrong or too complicated to implement. Instead, the failures all seemed to come back to much more prosaic stuff: personality conflicts, business plans, and the like. I met a mountain farmer who was a genius at working with plants— but who couldn't manage an intern to save his life. I learned of an organic food co-op—years in the making—that failed in six months due to a lack of business acumen. I saw many a nonprofit that wanted to lift low-income communities out of poverty, only to find themselves drawing the scorn and ire of the very residents they were trying to serve.

What was the deal? Was this world-changing movement really going to wither and die because of petty infighting and bad financial decisions? It was only as I dug deeper into my studies of permaculture that I began to understand that these challenges were also within the ability of the designer to solve. My mentors showed me how the same tools that we used to design homes and landscapes can be used to design businesses, economic systems, and community groups.

As I deepened my permaculture journey in my hometown of Denver, I saw no shortage of opportunities to begin thinking about designing these so-called *invisible structures*. As a budding educator, I used my understanding of permaculture to devise more effective and engaging workshops. As a member of a collective house, I used my knowledge of healthy ecosystems to think about creating a healthy community of housemates. I became involved in starting a nonprofit, with all the requisite legwork of raising money, forming a board, and running programming. The nonprofit happened to be based in an isolated and polluted Latino community, and part of our aim was to empower that community through developing a local food economy. And so I began a journey of understanding my own privilege and applying permaculture to dealing with systemic injustice.

The more I leaned on my understanding of invisible structures, the more clear the solutions seemed to be. More and more people came to me asking for advice about how to start their businesses or build community. And using my design skills, it was easy to help them uncover the answers. I began to regain the initial excitement I felt when first learning about permaculture. Maybe, I thought, we just need to redesign our relationships with each other in the same way we're redesigning our relationship to nature.

––––

When it comes down to it, the challenges of working with people are at the heart of figuring out how to live sustainably on this planet. As individuals, we can only accomplish so much—and in a world of seven billion and rising, nothing we can do will be large enough to make a difference without effective collaboration. Whether we're organizing a community garden, starting a business, mobilizing for political change, or just trying to become a better person, we encounter dense and knotty issues every day related to interpersonal dynamics.

Across the globe, courageous and dedicated leaders are delving into the core of these challenges, tinkering with "social technologies" that can untangle these knots of exploitative economics, systemic oppression, and interpersonal conflict. While every situation is different, there are recognizable patterns to both the problems and the solutions we usually encounter. And although these social technologies can't be seen or grasped in the same manner as a compost pile or wood stove, they are equally applicable to communities large and small, urban and rural, rich and poor.

This book is an attempt to comprehensively document many of these social technologies in one useful reference, in a way that that makes them meaningfully replicable in any number of contexts. *Change Here Now* is rooted in two related problem-solving approaches: permaculture design and pattern languages. I've found that both of these approaches provide helpful and complementary tools for dealing with the complex, confusing systems of human culture, allowing us to distill meaningful data out of the overwhelming noise of our day-to-day interactions. The introduction of this book offers an explanation of these two systems of thought for those readers who haven't encountered them. After that, I outline the structure of the solutions found in the book and give a few examples of how they might be used in your life or work.

The bulk of the book is devoted to the solutions themselves, which I've called *patterns*. The eighty-two patterns and design tools herein represent my best attempt at synthesizing some of the most important tools for successfully working with people to create a more thriving society. Note that I use the word *some*, not *all*; any number of the themes explored in this book could be developed into hundreds of sub-themes, and there are certainly important realms of the social experience not covered here. The content mostly sticks to my own experiences, which are necessarily limited, but I've tried to support my own convictions with evidence from three domains: natural systems, successful traditional cultures, and scientific research.

There's a wide breadth of territory covered, and hopefully it's sufficient to get your own gears turning. Much of the first third of the book discusses fundamentals of how human beings interrelate—what compels us to get along, the ideal number of people involved in various activities, and the like. The rest of the work focuses on specific areas of human interaction—exchanging goods and services (economics), how we make decisions in groups (governance), how we treat the marginalized in our culture (social justice). I hope you find the patterns as relevant and meaningful as I do.

ACKNOWLEDGMENTS

"Adam Brock" may be the name on the cover, but this book can hardly be called mine alone. Over the full decade that the ideas contained within these pages have been gestating, dozens, if not hundreds, of people have contributed in some way to their development.

My first permaculture teacher, Andrew Faust, gave me a role model in both agriculture and activism alike during a formative time in my growth. Peter Bane and Dave Jacke, two elders of the permaculture movement whom I've had the honor of being mentored by, both opened my eyes to the beauty and potential of pattern languages, as well as the power of permaculture to tackle social challenges. Eric Toensmeier gently planted the seed that these ideas could somehow be wrangled into a book during our time together at the thirteenth International Permaculture Convergence in Cuba.

Meanwhile, dozens of friends and colleagues have been patient and humble guides in helping me decolonize my own privileged mind. Rise Tren, Ashara Ekundayo, Shannon Francis, Pavlos Stavropoulos, Rafter Sass Ferguson, Karryn Olson-Ramanujan, Dani Slabaugh, Eutimia Montoya, Mike Wird, and Kendra Kreuger—you've all taught me much more than you probably realize.

My two brilliant research assistants, Susie Lewis and Mark Tebben, were invaluable to this endeavor. Besides their hours of tedious and confusing research, they both provided open ears and great feedback in what often felt like a lonely journey. Holly White, my illustrator, not only whipped up the brilliant diagrams and drawings you see in these pages, but an infectious enthusiasm for this work that kept me motivated when the going got tough.

Tim McKee and Ebonie Ledbetter, my editors at North Atlantic, both exercised much more flexibility and forbearance than I thought was allowed in their job description. My parents, Andrew and Laurie, and my partner, Dana, have all tolerated my obsessions and long writing sessions amazingly well, and their support has been invaluable.

Finally, I'd like to name all 122 friends, students, colleagues, family members, clients, and total strangers who contributed to my Indiegogo campaign, all of whom gave me a critical early sign that this project was worth going for. Their names read like my own personal zone of reciprocity, and I'm deeply grateful for their financial and emotional support: Deborah Lebow Aal, Kristin Alexander, Dominic Allamano, Michael Anderson, Cynda Arsenault, Ewelina Bajda, Ashley Basta, Jonathan Bates, Sarah Baxendell, Helen Behr, Bennett Black, Corin Blanchard, Natasha Blank, Nelson Bock, Andrew and Laurie Brock, Jeff Buck, Matthew Burawski, Graham Burnett, Les Canges, Christopher Canipe, Ann Cantelow, Raymond Caruso, Heather Christensen, Teri Ciacchi, Tristan Copley-Smith, Kate Croft, Scott Cutler, Ronnie Darling, Valerie Dawnstar, Mariel DeLacy, Naomi de Ville, Jessi DiTillio, Christopher Dixon, James Edwards, Avery Ellis, Sophie Ellison, Kate Ersing, Kate Farley, Matt Fetissoff, Fabio Fina, Amy Fortner, Jeremy Friedman, Kate Fritz, Jane Fruchtman, Nadia Gaona, Jason Gerhardt, Geoffroy Godeau, Coby Gould, Nancy Graham, James Hale, Paul Hetrick, Creighton Hofeditz, Megan K. Holcomb, Brittney Honkomp, Jennifer Jeffery, Mary Kay Jezzini, Laura Johnston, Kenneth Kanagaki, Emma Kaywin, Tara Kent, Jeremiah Kidd, Zach Klimko, Kristopher Korba, Kendra Krueger, Linda Kruhmin, Kathleen Landrum, Mickki Langston, Robert E. Law, Alison Alena Lewis, Eric Lewis, Susie Lewis, Katelyn Limke, Andrew Little, Hana Low, Brooks Luby, Kathleen Luttrell, Patricia Menzies, Lily Miezejeski, Marija Mikolajczak, Anne Misak, Judith F. Moran, Eryn Joy Murphy, Crystal Niedzwiadek, Elizabeth Nitz, Patty Nogg, Christopher O'Reilly, Oz Osborn, David Pailet, Andy Paluch, Ainslie O'Neil, Lee Recca, Kasie Roads, Michelle Robinson, Ross Rodgers, Abby Rosenbaum, Lance Rushton, Diego Sanchez Gomez, Caroline Savery, Lauren Scanlan, Ellis Scharfenaker, Elyssa Serrilli, Kimberly Shafer, Danielle Short, Leslie Sills McLaughlin, Kelsey Simkins, Kelly Simmons, Andrea Slinde, Sharona Thompson, Eric Toensmeier, Rise Tren, Gulden Deniz Ucok, Scott W. Vlaun, Mary Wagner, Holly White, Suellen White, Travis White, Bennett Williamson, Mike Wird, Michael Woods, and Lucie Worthen.

INTRODUCTION:
PERMACULTURE AND PATTERN LITERACY

PERMACULTURE 101

For a worldwide movement that's grown exponentially over the past few decades, permaculture is notoriously hard to pin down. Less a body of knowledge than a process for *using* knowledge, permaculture attempts to weave together fields as diverse as ecology, geology, history, and indigenous practices into a comprehensive framework for figuring out how humans can live indefinitely on this planet. As my colleague Rafter Sass Ferguson puts it, permaculture is, at its core, about meeting human needs while restoring ecosystem health—a radical proposition indeed in our hyper-destructive society.

Permaculture is most commonly introduced through a twelve- to twenty-one-day permaculture design course (PDC). Each PDC is taught differently, depending on the teacher's style and the local context—PDCs are taught in thousands of places around the world—but all adhere to the same general curriculum sketched out by Bill Mollison, one of permaculture's co-originators, in the late 1980s. At the heart of permaculture is a set of three ethics, a handful of principles, and a design process for applying those ethics and principles to just about any challenge you can think of.

David Holmgren, permaculture's other co-originator, developed an image of a flower to represent these key elements of the permaculture framework.

At the center of the flower are the three ethics of permaculture.

- care for the earth
- care for people
- fair share (also sometimes phrased as "redistribution of the surplus")

Surrounding the ethics, although still in the core of the flower structure, are the principles of permaculture. There are several sets of principles out there; the set that's most commonly referred to these days is Holmgren's list of twelve, first outlined in his 2002 book, *Permaculture: Principles and Pathways Beyond Sustainability:*

1. observe and interact
2. obtain a yield
3. catch and store energy
4. apply self-regulation and accept feedback
5. use and value renewable resources and services
6. produce no waste
7. design from patterns to details
8. integrate rather than segregate
9. use small and slow solutions
10. use and value diversity
11. use edges and value the marginal
12. creatively use and respond to change

Finally, the petals of the flower represent all the different areas in which permaculture can be applied, such as land and nature stewardship, built environment, tools and technology, culture and education, health and spiritual well-being, finance and economics, and land tenure and community governance. Others have added more areas. Holmgren's flower happens to have seven petals—but as with real flowers, the number of petals can vary widely, and the pattern still holds.

To continue the metaphor, practitioners of permaculture navigate through these petals of knowledge like a curious bee on the flower, identifying and solving design challenges holistically and creating connections between the petals as they go.

PHYSICAL STRUCTURES, INVISIBLE STRUCTURES

The ethics, principles, and design process give permaculturalists a flexible and powerful set of problem-solving tools that can be applied to just about anything. Practically speaking, however, those tools have thus far been applied relatively narrowly. For most of permaculture's history, its practitioners have tended to focus heavily on the petals of the flower connected with food production and land stewardship. The very word *permaculture* was invented as a portmanteau of *permanent agriculture* (it was later revised to *permanent culture*), and its co-originators were primarily concerned with how to derive a sustainable yield of calories from the land. And for good reason: the way a society gets its food determines nearly everything else about how it operates, and no culture can expect to last long without a sustainable way of feeding itself.

But in the process of developing sustainable agricultural systems, early permaculture designers quickly came across many non-agricultural questions: How can the shape of my house help extend the growing season? How can I capture the methane from animal manure to use as a cooking fuel? As a result, the standard permaculture curriculum has evolved into a thorough articulation of strategies for structures and building techniques, which draws from indigenous structures, contemporary advances in natural building, passive solar design, and renewable energy.

Similarly, permaculture has allied itself with the appropriate technology movement to pioneer new tools and rediscover old ones. These solutions—super-efficient stoves, bike-powered generators, soil-enhancing plows, and the like—allow us to meet our basic needs in a way that actually restores the landscape around us rather than depletes it. Unlike the flashy gadgets displayed at TED Talks and on tech blogs, these more humble technologies are based on renewable materials and easily fixable, human-scale systems.

And yet even this knowledge of buildings and tools was not broad enough. From the beginning, the originators of permaculture recognized that creating a "permanent culture" necessitated a redesign of more than just the stuff we can see and build. It also meant overhauling our economic and legal systems, governmental structures, educational attitudes, mass media, and modes of entertainment. For these, Bill Mollison applied the broad term *invisible structures* to denote that they were essential parts of any permanent culture but weren't easy to see.

Despite this initial acknowledgment, permaculture as a whole had relatively little to say about invisible structures for the first few decades of its existence. Bill Mollison's *Permaculture: A Designers' Manual*—still considered the ultimate text for die-hard designers more than twenty-five years later—spends a chapter discussing a few aspects of these invisible structures, and early design courses spent time discussing a smattering of social permaculture topics such as complementary currencies and ecovillages. Still, the intangible nature of invisible structures made them frustratingly hard to pin down and apply, and there was nothing like a systematic approach to teaching and designing with them. The bulk of theory and action within the permaculture community remained focused on obscure plant species, water-harvesting earthworks, passive solar design, and the like.

Fortunately, the last ten years have seen a sea change in permaculture's approach toward invisible structures. Increasing mainstream interest in sustainability made permaculture seem less of a fringe topic, and brought it a new and more diverse set of adherents—a crowd that that tended to be more urban and thus keenly interested in the social and economic aspects of permaculture. Meanwhile, the near-collapse of the global economy in 2008 and the recession that followed put economics front and center in the minds of many permaculture thinkers, as it did the rest of the population. Social movements like Black Lives Matter and Occupy brought a growing awareness of issues of inequality and systemic oppression in our society. With this lens, many permaculturalists began questioning the unintentionally oppressive nature of permaculture itself. Why, for instance, were nearly all of the best-known permaculture practitioners middle-aged white males? And how could we expect to train a diverse cross section of our society in permaculture when the cost and time requirement of a PDC was unrealistic for all but the wealthier members of society? Even the term *invisible structures* came under critique as sounding vague and even nefarious.

DESIGNING WITH SOCIAL STRUCTURES

Today, more and more in the permaculture community are turning their attention to social systems—and we're discovering that they might not be as slippery as we thought. In fact, our thirty years of lessons from the garden and landscape are surprisingly easy to apply to these social structures, and in more than just superficial ways.

To start at the center of the flower, two of permaculture's three core ethics—care for people and fair share—deal directly with how we interact with people. These ethics make it clear that we're obliged to consider ourselves responsible for the impact of our actions on our fellow humans. What's more, they offer potent seeds of an entire approach for doing so, one that upends many of our current cultural norms.

The permaculture principles, meanwhile, offer nearly unlimited relevance and insight into social dynamics, and many see this area as permaculture's fertile new edge. In 2007, for instance, David Holmgren and Rob Hopkins wrote an article that sketched out some ideas on how each of Holmgren's twelve permaculture principles apply to running a business. In her book *People and Permaculture*, Looby Macnamara has outlined how each principle relates to self-care and working in small groups. And across the globe, many more permaculture practitioners are figuring out how use their design skills to reinvigorate social structures in their own communities.

Whereas the ethics and principles offer general guidance in how to think about invisible structures, permaculture's design process provides much more specific tools. The "order of operations" suggested by the design process gives us a clear set of steps for going about our work, while many of the exercises used in the "analysis and assessment" phase help us ask the right questions and identify patterns that might otherwise be hidden.

A PATTERN LANGUAGE OF SOCIAL PERMACULTURE

As a flexible problem-solving framework, permaculture provides a solid foundation for analyzing social structures and coming up with an abundance of solutions. But how to best organize and share those solutions? A narrative won't do—the fluid lines of prose make it challenging to quickly find the exact information you're looking for. Nor does a simple encyclopedia-style format suffice—to present each solution as a discrete entity would diminish the cumulative value of the solutions used in conjunction with one another. What's needed is a way to give each solution its own distinct identity while still acknowledging the deep interconnections between it and many others.

For that task, I've chosen to adopt a format called a *pattern language*. On first encounter, that phrase often provokes a quizzical or confused look. How can patterns possibly form a language? What would that even look like? A library of plaids and zigzags, perhaps, or a set of pictographs made of spirals and circles?

Far from it. In disciplines as diverse as software development, architecture, and city planning, the concept of pattern language has come to denote a *framework for describing good design practices within a field of expertise*. Under this definition, each good design practice is a "pattern," which solves a particular design challenge that is common in that field. Patterns can offer solutions to broad design challenges or very specific ones, but either way, they aim to be as timeless and universally applicable as possible.

The concept of a pattern language first developed in the 1970s by a team of architects led by Christopher Alexander, who developed a set of 253 patterns for the built environment, which he described in a book called, simply enough, *A Pattern Language*. That landmark work, more than a thousand pages long, covered a broad range of conceptual territory from the size and shape of entire regions to how knickknacks are arranged on a bookshelf.

A Pattern Language inspired a generation of architects interested in vernacular building. But its influence was far greater than that. Relatively quickly, holistic thinkers in a variety of fields began to see that using pattern language thinking was a powerful tool to solve all kinds of problems that had nothing to do with buildings or urban planning. Computer programmers saw the potential of pattern languages for efficiently writing code and developed multiple sets of pattern languages for specific programming applications. Under the direction of professor Douglas Schuler, the Public Sphere Project developed a pattern language for communications media—much of which was published in 2008 under the title *Liberating Voices: A Pattern Language for Communication Revolution*.

Permaculturalists have also had a productive overlap with pattern languages. Dave Jacke and Eric Toensmeier developed a pattern language for forest gardening in their two-volume *Edible Forest Gardens*, while Peter Bane has one for garden farming in his *Permaculture Handbook*. More recently, Karryn Olson-Ramanujan has developed one for women in permaculture, and several other permaculture designers and teachers have adopted pattern language thinking for their own specialties.

PATTERN FORMAT

No matter which subject a pattern language describes, a pattern tends to follow the same general rules, first used in Alexander's original work:

- A pattern has an easy-to-remember and highly descriptive *name*. It must be general enough to be applied to very different systems within its context, but still specific enough to give constructive guidance. For instance, Alexander's pattern A PLACE TO WAIT addresses bus stops in the same way as waiting rooms at a doctor's office, while still proposing helpful and constructive solutions.

- A pattern must characterize the *problems* that it is meant to solve, the *context* or situation where these problems arise, and the *conditions* under which the proposed solutions can be recommended.

- A pattern provides *examples* (best practices) of successful use of the pattern in the real world.

- A pattern will describe *relationships* to other patterns in the language, both larger and smaller.

Contrary to the common definition of *pattern,* the patterns in a pattern language aren't necessarily visual. Instead, a pattern can refer to any set of conditions that are frequently repeated. In Dave Jacke and Eric Toensmeier's *Edible Forest Gardens,* for instance, the pattern STAGGERED HARVESTS, CLUSTERED HARVESTS cautions the designer to plant trees and shrubs that yield at various times of the year, lest they find themselves deluged with a dozen kinds of fruit come September. STAGGERED HARVESTS, CLUSTERED HARVESTS doesn't have an immediate visible form, but it clearly qualifies as a pattern: understanding its near-universal relevance makes for a more successful forest garden design.

What's more, the patterns gain their true power in association with one another. Just like we commonly link certain words together in English to form phrases and sentences, any given pattern in a pattern language is associated with related patterns at larger and smaller scales. The result is a densely interlinked web of patterns, any which of can be drawn from to best suit a particular context.

In a real-world design project, a subset of relevant patterns from the language can be applied to create a set of specific design solutions for that project. For example, homeowners wishing to add a second-floor deck might consult *A Pattern Language* and come up with a dozen patterns that provide insight into their design. Pattern number 62, HIGH PLACES, alerts the designers that their deck might be more than a mere indulgence—as Alexander puts it, "the instinct to climb up to some high place, from which you can look down and survey your world, seems to be a fundamental human instinct." From there, PUBLIC OUTDOOR ROOM (69) describes the important social role played by outdoor spaces adjacent to buildings, while SOUTH-FACING OUTDOORS (105) gives clues about the deck's ideal orientation. ROOF GARDEN (118) suggests that adding some plants might liven up the space; SIX-FOOT BALCONY (167) and SOLID DOORS WITH GLASS (237) provide specific direction about the deck's size and materials.

THINKING IN PATTERN

Just like permaculture, pattern languages have proven themselves to be an enormously flexible design tool for thinkers on the cutting edge of their respective fields. But while the idea of a pattern language is a relatively recent meme, the truth is that humans are hardwired for pattern recognition. In the same way that permaculture is a contemporary revamp of timeless indigenous wisdom, patterns and pattern languages have been used to solve problems for thousands of years. Yoga, for example, can be seen as a pattern language of *asanas,* or poses, each one designed to alter the body in a specific way. Depending on the goals and skill of the practitioner, individual *asanas* are combined into sequences, or "flows," to achieve an effect that is greater than the sum of their parts. Similarly, mathematical proofs can be considered patterns, each of which has been combined over the centuries to develop theorems of greater and greater sophistication. In the realm of entertainment, the common beats, melodies, lyrical themes, and instrumental textures of pop music form their own pattern language—itself split into genres and subgenres, each of which is instantly recognizable to anyone with a favorite radio station.

Of course, not every situation is as easy to apply existing patterns to as yoga or pop music—and after multiple generations of disuse, the pattern-recognition parts our brains are sorely out of shape. But with a little practice, thinking in pattern languages becomes an incredibly useful and beautiful way of seeing the world. The more familiar the patterns become, the more you'll start to notice them in your everyday life, sometimes in the most unexpected places. And before too long, you'll begin to discover your own patterns and form a personal pattern language relevant to your life. This overall process of learning to correctly identify and apply these patterns is often dubbed *pattern literacy.*

HOW TO USE THIS BOOK

Change Here Now is intended, first and foremost, as a reference. While it can be read cover to cover, the goal is for the book to be used in the context of specific projects. As such, there's no requirement for you to start at the beginning and work your way through—it's unlikely that all the patterns will be relevant, or even interesting, to every user. Like an atlas, this book is meant to show you the landscape and give you the tools you need to engage with it, rather than dictate exactly where to go. I believe it can be useful whether you're navigating toward a specific destination or meandering about in exploration. To show you what I mean, let's follow a couple of hypothetical readers.

Let's say, for example, that your destination is starting or improving your own SMALL BUSINESS. You might start at the table of contents and pick a few specific patterns of interest to you and read only those—such as SMALL BUSINESS, MEASURING SUCCESS, and REDUCE THE NEED TO EARN—and then answer the "applying the pattern" questions at the end of each. You may also jump to the CAPITAL ANALYSIS and BUSINESS MODEL CANVAS design tools and use them to evaluate your business plans or generate new ideas. At this point, you may have found the specific tools you need, and you put the book down.

On the other hand, you may have picked this book up because of a general interest—for example, in activism. The first pattern you read might be NONVIOLENT STRUGGLE. While reading that section, you come across the related pattern of TELLING THE STORY and read that one next. From there you could jump back to NONVIOLENT STRUGGLE, go to a pattern related to TELLING THE STORY, or start over from an unrelated pattern. Eventually you might find yourself using one of the design tools, such as the POWER ANALYSIS, as part of your exploration.

Of course, you can also read this book cover to cover, but I won't be offended if you don't. The point is that there's no one right way to use it, so don't feel constrained by the way I've laid it out.

The patterns for this book follow this format as closely as possible.

- *Title.* The names of individual patterns are always displayed in small caps for easy identification.

- *Summary.* This is a one- or two-sentence summary of the pattern, designed to help the reader quickly identify what it's about.

- *Discussion.* This section describes the problem that the pattern is trying to solve and makes the case for the pattern, pointing to natural systems, indigenous societies, and present-day case studies as evidence. It sketches out the appropriate context in which the pattern is to be used, and it discusses the conditions that make it effective or ineffective.

- *Further learning.* This section lists additional resources for exploring the content of the pattern in more depth.

- *Applying the pattern.* This is a set of questions for the reader about how to apply the pattern in his or her own designs.

PART 1

Vision for a Permanent Culture

What does your perfect world look like? I'm not talking about a less-bad world sketched out in policy prescriptions or optimistic statistics. Nor am I referring to a technological wonderland envisioned by some twentieth-century sci-fi author or twenty-first-century tech entrepreneur. No, I mean the world that *you,* and only you, can envision—the world that you know to be the fulfillment of humankind's highest potential as a species.

For me, that world is one in which every person performs meaningful labor. Where every family has the ability to prosper if they work hard. Where one person's success doesn't mean another's oppression. A world where elders are revered and women are empowered, and where a multiplicity of skin tones, ethnic traditions, and gender identities are able to thrive. It's a world where local communities have control over their own affairs and manage them responsibly, with their grandchildren's grandchildren in mind. Where communities are seamlessly embedded within the ecosystems around them. It's a world that understands and respects natural limits on local and global scales, a world that's learned how to balance individual agency with collective responsibility for each other and our shared home.

Perhaps your perfect world looks different. Each one of us, after all, has our own priorities of growth and change. Our imaginative impulses send us in all kinds of different directions, and our life experiences give us vastly different perspectives on society's problems and opportunities. Regardless of the specific substance of your perfect world, however, it probably seems pretty distant right now. From the ballot box to the global climate, we live in a time of unparalleled turmoil. Every day seems to bring news of another act of unprecedented violence, another natural disaster, a worsening of one ongoing crisis or another. Under these circumstances, visions of a perfect world might seem not only far-fetched but also embarrassing to even contemplate.

Yet it's now, more than ever, when we need these visions to guide us. It's true that things are likely to get worse before they get better. Much of our vision will remain unrealized during our lifetimes, and perhaps for several generations to come. But whether or not we even "get there" at all is only part of the point. Because back in the here and now, we need goals to guide our actions, targets to rally around. And if all we're striving for is "less bad," then that's all we can ever hope to achieve. This book makes the case that no progress—incremental or revolutionary—can occur without a long-term vision of what we're after. This first section of the book lays out a series of patterns explaining one possible vision, guided by a few core premises.

Premise number one is that *humans are part of nature, and nature creates abundance.* As much as we like to tout our own exceptionalism, it's hard to deny that *Homo sapiens* is just one species of millions, all of us sharing the thin crust of a planet hurtling through cold space. Without collaboration and stewardship of that thin film of life, we're toast. Fortunately, we're surrounded by ecosystems that, despite challenging conditions, have managed to thrive for billions of years. Abundance is what nature does best, and it's used that abundance to weather untold challenges over the eons.

Humans are part of nature—and always have been. But despite having nature's abundance on our side, our operating system has been infected with code that erodes this abundance. That brings us to the second premise, that *our current political-economic system is unsustainable and headed toward collapse.* Like a parasitic virus destroying its host, our elite-controlled global economy is consuming the very foundations of life we need to survive: natural resources like fossil fuels and fresh water, to be sure, but also local economies, networks of mutual aid, and shared narratives of meaning. These parasitic dynamics have been operating for decades—in some cases, centuries—but in the last several years they've become increasingly impossible to ignore. Our addictions to control and growth are still largely absent from civil discourse, but they're lurking in the subtext of just about every headline. Across the globe, example after example of civil unrest, repressive regimes, and economic instability can be tied to the social and environmental stress caused by attempting infinite growth on a finite world.

Recognizing the dire situation we're in, tens of millions of people across the world have dedicated their time and money to addressing issues of violence, poverty, climate change, and resource depletion. Yet many contemporary efforts at social change are atomistic—they try to change individual issues, one by one. Many of these solutions have become vital stopgaps, slowing the spread of our planetary virus. Many others, by focusing so narrowly on one challenge, have created side effects that actually make other problems worse. But even if they all worked exactly as intended, these solutions just don't add up to the deep change that we need. That's where the third premise comes in: *permaculture design and pattern languages give us the conceptual tools for transcending the challenges we face as a society.*

By drawing on ecosystems for inspiration and applying a rigorous and methodical problem-solving process, permaculture design shows that it's indeed possible to create twenty-first-century communities that work in concert with nature's abundance. And by organizing potential solutions into a networked library of patterns, Christopher Alexander's pattern-language framework provides us some essential shortcuts in the complex, messy work of healing communities. Together, they invite us to approach our civilizational crisis from the "top of the watershed," where it's clear that our myriad challenges are all symptoms of the same fundamental disconnection. In that vein, the first section of this book works at a high level. There are few specific, practical solutions in these first patterns, but they are critical in laying the conceptual foundation for those that appear later.

As the first pattern in the book, THE LONG GAME serves to ground the social designer in the vastness of "deep time," reminding us that events within our own lifespans are but footnotes to much larger cycles of growth and destruction. Next, BIOPHILIA explores the importance of having healthy relationships with other species. INTERDEPENDENT COMMUNITIES takes a broad look at how humans work together, making the case that true communities are ones that truly need each other. THE RIGHT SIZE and RELATIONSHIP ZONES explore the question of scale, using biology and neuroscience to question the current size of our institutions and to propose a more humanist restructuring.

DETHRONING THE ANTIMARKETS lays out our present economic situation, in which a powerful few are systematically plundering the wealth of the many for their own short-term benefit. COMMONING and SUBSIDIARITY, meanwhile, sketch out an alternative framework in which small, relatively autonomous communities are empowered to create prosperity themselves. ZONES OF AUTONOMY delineates the importance of creating islands of resistance in our present sea of destructive institutions, while GOING HOME makes the case for reclaiming the dying art of staying put.

Finally, the last three patterns in this section touch on our individual attitudes in creating lasting change. THE EDGE OF CHANGE reminds us that our most effective work lies at the intersection between the ideal and the possible. MULTITUDES OF KNOWING posits that scientific knowledge is just one of several important modes of truth. And FEAR BURNS BRIGHT, HOPE BURNS LONG brings things full circle by stressing the importance of positive visions.

1. THE LONG GAME

Meaningful change is a long process, often outlasting our own lifespans. Practice patience and recognize the importance of small victories.

Never mistake a clear view for a short distance.

—Technology forecaster Paul Saffo

Five centuries ago, in the midst of the Protestant Reformation, there was a small sect of radicals—the fringe of the fringe—called the Anabaptists. Unsatisfied with the bold proposals of Martin Luther and his followers, this ragtag group of Christians called for the separation of church and state, free education, the abolishment of corporations, and a guaranteed income. In response for these heretical views, the Anabaptists were ruthlessly persecuted by the Catholic government and ridiculed even by their fellow reformers. In hindsight, it's clear that the Anabaptists had a profound influence on progressive thought. But many of their ideas took centuries to gain widespread support, and from the perspective of the movement's founders, their cause was a resolute failure.

The story of the Anabaptists illustrates the peculiar nature of THE LONG GAME: the manner in which crazy ideas become mainstream. Every SACRED ACTIVIST has a PERSONAL VISION of a future that may seem wildly impractical today. Broader trends might be moving in the opposite direction from what we know to be important and true, and the necessary resources never seem to show up. In some cases, we may spend decades watching our cherished goals slide farther and farther away from THE EDGE OF CHANGE.

But while our own lifetimes may feel impossibly long, the truth is that eighty years is but a single narrow ring in the sturdy tree trunk of human experience. Even the storied history of civilization, beginning with the dawn of agriculture a dozen millennia back, represents just 1 percent of the history of anatomically modern human beings. And the human experience is only a blink of an eye in the multibillion-year saga of planet Earth. The concept of "deep time" is often invoked by geologists, archaeologists, and philosophers intent in lifting our gaze past the next election cycle or quarterly earnings report. Today, the institution most successfully bringing attention to deep time is the Long Now Foundation, founded by pioneering environmentalist Stewart Brand. Since 1996, the Long Now Foundation has launched a series of thought-provoking projects—a ten-thousand-year clock, a lecture series on long-term thinking—designed to stretch our thinking toward the distant future.

Of course, in a time when billions of people are suffering from injustice and millions of acres of wilderness are imperiled in the very short term, contemplating ten-thousand-year time horizons can seem callous and absurd. The radicals in our communities (and in our own heads) may argue for immediate revolution—and in some cases, CREATIVE DESTRUCTION is indeed the order of the day. But the rest of the time, the elders in our midst are there to remind us that the most healthy and lasting social change can take many generations to transpire. A social or political revolution may occur in a matter of months, but it takes years to purge a society of the grudges spawned by that revolution. A hundred trees can be planted in a few days, but it will take fifty years for those trees to become a forest.

There's no way around it—the work of healing our society is a marathon, not a sprint. There are no shortcuts, no quick fixes to nurturing a healthier planet. That doesn't mean that our incremental actions don't matter—in fact, they matter now more than ever. The choices we make today, perched as we are at the pinnacle of Western civilization, will reverberate long after anyone is around to recall why those choices were made in the first place. As with the Anabaptists, the innovative ideas that are ridiculed today might become the unifying cause of the next generation. The REGENERATIVE ENTERPRISES we launch next year might meet the basic needs of our great-grandchildren. And the earthworks we shape over the next decade will capture rain and restore nutrients in the soil for millennia.

But only if we plan for the long game. That means studying how the deep past brought us to where we are and contemplating the ripples of our choices into the deep future. It means cultivating grounding rituals to connect our work with larger structures of meaning. It means remaining steadfast in our convictions, despite the rejection we face in the present moment. It means LETTING LOOSE to celebrate the small wins and taking breaks to decompress and rest. Perhaps most importantly, it means practicing patience, forgiveness, and grace—both for the shortsightedness within ourselves and in those around us.

FURTHER LEARNING

The Long Now Foundation, "Seminars About Long-Term Thinking" (podcast), http://longnow.org/seminars/podcast.

APPLYING THE PATTERN

What can you learn about the histories of your community? Who laid the groundwork for the work that you and your organizations are doing? What might the legacy of that work be one hundred or five hundred years from now? How many literal and metaphorical trees have you planted? How can you integrate the contemplation of deep time into your SACRED ACTIVISM?

2. BIOPHILIA

Humans coevolved with other species, and we are not whole without their presence.

For a new generation, nature is more abstraction than reality. Increasingly, nature is something to watch, to consume, to wear—to ignore.

—Richard Louv, *Last Child in the Woods*

Few shifts in our species' history have been more profound than the reorientation of our habitat from diverse ecosystems to human-created environments. After living, since time immemorial, in daily relationship with innumerable forms of life, our connection with plants and animals is now drastically limited, and largely voluntary. For the most part, this was a deliberate shift: an attempt to insulate ourselves from the difficulties and unpredictability of ecosystems. But for all the benefits gained by keeping nature at arm's length, its absence from our lives has left a gaping hole. Like children raised without the touch of our mothers, we move through life with a vague but pronounced alienation, a yearning for something we've never known.

For most of human history, "nature" as a concept didn't exist, since there was nothing that wasn't nature. Our familiar Western distinctions between humanity and nature, savage and civilized, were part of a restless continuum that refused simple categorization. Until agriculture began a feedback loop of urbanization and ecological simplification, our calories, medicine, fiber, fuel, and building materials were secured through engaging with and, in some cases, dramatically reshaping intact ecosystems. And on a more abstract level, our collective sense of meaning and story was intimately tied to natural rhythms. From the Ayllu cosmology of the Andean Quechua to the Tibetan Bon religion to Igbo deities of West Africa, nonagricultural societies have tended to see forces of nature as deities with their own personalities and predilections.

Even as recently as the founding of our country, many leading scholars viewed a connection to the land as vital to a flourishing society. Prominent Enlightenment-era thinkers, including Thomas Jefferson, John Locke, and Benjamin Franklin, subscribed to the economic philosophy of physiocracy, in which the health and liberty of a culture are determined by the health of the soil. "Cultivators of the earth are the most valuable citizens," proclaimed Jefferson in a 1785 letter to John Jay. "They are the most vigorous, the most independent, the most virtuous, and they are tied to their country and wedded to its liberty and interests by the most lasting bonds."[1]

But as America became urbanized and industrialized, Jefferson's words fell more and more out of step with the times. In his bestselling book *The Last Child in the Woods,* journalist Richard Louv traces the evolution of Americans' relationship to nature through three distinct post-physiocratic phases. Nineteenth-century explorers and pioneers took a *utilitarian* approach, seeing nature as a wild frontier to be tamed and exploited. With the rise of transcendentalist thinking, streetcar suburbs, and America's first national parks, nature was *romanticized* as a place of inspiration and beauty. And today—despite the influence of a varied and powerful environmental movement—most Americans treat nature as an *afterthought,* with grave consequences for our well-being.

Louv coined the term *nature deficit disorder* to describe the many ways this current disconnection is damaging to our collective and individual psyches. And while the term itself has yet to be recognized by the medical establishment, its symptoms are well documented. A 2015 study published in *Nature,* for instance, estimated that living on a block with ten more trees has the same effect on our health as a $10,000 raise or being seven years younger.[2] Numerous studies have shown positive benefits on our mental health as well, from reducing stress levels to improving our memory, creativity, and generosity.[3]

Some of us, of course, *have* been able to maintain regular access to nature, even if only in a superficial manner. Americans on the higher rungs the economic ladder are more likely to live in places with tall, shady street trees, nearby park space, and lush backyards. And many of us, when we wish to escape our urban and suburban habitat, can find the time and disposable income to take camping and skiing trips. But like so many elements of a healthy lifestyle, these opportunities have become stratified by class. The environmental justice movement of the 1980s and 1990s demonstrated that poor and minority communities bore the brunt of environmental pollution, and numerous studies have confirmed the disproportionate access of white affluent communities to green space and wilderness activities. A 2011 study commissioned by the National Park Service, for instance, found that, even as America's population becomes increasingly diverse, an astonishing 80 percent of visitors to national parks across the country are white.[4]

From the perspectives of both public health and social justice, it's clear that increased contact with nature will benefit our society as a whole. But there's yet another rationale for a deeper union with living systems: besides making us feel better physically and emotionally, natural systems embody ways of being that we desperately need to solve the greatest challenges of our time. Civilization has allowed us to turn our backs on the wilderness, but we can never fully leave it behind. For all the singular characteristics of our strange species, we're ultimately just another animal, embedded in a web of interdependent relationships like any other. And if we're to remain on this planet for very long, we'll need to temper the lessons learned in twelve thousand years of civilization with those gained by three billion years of evolution. In the breathtaking diversity, creativity, and resilience of other species and their mutual interactions, we can learn just about everything we need to solve the problems we've created for ourselves.

FURTHER LEARNING

Louv, Richard. *Last Child in the Woods*. Chapel Hill, NC: Algonquin Books of Chapel Hill, 2005.
Wilson, Edward O. *Biophilia*. Cambridge, MA: Harvard University Press, 1984.

APPLYING THE PATTERN

In what ways do you regularly interact with the "natural" world? How might you better integrate nature or wilderness into your community? How accessible is nature and the great outdoors to you? If you have easy access to nature, how could you use your privileges to work for easier access for all?

3. INTERDEPENDENT COMMUNITIES

Authentic communities are ones that need each other.

We are social creatures. Community is woven into the very fabric of what it means to be human. Today, however, we are suffering a crisis of community. Car culture and the design of the modern suburb keep us separated from one another in boxes of wood, glass, and steel. Ever-increasing mobility means that we scarcely put down roots in a place before packing up and moving somewhere else. And the dynamics of the global ANTIMARKET, pushing toward ever-greater efficiencies, have obliterated many of the vital interpersonal transactions centered on love.

It's one of the great ironies of our age that, even as we find ourselves more connected to the entire globe than ever before, we've lost meaningful connections with the people right around us: coworkers, neighbors, and even friends and family. The result, as documented in works like Robert Putnam's *Bowling Alone*, is a society that has become distressingly listless and alienated.

A better world isn't possible without a recalibration of these relationships. We need to reknit the fabric of community, starting at the small scale and working outward. But before we extol the benefits of any and every attempt at "community building," it might be helpful to examine just what we're aiming for.

Ask most people what a community is, and they'll say something like "a group of people living in the same place," or "people that have a particular characteristic in common." Simple enough. But if our goal is *healthy* communities, these definitions prove sorely lacking. For starters, merely living in the same area is no longer enough to guarantee any kind of connection; many folks living on the same block may have never even met.

How about communities of shared interest? These days, thanks to the internet, we're able to form relationships with all kinds of geographically disparate people who share our passions. I feel fortunate to have dozens of connections around the globe who can give me advice about allyship, natural building, or teaching techniques. But these connections of mutual interest run only so deep, and they can't be counted on to provide true security or lasting meaning. For example, I wouldn't feel comfortable turning to my online community for relationship advice or a personal loan.

So if neither physical proximity nor shared characteristics are adequate qualifiers for meaningful community, then what is? As is often the case in permaculture, using the natural world as a guide gives us some helpful clues. In nature, communities are frequently formed among members of a given species. But even more important are the communities formed *between* species in a larger ecosystem. Indeed, a natural system gets its strength from the diversity of species present. That strength is formed over a long, long time, as each species slowly weaves a web of relationships with others in the system. And while most of those relationships are ones of mutual collaboration, there are also interactions of competition, predation, and parasitism—all part of the larger goal of dynamic stability. At the end of the day, what makes ecosystems last is the quality of *mutual interdependence*. Whether any two species are "friends" or "enemies," all the species in an ecosystem ultimately depend on a healthy network of relationships in order to survive. And in the proper relationship, a community of diverse species can weather the ups and downs of drought, fire, or climate change to last for millions of years.

Likewise, the communities of human beings that work—the ones that form close, long-lasting connections and that accomplish great things—are the ones that actually need each other in very basic ways. What brought communities together in the past was the necessity to cooperate in the face of threats from weather, wild animals, or other people. And even today, some of the strongest communities are organized around mutual aid—consider recent immigrants sending money to relatives back home or small-town residents banding together to fix an irrigation ditch.

Once we shift the focus away from proximity and shared characteristics, and toward interdependence, *community* takes on a different meaning. Members of interdependent communities don't need to share similar values. They might not look or act alike. They don't even have to be interested in the same things. They just have to need each other.

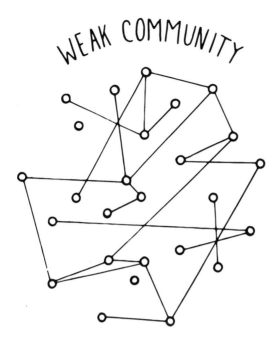

WEAK COMMUNITY

• lacking strong connections

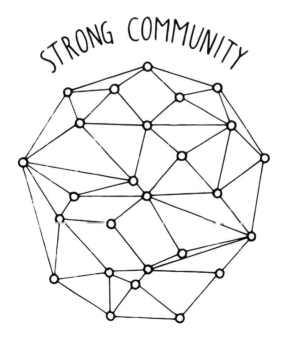

STRONG COMMUNITY

• mutually interdependent

• diverse

• often organized around aid

All of which sounds great in theory. But what does it mean for helping us to move beyond superficial "community-building" strategies and to start actually creating communities of mutual interdependence? For starters, we can each, as individuals, make conscious choices to rely on our neighbors more. We can take stock of the people and organizations we currently depend on to live our lives—which, more often than not, are faceless corporations—and try to replace some of those relationships with connections to people and businesses closer to home. We can invite our neighbors to our home to share a meal. We can rally our friends to build a chicken coop or community bulletin board, in the grand tradition of GADUGI. We can organize tool libraries to share our drills and wheelbarrows, and hold fundraisers to help those struggling with medical issues. We can form childcare cooperatives, carpool systems, and lending circles. And that's just the beginning.

FURTHER LEARNING

Berry, Wendell. *What Are People For?* Berkeley, CA: Counterpoint, 1990.

APPLYING THE PATTERN

To what extent are your needs for food, shelter, clothing, entertainment, and meaning met from within your community? To what extent are you meeting the needs of your community? Are there others living nearby who seem to model INTERDEPENDENT COMMUNITIES? What opportunities are there in your area to increase the number of direct relationships and facilitate greater interdependence among community members?

4. COMMONING

For centuries, large-scale forces of government and business have appropriated community-held land, knowledge, and relationships. Commoning is the vital process of reclaiming these forms of wealth for our local communities.

How wealthy are you? At first glance, the question seems relatively straightforward, if a tad impolite. With so many of our needs mediated through a single, centrally issued currency, describing our wealth is a matter of simple arithmetic: adding up our bank accounts and investments (if we're fortunate enough to have any) and subtracting our debts (if we're unfortunate enough to have any). The same logic applies to companies, cities, nations, and even the entire global economy. It's a given that the primary indicator of our overall well-being is our economic condition and that that condition can be reduced to a single number.

If only it were so simple. As soon as we leave our spreadsheets behind and enter the tangled mess of reality, we see that wealth takes many shapes and forms, from the richness of our topsoil to the strength of our friendships. Indeed, it is these non-monetary forms of wealth that represent our ultimate bounty: money itself is useful only inasmuch as it can be exchanged for the food, shelter, and meaning we actually desire. And while our current monetary arrangement makes wage slaves of us all, it's hardly a prerequisite for a thriving local economy.

Throughout most of human history, formal currencies served as instruments of taxation and long-distance trade, but they played a relatively minor role in the everyday creation and exchange of wealth. Instead, prosperity was ensured through an astounding diversity of informal and semiformal arrangements of THE GIFT, bartering, and HEIRLOOM CURRENCIES, each one evolved to fit the culture and resources at hand. These arrangements—developed, managed, and maintained by the people that benefit from them—are often referred to as *commons*.

To pick one example among dozens, Hawaii's indigenous *Ahupua'a* system demarcated communities based on the wedge-shaped watersheds that surrounded each island's central volcano. With fresh water and rainforests at the top of the watershed and agricultural flatlands and fishing areas below, each *Ahupua'a* was more or less self-sufficient and was expected to look after itself. There was no private property in this system, and the *Ahupua'a* was monitored by chief-appointed overseers and maintained by a strict cultural code called *kapu*, which discouraged over-harvesting.

On the other side of the globe, the forested areas surrounding medieval European villages were also managed collectively as commons. Peasants relied on their nearby forests, where they foraged for food and medicine, hunted game, and harvested wood for fuel and timber, and their shared need to prevent over-harvesting reinforced a sense of INTERDEPENDENT COMMUNITY.

But as the Renaissance led to the emergence of debt-based currencies and antimarkets, a new set of incentives took hold. Merchants and rulers sought to convert these forms of informal, local wealth to something that could be quantified, taxed, and—more often than not—usurped. And so began the "enclosure of the commons," a process of converting public goods into private commodities that, to this day, continues to shape our economic reality.

FORM OF WEALTH	INDICATORS WITHIN A GROUP	INDICATORS WITHIN A COMMUNITY	HUMAN POLYCULTURE ROLES	RELATED PATTERNS
Natural Capital				
NATURAL The wealth of nature, including all the species, processes, and matter that humans depend on for our survival.	How often does our group interact with other species? What might we gain from deeper or more frequent contact with natural systems?	How clean are our water supplies? How vulnerable are we to heat waves, drought, flooding, and other symptoms of climate change? How healthy are our soils? What is the biodiversity of our local ecosystems? Are there thriving communities of local farmers?	Translators Mavens	BIOPHILIA ISITES LEADERSHIP FROM WITHIN

FORM OF WEALTH	INDICATORS WITHIN A GROUP	INDICATORS WITHIN A COMMUNITY	HUMAN POLYCULTURE ROLES	RELATED PATTERNS
Material Capital				
 MATERIAL The physical wealth accumulated by humans: buildings, transportation and energy infrastructure, and durable goods like vehicles, tools, and furniture.	Do we have clean, secure, and appropriately sized spaces to meet and work? Do we have the necessary supplies to inspire creativity and accomplish quality work?	Is our housing durable, beautiful, and affordable? Is our energy infrastructure decentralized and running on renewable sources? Is our transportation infrastructure durable, clean, and community owned?	Mavens Helping hands	INFRASTRUCTURE COMMONS SLOW CITIES GADUGI BREAKING BREAD THE GIFT LETTING LOOSE RITES OF PASSAGE PRACTICING GRIEF
Experiential Capital				
 EXPERIENTIAL The wealth of embodied knowledge gained from from practice of a specific discipline, skill, or craft	What diversity of skills are represented among group members? What skills are lacking?	Is there a core group of long-time community members? Is vocational training readily available?	Mavens Helping hands Elders	STEWARDSHIP REGENERATIVE MANAGEMENT LEADERSHIP FROM WITHIN

FORM OF WEALTH	INDICATORS WITHIN A GROUP	INDICATORS WITHIN A COMMUNITY	HUMAN POLYCULTURE ROLES	RELATED PATTERNS
Social Capital				
SOCIAL The wealth gained from having diverse and meaningful relationships among members in a community.	Do group members have social or professional connections to other key individuals or groups? Do we share a sense of trust in each other? Are conflicts addressed as they come up, and are they resolved in a healthy and productive way?	Does the community have a culture of hospitality and mutual aid? Do community members experience frequent chance encounters with acquaintances? Are there COMMONING initiatives?	Graces Network weavers Translators	INTERDEPENDENT COMMUNITIES INTIMACY THROUGH ADVERSITY GADUGI BREAKING BREAD THE GIFT LETTING LOOSE RITES OF PASSAGE PRACTICING GRIEF
Cultural Capital				
CULTURAL The wealth of shared experiences of a community, expressed through stories, songs, rituals, foods, clothing, and more.	Has the group gone through a process of NAMING NORMS? Does it have informal traditions or inside jokes? What perspectives are missing?	Do community members come from diverse backgrounds? Do community members feel comfortable expressing their traditions?	Griots Elders Radicals	RITUAL AND CEREMONY SANKOFA

FORM OF WEALTH	INDICATORS WITHIN A GROUP	INDICATORS WITHIN A COMMUNITY	HUMAN POLYCULTURE ROLES	RELATED PATTERNS
Intellectual Capital				
INTELLECTUAL The wealth of ideas, facts, and knowledge generated by individuals and groups.	Does the group have all the information it needs to make wise decisions? What expertise is missing?	Does the community have access to quality libraries and educational opportunities? Are there local efforts of scientific inquiry?	Mavens Mentors	MULTITUDES OF KNOWING DOCUMENT THE PROCESS
FORM OF WEALTH	INDICATORS WITHIN A GROUP	INDICATORS WITHIN A COMMUNITY	HUMAN POLYCULTURE ROLES	RELATED PATTERNS
Spiritual Capital				
SPIRITUAL The internal well-being gained from finding a satisfactory place within larger narratives of meaning.	Does the group make efforts to connect its day-to-day work to larger trends, movements, and values? Does the group place an emphasis on self-care? Does the group engage in RITUAL AND CEREMONY?	Is there a culture of reverence, faith, and humility? Are there elders or other spiritual leaders in the community? Are there places to pray or contemplate?	Elders Graces	RITES OF PASSAGE TELLING THE STORY PERSONAL MYTHOLOGY

FORM OF WEALTH	INDICATORS WITHIN A GROUP	INDICATORS WITHIN A COMMUNITY	HUMAN POLYCULTURE ROLES	RELATED PATTERNS
Financial Capital				
FINANCIAL The wealth gained from the ability to translate and exchange other kinds of wealth.	Does the group have a clear and accurate budget? Does it have adequate financial resources to cover the budget?	Does the community have successful SMALL BUSINESSES patronized by community members? Do community members employ HEIRLOOM CURRENCIES to meet their needs? Are they supporting each other through IMPORT SUBSTITUTION?	Network Weavers Servant Leaders	DETHRONING THE ANTIMARKETS FINANCIAL RAM PUMPS HEIRLOOM CURRENCIES COMMUNITY-SUPPORTED ENTERPRISE

The results are tragically familiar: theft of indigenous land, the logging of forests, the leveling of mountaintops, the enslavement of the innocent, skyrocketing property values, and the privatization of everything from railroads to prisons to armies. As if these injustices weren't enough, centuries of enclosure have plundered even our mental landscapes. As leading commons theorist David Bollier explains, "If the processes we are involved in are primarily mediated by money and can be easily measured and calculated, then we become traders or transactionists. We experience ourselves as customers or producers and come to build an identity and culture around those practices.... Pressed into using market-oriented infrastructures and social habits, we practice the role of *Homo economicus* daily, like actors rehearsing their roles or musicians practicing their parts, often driven by institutional priorities, political considerations, media spectacles, and the artistically contrived illusions of advertising."[5]

But for all their current strength, the dynamics of enclosure face some powerful headwinds. Climate change, political resistance, financial recklessness, and any combination of other factors may well succeed in DETHRONING THE ANTIMARKETS. And in their place, we have the opportunity to do what humans have always done: use the commons to provide for ourselves.

In 1968 Garrett Hardin famously argued in "The Tragedy of the Commons" that collectively managed resources were destined to be undone by freeloaders. But while Hardin's tragedy remains vibrant in the popular imagination, its core thesis has long since been disproven. Scarcely twenty years after Hardin's essay, for instance, Elinor Ostrom won the Nobel Prize in Economics for her systematic studies of successful commons throughout the world.

Today, despite the pervasiveness of antimarkets and the pressures of enclosure, innovative commons are starting up all around us. Wikipedia has become a vast commons of knowledge, while the open-source software and hardware movements are shifting tools and technologies away from the market-driven model. Community-scale utility systems are putting everyday citizens in control of their power and water. The Creative Commons licensing system is inverting the protectionist mentality of traditional copyright law, allowing content creators to maintain credit for their work while opening it up to co-creation to a degree that suits their needs.

Some communities have developed entire networks of commons, creating webs of mutual interdependence that weave together natural resource management, job creation, and community cohesion. The Cecosesola network of cooperatives in western Venezuela employs more than a thousand people through a network of farms, healthcare providers, retail stores, and a credit union, serving tens of thousands of citizens. Across the Atlantic, in the Basque Country of northern

EIGHT FORMS OF CAPITAL

While the word *capital* generally refers to monetary assets, more and more people have begun employing the term to describe forms of stored value not captured by balance sheets. Ecological economists, for instance, commonly refer to *natural capital*, while sociologists discuss a community's health in terms of its *social capital*. In 2009, permaculturalists and entrepreneurs Ethan Roland and Gregory Landua devised a framework of eight forms of capital that they identified as necessary for a healthy society.

The chart on pages 16-20 is adapted from their 2013 ebook *Regenerative Enterprise: Optimizing for Multi-Capital Abundance.* Roland and Landua's chart provides an elegant and easy way to understand multiple forms of wealth—but don't let it stop you from reorganizing or identifying your own forms of capital.

Spain, the famed federation of Mondragon cooperatives has been slowly building an entire "society of the commons" encompassing dozens of multimillion-dollar businesses that span the sectors of education, retail, manufacturing, and banking. Even here in hyper-capitalist America, the endurance of rural commons like volunteer fire departments and irrigation districts prove their ability to meet local needs in areas left alone by both the markets and the state.

By their very nature, successful commons can't be prescribed from the top down by experts or policymakers. Rather, they must emerge as grassroots efforts from the communities they are designed to serve. For this reason, commons resist the sort of explosive growth that attracts headlines and big investment. But look beyond the policy papers and stock-exchange listings, and commons of all kinds can be found thriving, acting as what commons theorist Friederike Habermann calls "peninsulas against the current."[6] By blurring the boundaries of public and private, tangible and intangible, COMMONING rewires our binary-trained brains and opens up new possibilities of engagement with our neighbors. As Bollier puts it, "commons do not only produce what we need, they shape who we become: our values, practices, relationships, commitments and very identity."[7]

FURTHER LEARNING

Bollier, David, and Silke Helfrich, ed. *Patterns of Commoning.* Amherst, MA: The Commons Strategies Group, 2015.
Donahue, Brian. *Reclaiming the Commons: Community Farms and Forests in a New England Town.* New Haven, CT: Yale University Press, 2001.

APPLYING THE PATTERN

What are some common resources currently in your community? What common resources that existed in the past have since been privatized? Can you identify opportunities for COMMONING in your community? You may find it helpful to perform a CAPITAL ANALYSIS as part of applying this pattern.

5. THE RIGHT SIZE

Many of our current institutions and communities have become too large to function well. Replace these systems with ones that function at the appropriate scale.

Every system in nature has an optimal scale. There are reasons why solid planets don't get much larger than our own and why gaseous planets tend to be ten to one hundred times the size of solid ones. There are reasons why we don't see whales the size of shrimp, or—thank goodness—cockroaches the size of elephants. Scientists call these reasons *limiting factors*. In the celestial realm, limiting factors generally have to do with the laws of physics, while in biology, size and population are kept in check by things like predators, disease, and nutrient availability.

Humans are also subject to limiting factors: we don't live much longer than one hundred years or grow much taller than six or seven feet. But over the last ten thousand years, we've waged a systematic campaign against every limiting factor getting in our way. Too cold to survive in the temperate regions? Twirl some sticks and voilà—fire! Not enough calories available in the environment? Let agriculture take care of that. Epidemics of infectious disease? No longer a big deal in the overdeveloped world, thanks to antibiotics and other medical interventions. Even the limiting factor of the earth's annual biomass production has been surpassed by the skillful manipulation of long-dead organic matter— what we commonly refer to as fossil fuels.

The result is our global metaorganism of eight billion and rising, the likes of which this planet has never seen. We have megacities of fifty million and companies that employ hundreds of thousands. Our most popular websites have over a billion daily users. We've successfully transcended the limiting factors that used to keep us in measly tribes, and the global scale of our institutions stands as a testament to our success.

Or so the story goes. But a number of holes have begun to appear in that story—and they have grown too large to be ignored. For one thing, the benefits of all that progress have never been evenly distributed. For every intellectual of ancient Athens or Tenochtitlan, there were thousands of people, enslaved and "free," toiling away in fields, armies, and mines. And for every contemporary millionaire CEO, there are thousands of workers in cubicles and sweatshops whose labor keeps the profits rolling in.

Meanwhile, even our legitimate triumphs over nature's limits are starting to seem dubious and temporary. Fossil fuels are becoming harder and harder to tap, and their combustion is throwing our very climate into a tailspin. Increasingly virulent pathogens are resisting our latest antibiotics. Another narrative has begun to emerge, one that asks if we've actually outsmarted limiting factors or just temporarily kept them at bay. Perhaps, when it comes to our long-term survival, bigger isn't better after all.

Today, we've found ourselves faced with a challenge that few, if any, species have ever had to consider—that of voluntarily setting limits to our growth. If "bigger is better" is no longer the rule of the day, then what is? What scales are actually the right ones for human systems? To begin with, it's important to recognize that every system has a minimum and maximum viable size—let's call them *floors* and *ceilings*. In the case of human systems, floors represent the smallest viable group size for a given behavior to occur. Two's company, three's a crowd, a couple hundred is a viable gene pool, and a few thousand are necessary to keep a language alive. Ceilings, meanwhile, are usually set by the physical limitations of our bodies, minds, and the environment in which we're embedded. The size of a nuclear family, for instance, is limited by a child's gestation period, while our brains are capable of recognizing only a couple thousand faces.

As social designers, the key to establishing appropriate scale is finding the right ceilings and floors for the task at hand. And one of the first places to look is other social organisms, of which there are many in the animal kingdom. Some of the most well known are the social insects: bees, termites, and ants. Together, they are some of the most successful species on the planet, both in terms of longevity and numbers. An individual colony of social insects can number in the millions, roughly the same scale that we humans are currently organizing ourselves into cities.

At first glance, insects might sound like a great model for us to emulate. Indeed, much has been said of the uncanny collective intelligence of ant and bee colonies. But it's important to consider *how* the social insects work together. In contrast to human beings, insects aren't self-aware. As far as we know, they don't have emotions, and their tiny brains are limited to processing small quantities of data. Those factors, for them, work great: insect colonies are organized into strict caste systems, with each individual groomed from birth to perform a specific, specialized role in the colony. In a beehive, for instance, there are worker bees that build and maintain the hive structure; drones, male bees whose primary purpose is to inseminate the queen; and then there's the queen herself, who exists only to lay eggs for the continuation of the hive.

So the key to the great numbers of social insect communities, it seems, stems from extreme specialization and efficient communication systems. But what about social animals more similar to us—ones that exhibit emotion and individual intelligence? Among mammals, the upper limit of gatherings is the range of ten thousand or so. Large ungulates like buffalo form temporary herds when migrating from place to place, while prairie dogs can assemble colonies of thousands that stretch for acres. More commonly, however, social mammals form smaller packs of eight to forty individuals, organized around bonds of kinship. Just like in the social insects, there's a hierarchy in these packs. But for mammals, the hierarchy is much more loose, with each animal able to shift places, depending on outside conditions. Roles within each level of the hierarchy are also more fluid—sometimes a lioness will take care of her young, at other times, she will go out for the hunt.

So how does all this apply to human groups? While it's wise not to over-apply ecological analogues to our own society, the group sizes of social animals nevertheless give us clues about the kinds of interactions that happen at different scales of community. In particular, it seems meaningful that most animals that permanently gather in large groups have little agency. There appears to be a tradeoff, in other words, between the total size of a community and the relative choice available to each member of that community. The larger the group, the less freedom any individual has to choose his or her role within that group. If the insects are any indication, this is an inherent property of large groups, not a mere quirk of our present-day arrangements. There might just be no way to have our cake and eat it too—to permanently gather in the millions while truly allowing for the individual freedoms we cherish.

APPLYING THE PATTERN

Think about the institutions and social systems you interact with—employers, organizations, cities, and so forth. How do their actual sizes compare with what you see as appropriate ceilings or floors? What would it look like to transform them into an appropriate size? How can the patterns of RELATIONSHIP ZONES inform that transformation?

6. RELATIONSHIP ZONES

Our brains are structured to engage with different sizes of groups in different ways. Our institutions should be aligned with these physiological thresholds.

From kindergarten classes to political parties to Bible study groups to hunting expeditions, *Homo sapiens* sorts itself into groups of nearly unimaginable diversity. But for all their variation in purpose, nearly all of these social institutions rely on one of a handful of kinds of relationship between their members. Close-knit groups like fraternities and sororities are rooted in deep emotional intimacy, while many social and business groups rely on relationships based on collaboration or camaraderie. Groups of mutual interest merely require shared identity to function, but institutional groups like public schools or the armed forces rely on various forms of implicit or explicit coercion. Each of these relationships has its place, and each one works best at a different scale. Few of us, after all, have the time or emotional space to have dozens of best friends, and it would be impossible to design and build a skyscraper with only five people.

But while we know that closer relationships mean smaller groups, the exact bounds can seem quite blurry. Should a book club be capped at six or open its membership to anybody who wants to join? Does it make a big difference for a classroom to have twenty-five students instead of forty? How does the culture of a social movement change when it grows from a small cadre of die-hards to a movement of hundreds or thousands? Finding the optimal size for each group is critical to that group's success. And while this challenge has vexed philosophers, rulers, and management consultants for millennia, the last few decades have seen a growing body of neurological research that might finally be answering it with some kind of authority.

Thirty years ago, British professor of evolutionary psychology Robin Dunbar was studying social organization among various primate species. Why was it, he wondered, that gorillas gathered in groups of five to ten, while chimps seemed to prefer clans of fifty or more? Eventually, Dunbar found a clue in the neocortex, the part of the brain responsible for social and emotional processing: there appeared to be a strong correlation between the size of a primate's neocortex and the maximum size of group networks in that species. With this relationship in mind, Dunbar next turned his attention to our own species, hypothesizing that the size of the human neocortex would limit our stable social networks to roughly 150 people. Above that number, he reckoned, our brains simply can't keep up with the number of connections necessary to maintain stable relationships, so we require rules or laws imposed from above to keep large groups functioning.

The anthropological and archeological evidence appeared to confirm Dunbar's neurologically derived number. Across the globe, both ancient and modern tribal networks usually cap their numbers between one hundred and two hundred, and numerous studies of contemporary society show similar numbers in social networks and organizations.

Of course, plenty of human groups fall nowhere near 150 people. Gatherings can occur at nearly any scale, from nuclear families of three to six to standing armies in the tens of thousands. But as Dunbar and his peers continued their research, they discovered that each of these scales also exhibited remarkable consistency in their numbers. From Masai hunting bands to suburban soccer teams, there seemed to be a whole series of key sizes for different kinds of groups. What accounts for these built-in standards for optimal group size? In a 2005 paper, Dunbar and his colleagues posit that, just as 150 serves as the neurological threshold to relationships of mutual aid, each kind of relationship has its own optimal size rooted in the structure of our brains.[8]

THE ZONE OF INTIMACY (3–10)

For most of us, the great majority of our time spent in groups is spent in small groups. We may attend occasional rallies and parties, but most of our actual socializing is with a few close friends. We may work for a large organization, but most of the work is done by small teams. And even for the largest families, most gatherings and outings happen with a handful of people.

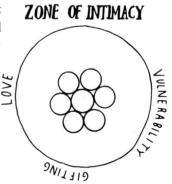

Perhaps the most important set of individuals that comprise a zone of intimacy is what social psychologists term our *support clique:* those who see us at our most vulnerable. When we're in the presence of those closest to us, we're willing to cry, express our deepest anxieties, and share our darkest secrets. Most of us have three to five people in our support clique (a 1998 survey pegged the average at 3.3), and it's usually composed of some combination of parents, siblings, romantic partners, and the closest of friends. Support cliques are defined by love. We freely share our time, attention, and goods with them without any expectation of reciprocation. In a sense, THE GIFT is the currency we use to express that love.

The zone of intimacy shows up in other spheres as well. The HUMAN POLYCULTURE is the family-sized group with which we engage in collaborative action. Regardless of how large our companies, volunteer groups, and activist networks may be, chances are that most of our day-to-day collaborative activities happen in groups of three to seven.

THE ZONE OF TRUST (10–25)

The next circle out encompasses those whom we contact on a regular basis and share special ties with: relatives, friend groups, and perhaps some close colleagues. Sociologists call this circle our *sympathy group* and cite social surveys across the globe showing that it consistently has ten to fifteen people at any given time. While we might not share the most intimate details of our lives with those in our zone of trust, we're likely to keep them updated on the ups and downs of our lives, such as struggles at work, vacations, and our romantic status. As Dunbar points out, groups of ten to fifteen are frequently found in contexts "where very close co-ordination of behaviour is required: juries, the inner cabinets of many governments, the number of apostles, the size of most sports teams."[9]

ZONE OF TRUST

THE ZONE OF COOPERATION (25–50)

For most of human history, humans lived in traveling bands of foragers that frequently numbered between thirty and fifty people—a range that apparently represented the narrow window between self-sufficiency and social stability. As humans settled in towns and cities, these clan-sized groups remained an important unit of society. The members of each such group assisted one another with the operations of the HOUSEHOLD ECONOMY: looking after one another's children, tending to the sick or elderly, and trading surplus harvests or skills.

Today, with the household economy waning in importance, cooperative groups of thirty to fifty have become much less important to our domestic lives. Still, groups of a few dozen members remain important in our social, cultural, and political institutions. Most classrooms have between twenty and forty students, and the basic combat unit in the U.S. Army, the platoon, consists of sixteen to forty-four soldiers. Within business and social movements, HUMAN POLYCULTURES of five to seven people are often woven together as coalitions or a series of departments within a larger organization. And for groups practicing consensus as THE RIGHT WAY TO DECIDE, the zone of cooperation represents the largest practical size, if every individual's opinion is to be effectively heard and integrated. Beyond thirty or so people, NURTURED NETWORKS are better off shifting to CONSENSUAL HIERAR-CHY, delegating authority over certain areas to group members whom they trust.

THE ZONE OF RECIPROCITY (50–150)

At the next level up, we arrive at Dunbar's best-known number: 150. As the neurologically derived limit to stable relationships, this is the upper bound of any network held together by favors and mutual expectation. The earliest farming villages were typically around this size, as were army companies from Roman times onward. Even in the social

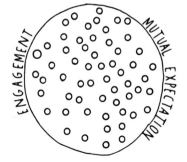

network era, the figure holds strong: recent studies have found that the median Facebook user has around two hundred friends, and even "power users" with many more friends engage with only 150 or so on a regular basis. For the same neurological reasons, 150 is also the maximum size of CONSENSUAL HIERAR-CHY, in which servant leaders know and engage with all the members of their organizations.

While the zone of reciprocity represents a key threshold in human communities, it should hardly be considered an upper limit to our groups. In fact, the need for larger groups is encoded in our very DNA: in addition to being the maximum size of mutual relationships, 150 is also the approximate minimum size of a healthy gene pool.

THE ZONE OF RECOGNITION (150–1,500)

Our neocortex may limit the size of *recip-rocal* groups to around 150, but that hasn't stopped us from creating groups based on other kinds of relationship. Even if we can't maintain stable social relationships with more than a couple hundred, most of us have the ability to recognize the faces of hundreds more. Within this fertile territory of 150 to 1,500 or so people, we've found our-selves bound together by shared cultural narra-tives: believing in the same gods, speaking the same language, dressing in the same style. These narratives replace the glue of personal relationships, allowing larger groups to maintain a solid identity despite the fact that not all members know each other.

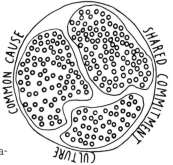

In the absence of the accountability engendered by personal relationships, these larger groups tend to require other forces to maintain group cohesion and stability. Often, these forces are subtle and largely voluntary—groups might stick together because of a commitment to a common cause, for instance, or because they share a set of traditions. In many cases, though, large groups remain united by becoming more formal and institutionalized, developing written rules and regulations that carry the threat of expulsion if violated.

Groups of this size are large enough to contain identifiable cliques, CAU-CUSES, and other forms of subcommunity. In an industrial economy, the zone of recognition is the minimum threshold for IMPORT SUBSTITUTION, in which SMALL BUSINESSES band together to meet each other's basic needs. And while groups of a few hundred are too large for consensus, they're often well suited to other forms of direct democracy, as evidenced by the city-states of ancient Greece or the town halls of eighteenth-century New England.

THE ZONE OF SUSPICION (1,500 AND GREATER)

What happens in groups that exceed the number of faces we can recognize? Those around us become strangers. Our disposition toward those strangers can vary, depending on our (and the strangers') age, gender, race, and many other factors. But one thing remains constant: without being able to recognize faces, we have no way of knowing how long they have been around, if they are friends or foes. Frequently, therefore, we default to stereotypes, judging strangers by their age, skin color, clothing, or whatever else we can discern.

Institutions that exceed the zone of recognition strain the limits of CONSENSUAL HIERARCHY, instead becoming formalized bureaucracies that most participants have little control over. Without a personal connection HUMANIZING THE OTHER, leaders are no longer accountable to the needs of everyone in the group, and norms become increasingly standardized to maintain efficiency. Like bees in a hive, participants give up a significant amount of their autonomy and creativity to participate.

Of course, groups that number in the thousands also have many advantages. It is only well-organized settlements of this size—cities—that can provide enough stimulation and specialization to power the churning engine of novelty that drives our society forward. From the great pyramids to space flight, humanity's most complex endeavors become possible only with the careful coordination of thousands. For the price of submission to the rules, well-organized groups of one thousand to ten thousand can have a meaningful impact on the local economy and culture at large.

Still, the agency issue remains. Christopher Alexander sums it up: "Individuals have no effective voice in any community of more than 5,000–10,000 persons."[10] Wherever possible, then, it's ideal to apply the principle of SUBSIDIARITY and split communities at this scale in to semiautonomous CAUCUSES.

APPLYING THE PATTERN

What sizes are the groups that you're a member of? The communities you're a part of? How many people do you interact with on a regular basis? Do the sizes match the zones above? Do you think your groups are THE RIGHT SIZE, or should they be adjusted? How would you redesign them in order to be more appropriately sized?

	ZONE OF INTIMACY	ZONE OF TRUST	ZONE OF COOPERATION	ZONE OF RECIPROCITY	ZONE OF RECOGNITION	ZONE OF SUSPICION
Approximate Size	3–10	10–25	25–50	50–150	150–1,500	1,500+
Types of Relationship	People you love	Close friends	Friends	Acquaintances	People you recognize	Strangers
Institutions	Households, HUMAN POLYCULTURES	Sports teams, juries, boards of directors	SMALL BUSINESSES, blocks, army platoons, classrooms	Parliaments, business polycultures	Neighborhoods	Armies, school districts
Emergent Properties				Healthy gene pool	IMPORT SUBSTITUTION	Linguistic dialect
Currency	THE GIFT	Gift and barter	Barter	HEIRLOOM CURRENCY	HEIRLOOM CURRENCY	HEIRLOOM CURRENCY or national currency
Physiological Limits	Number of people that we can unconditionally love		Size of extended family, limits of close relationships	Number of stable social relationships we can maintain	Number of faces we can recognize	
Governance Methods		Decisions by consensus, hierarchy, or informal methods	Maximum size for networks, consensus decision making	Direct democracy, councils, CONSENSUAL HIERARCHIES	Representative democracy, CONSENSUAL HIERARCHIES	Forced hierarchies, bureaucracies

7. SUBSIDIARITY

The most resilient and just systems are those that are managed at the smallest practical scale.

The canyons and mesas of the Southwest United States have long been admired for their austere beauty. Water may be scarce in the desert landscape, but it is also a powerful agent of change, sculpting the stark landforms that the Southwest has become known for. In places without much topsoil or vegetation to catch precipitation and allow it to sink into the land, water quickly gathers in rills, streams, and rivers, pouring through arroyos and canyons, gathering speed and force as it goes. In these ecosystems, even a mild thunderstorm can quickly cause a flash flood, scouring away already-fragile soil and further deepening the feedback loop.

As it turns out, power flows through societies just like water in the desert. Multinational corporations and autocratic governments have their own internal momentum, using their vast resources, psychological manipulation, and the implicit or explicit threat of violence to consolidate their strength. Of course, these rivers of power can be directed toward important and meaningful ends—providing a social safety net, for instance, or investing in new technologies. But all too often, vast hierarchies serve to erode the lifeblood of the rest of society, depriving individuals and smaller institutions of their self-determination.

In today's world, it's not hard to see how the formidable canyons of power are cutting deeper and deeper into the fragile landscape of community. For decades, thriving local economies have been systematically uprooted by cutthroat corporations. Our elected officials are expected to represent larger and larger numbers of people, while being glad-handed by special interests into policies that favor short-term profit over long-term prosperity.

Erosive forces like these are powerful and self-reinforcing—but they can be reversed. In the desert Southwest, indigenous peoples, thoughtful ranchers, and permaculture designers have all learned how to bring life back to the desert, by slowing, spreading, and sinking the flow of water, starting at the top of each watershed. By building simple but durable earthworks at the source of every trickle, water's fury can be subdued, giving it time to sink into the soil and nourish new plants. As these plants mature, they stabilize the soil, slow down the raindrops, and attract insects, birds, and rodents. The spiral of erosion is converted into a SPIRAL OF ABUNDANCE.

A similar approach applies to arresting the erosive consolidation of power. Placing authority "high in the watershed"—in the hands of many small, local communities—prevents power from becoming too large and fast to manage. Instead, our collective efforts can be put to use where it really matters: working together to ensure the health of the people and species around us.

HIERARCHY

power is concentrated at the highest level

SUBSIDIARITY

power is concentrated at the lowest level

Ironically, one of the best-known articulations of this philosophy comes from an institution infamous for its hierarchy: the Roman Catholic Church. During the late 1800s, as robber barons flexed their capitalist muscles and Marxist visions of a proletariat revolution were gaining adherents, church reformers began to articulate a "third way"—a doctrine they called *subsidiarity*.[11] In contrast to both laissez-faire capitalism and state-managed socialism, SUBSIDIARITY called for social challenges to be addressed *at the most local level practical,* with central authorities playing a supporting role rather than a primary one.

Throughout the following century, as the clash of free markets and state autocracy intensified, the quiet voice of SUBSIDIARITY seemed to get lost in the din. For all their differences, both sides of the Cold War effectively ceded control over society to large institutions; the question was whether business or government held the upper hand.

Today, however, local and decentralized movements appear to be staging a comeback. In fact, SUBSIDIARITY might be one of the few things that reformers on both ends of the political spectrum can agree on. With federal governments hamstrung by inefficiency and corruption, cities have begun to take the lead as problem-solving agents. And if there's anything that the Occupy movement, the Tea Party, the peer-to-peer revolution, and the Arab Spring have in common, it's a fierce desire to reassert local control in the midst of repressive, top-heavy institutions. Even our shifts in food and fashion are pointing toward a desire for a life that's more local and handcrafted.

What would a globally connected world that works according to SUBSIDIARITY look like? For starters, more government programs might be shifted toward states and municipalities, with a corresponding shift in tax allocation. Local communities could operate under an ethos of CITIZEN GOVERNANCE, with local citizens helping to determine budgets, land-use planning, and infrastructure investments. From an economic perspective, the relative strength of antimarkets would be drastically curtailed in favor of local business guilds, each composed of a network of REGENERATIVE ENTERPRISES. HEIRLOOM CURRENCIES would keep wealth circulating within the community and would allow us to properly value the domestic and caregiving activities that our current economy ignores. And institutions throughout society, from sports teams to elementary schools, would embrace the guidelines of CONSENSUAL HIERARCHIES and NURTURED NETWORKS. The specifics, of course, would vary wildly from place to place—indeed, that's the point of SUBSIDIARITY. But across all communities, SUBSIDIARITY would be implemented with the recognition that the solutions our society's needs must be crafted with love. And it's hard to love something distant.

FURTHER LEARNING

De Tocqueville, Alexis. *Democracy in America.* Translated by Gerald Bevan. New York, Penguin, 2013.

APPLYING THE PATTERN

Can you identify canyons of power or wealth flowing out of your community, such as large corporations, big government, and extractive industries? For each example you identify, list ways in which that flow could be slowed, spread, or sunk. Are there any people or organizations already slowing, spreading, or sinking power in your community?

8. DETHRONING THE ANTIMARKETS

Free markets of local small businesses are a remarkably efficient way to distribute prosperity throughout a community—yet our economy is dominated by an array of state-supported oligopolies that erode community wealth. The scales favoring these "antimarkets" are in need of rebalancing.

> *The fact that corporations were invented should alone empower us to reinvent them to our liking.*
>
> —Douglas Rushkoff

The twentieth century's grand political narrative was the ideological clash between big-government communism and free-market capitalism. Like any good narrative, it had its share of unexpected plot twists and compelling characters on both sides. But by the turn of the millennium, the story appeared to be reaching a triumphant conclusion. Reagan and Thatcher led a wave of tax cuts, free trade, and deregulation in the West, communism collapsed, and the increasingly globalized world began a sustained run of growth and prosperity. The capitalists appeared to have prevailed.

In the twenty-first century, communism has been all but discredited as a viable economic arrangement. But as the failures of trickle-down economics grow more apparent and as economic inequality rises to the top of the political agenda, a new and equally epic showdown is emerging around the future of capitalism. In this confrontation, a new set of questions is emerging: How much influence should corporations be able to wield over our governments and our economy? Is economic growth necessarily correlated with actual prosperity? And what system of exchange is best suited to prosperity in THE LONG GAME?

In his book *A Thousand Years of Nonlinear History,* ecological historian Manuel De Landa uses an unconventional dichotomy to show that these questions have been with us all along. Rather than lump capitalist economies into one category and communist economies into another, De Landa distinguishes between bottom-up and top-down economic activity.

According to De Landa, the free market—as taught in Economics 101—qualifies as bottom-up economic activity, and it works a lot like an ecosystem. These "true" markets, formed from small, family-owned businesses engaging in vigorous trade and competition, are innovative, self-balancing, and somewhat messy. They also have properties of what systems thinkers call *emergence*, exhibiting hive-mind behaviors that can't be explained by the actions of individual businesses alone. As many mainstream economists have been saying for decades, these bottom-up markets are indeed a remarkably effective way to meet a community's needs.

The thing is that most of today's markets are not bottom-up. After forty years of neoliberal policy, our economy is dominated by multinational corporations—organizations that no more resemble the SMALL BUSINESSES of true markets than a gleaming skyscraper resembles a bungalow. Our food is grown by agribusiness corporations and shipped to big-box retailers. Every morning, we drive away from our corporate-built homes in our corporate-made automobiles and go off to work so that we can pay our mortgage to corporate banks.

Increasingly, these corporations function as oligopolies, with a handful of organizations controlling most of an industry's market share. From a systems thinking perspective, these players are not bottom-up networks at all, but rather classic hierarchies—powerful, rigid, efficient, and slow to change. Whereas market forces price goods and services based on competition, oligopolies fix prices and generally thrive by using their outsized influence to bend government policy to their will.

MARKETS	ANTIMARKETS
Many SMALL BUSINESSES in the same industry	Industry dominated by a few large businesses (oligopoly)
Owned by community members	Owned by shareholders or the government
Sets prices through supply and demand	Sets prices through price fixing
Held accountable via community feedback	Held accountable via regulation
Designed to meet real needs of community	Designed to maximize profit
Restores non-financial capital	Erodes non-financial capital

De Landa calls these oligopolies *antimarkets* and traces their development all the way back to traders of luxury goods in medieval Europe. "As far back as the thirteenth century, and in all the centuries in between," he explains, "capitalism has always engaged in anti-competitive practices, manipulating demand and supply in a variety of ways. Whenever large fortunes were made in foreign trade, wholesale, finance or large scale industry and agriculture, market forces were not acting on their own, and in some cases not acting at all."[12]

Antimarkets, in other words, actively discourage competition, swatting down Adam Smith's invisible hand in favor of economic conditions that keep them firmly in control. Whereas markets are predicated around meeting the real needs of communities and use currency as a means of exchange, antimarkets see actual goods and services as a mere vehicle for growing their pile of currency. Today, antimarkets are so entrenched that our primary gauge of the economy's health—the stock market index—measures only the relative well-being of antimarkets. It's as if the rest of the economy doesn't even exist.

Given the feedback-loop dynamics employed by antimarkets, our current corporate-dominated arrangement may seem inevitable. But in fact, the history of capitalism has seen a continual battle between small-business markets and corporate oligopolies. After the railroad and steel corporations came to dominate the Gilded Age of the late nineteenth century, a populist backlash led to "trust-busting" reforms designed to keep antimarkets from getting too large. By the New Deal era, legislation such as the Robinson-Patman Act was passed specifically to hinder the formation of chain stores that would put small, independent stores out of business. This law—and many others like it passed after World War II—remained in place until deregulation began in the 1980s.

Today, the popular sentiment is once again shifting away from corporate oligopoly. Lobbyists and corporate executives may claim otherwise, but there's every reason to assume that true markets—small, locally owned companies engaging in competition and trade with one another—are ideally suited to lead the way toward a more equitable and environmentally aware economy. In order to create those conditions, of course, we'll need legislation at the local, state, and federal levels. Antitrust laws must be strengthened, corporate tax incentives must be pulled back, and antimarkets must be held more accountable to the workers and communities that they depend on. At the same time, we'll need to rebuild local economies in the many communities that chain stores have hollowed out. This may mean a renewed focus on entrepreneurship and business development, as well as the creation of novel structures like HEIRLOOM

CURRENCIES. Finally, we'll need to build a social movement of consumers committed to avoiding antimarkets through COORDINATED NONCOMPLIANCE, "buy local" campaigns, and myriad other tactics.

It's possible that one day, several generations from now, we'll conclude that antimarkets are simply too dangerous and ineffective to be allowed, and they'll join feudalism, communism, and slavery in history's compost pile. Or perhaps we'll discover that the tension between markets and antimarkets is actually a necessary and healthy one and that antimarkets just need to be kept in check. Either way, we can look forward to focusing our efforts on neutralizing antimarkets for a long time to come.

FURTHER LEARNING

De Landa, Manuel. *A Thousand Years of Nonlinear History*. Brooklyn, NY: Zone Books, 1997.

Piketty, Thomas. *Capital in the Twenty-First Century*. Translated by Arthur Goldhammer. Cambridge, MA: Harvard University Press, 2014.

APPLYING THE PATTERN

Which of your daily needs are met through markets and which are met through antimarkets? How has your livelihood engaged with markets and antimarkets? What has been your experience of the benefits and drawbacks of each? What are a few specific ways you can shift your behavior to support markets?

9. ZONES OF AUTONOMY

Before they can spread to society at large, beneficial ways of living may need to be incubated in a space that is socially, legally, or geographically separate.

Accroding to the rules of our current society, profit trumps justice and health, hands down. In the vast majority of situations, antimarket forces of commodification prevail over citizen-driven acts of COMMONING—not because they are inherently better, but because of the way the game is currently rigged. This tyranny of the present could significantly narrow any future solutions. Unless we provide protection from antimarket forces, our manifestations of a different world will either wither into obscurity or become co-opted by agents of profit.

Farmers and gardeners face a similar dilemma in their fields every year. If directly seeded into the soil, many of the crops they want to grow would fail to outcompete their aggressive but useless neighbors—what we usually call *weeds*. In order to give the crops a competitive advantage, humans start their plants under protected conditions: planting them indoors so they don't freeze, giving them rich soil free of other seeds, and watering them on a regular basis to reduce stress. Only once the seedlings are large enough to hold their own are they placed in the field.

Just like tender plants, social solutions often need incubation to thrive—places where the "outside" rules don't apply, where participants are free to practice alternative ones instead. This idea was memorably articulated by anarchist author Hakim Bey in his 1990 book *The Temporary Autonomous Zone*. In that book, Bey posits the temporary autonomous zone (or TAZ) as "an uprising which does not engage directly with the State, a guerilla operation which liberates an area (of land, of time, of imagination) and then dissolves itself to re-form elsewhere/elsewhen, before the State can crush it."[13]

Given Bey's orientation as an anarchist, his TAZ is necessarily political in nature. But the concept can be extended to many aspects of human life. For young adults fortunate enough to have the resources and test scores, for instance, college is an autonomous zone during their life cycle, an intermission between the sheltered environment of childhood and the responsibilities of adult life. During the four years of undergraduate education, it's common to try on various identities, groups of friends, and intellectual pursuits without the pressures of needing to adhere to a long-term path.

Certain kinds of annual celebrations serve as autonomous zones as well, providing a release valve for behavior that's off-limits the rest of the time. In India—where intoxication is shunned and sexuality is frequently repressed—the Holi festival gives young adults license to throw food coloring at one another and drunkenly grope each other's bodies. Back in the Americas, Mardi Gras and Carnaval have served similar roles for some segments of the population for generations, while more modern festivals like Burning Man do so for others.

Since Hakim Bey's initial articulation of the TAZ, it's become clear to him and to others that autonomous zones need not be temporary. From Amish settlements of the Midwest to contemporary ecovillages, centuries of utopian movements have sought to establish long-term autonomous zones. Many were quick to collapse under the weight of their own ambitions—as it turns out, starting a new society from scratch is remarkably challenging. But some have managed to persist for decades or even generations, influencing the culture at large along the way. Israel's Kibbutzim, for instance, have been home to tens of thousands of idealists for nearly a century. During that time, they have raised some of Israel's leading thinkers and invented drip irrigation, among many other contributions to society at large.

While many autonomous zones experiment with new ideas, others provide refuge for ancient ones. In a time when few corners of the globe are free from exploitative human impact, national parks and nature reserves function as autonomous zones where other species can thrive in (relative) isolation from *Homo sapiens*.

In theory, Native American reservations are permanent autonomous zones as well. But in reality, they have functioned more like prisons, separating indigenous cultures from their ancestral land, denying them access to resources, and hosting decades of misguided attempts at assimilation. A more holistic attitude has prevailed in the Peruvian Andes, where a permanent autonomous zone was established in 2000 through an innovative legal structure called an Indigenous Biocultural Heritage Area. Parque de la Papa, or "Potato Park," is a fifty-square-mile zone intended to preserve fragile ecosystems, crop diversity, and indigenous culture all at once. Quechua villages inside the park have the authority to govern themselves, and are entrusted with preserving the nine hundred varieties of potatoes they have domesticated over centuries of continuous agriculture.

Each of these examples points toward a set of common attributes of well-functioning autonomous zones. Whether temporary or permanent, whether managed by Quechua elders or idealist hippies, autonomous zones all require a few key conditions to thrive:

- Members of the autonomous zone must have a *shared vision* as well as a system of governance that reflects and effectively advances that vision.

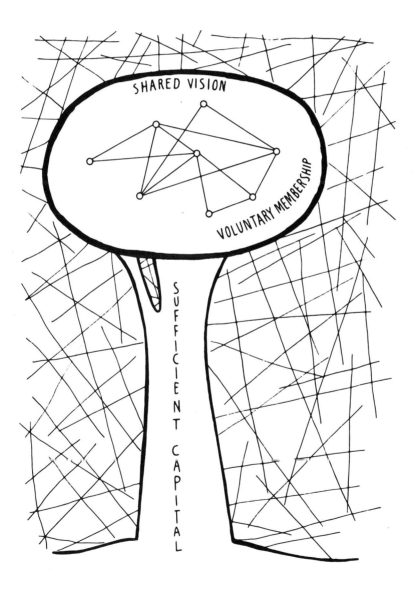

- Membership must be *voluntary*. The members must be there by their own volition—and fiercely committed to the ideals of the group.
- The autonomous zone must have sufficient *capital*—living, social, intellectual, financial, and otherwise—to sustain itself, as well as to defend itself from the inevitable attempts by antimarket forces to control it.

FURTHER LEARNING

Bey, Hakim. *T.A.Z.: The Temporary Autonomous Zone, Ontological Anarchy, Poetic Terrorism.* Brooklyn, NY: Autonomedia, 2003.
Christian, Diana Leafe. *Creating a Life Together.* Gabriola Island, BC: New Society, 2003.

APPLYING THE PATTERN

What autonomous zones have you experienced in your life? How have they influenced your values and ideas of what's possible? What elements of your PERSONAL VISION might benefit from incubation in an autonomous zone? What kind of isolations might they require—economic, geographic, social, and so forth? Are there any autonomous zones that are already incubating ideas or projects aligned with your values?

10. GOING HOME

Every person needs one community that he or she can call home, where he or she feels safe, supported, and connected.

Wisdom accumulates in a community the way fertility accumulates in soil.

—Wendell Berry

Historically, people throughout the globe were so bound to their territory that their identity was inseparable from the place they were from. But no longer. Today, our connection to place seems to be eroding as quickly as the topsoil of an overworked farm. Just as frequently tilled soil loses its biodiversity and long-term fertility, a community where residents come and go on a whim lacks the networks of mutual aid that are a precondition for INTERDEPENDENT COMMUNITIES.

In the last century or two, it's become common for us to hop from place to place like stones skipped on a pond, crossing state and even national boundaries with ease. Car and air travel have lowered the time and expense of such journeys, and modern technologies like air conditioning, watershed engineering, and artificial fertilizers have opened up whole new areas to human habitation on a massive scale. Meanwhile, mass media and globalized businesses have made moving less intimidating by lowering the cultural barriers to relocation and making it easy to remain connected to those we left.

The benefits of living in such a mobile society have been promoted for centuries—greater opportunity, freedom from persecution, better weather. But what are the tradeoffs? What have we lost by becoming urban nomads? According to a growing body of thinkers, a lot. Perhaps too much.

One unfortunate consequence of all this moving around is homogenization. When people stay put and are relatively isolated from others, they develop unique ways of speaking, thinking, creating, and working. That's how Latin differentiated itself into French, Spanish, and Italian, and how every Native American tribe in the Pacific Northwest ended up with a different set of iconography for their art. Geographers call this special something that makes a place unique its *genius loci*—literally, "the wisdom of place."

Today, *genius loci* is an endangered species. As we continue to globalize, we're losing unique musical traditions, languages, folk remedies, land management practices, and more at an alarming rate. The homogenizing influence of the capitalist economy has been like taking a blender to a salad, turning a rich array of cultural flavors, colors, and textures into a bland mush.

But our lack of connection to place is about more than mere cultural homogenization. The loss of *genius loci* also has profound consequences for our relationship with the natural world. An itinerant society isn't able to perceive the long-term rhythms of a place—how frequently it experiences extreme weather events, for example, or the intricate ways in which the various plants and animals in the ecosystem keep each other in check. Without this knowledge, we often cause great harm to ourselves and other species by trying to fit in—or, more commonly, by changing the ecosystem around us for our short-term convenience.

My own hometown, Denver, is chock full of examples of this ecological ignorance. When white folks first settled here 150 years ago, for instance, they chose to build their shacks in what appeared to be an ideal spot: a flat area at the confluence of the Platte River and Cherry Creek. But, as the Arapaho and Cheyenne tried to warn them many times, the high plains ecosystem was one adapted to seasonal flooding of those waterways. As the snowmelt came out of the mountains every spring, the Platte routinely breached its banks, sometimes reaching a mile wide. The settlers soon found this out, of course, but rather than relocate, they dug in their heels and embarked on an eighty-year effort to dam and channel the Platte to control its flow. It wasn't until the mid-twentieth century that the danger of regular flooding had passed—and only at great cost to ecosystems upstream and downstream, whose source of life had been irrevocably altered.

The bottom line? Until at least some of us rediscover what it means to become native to a place, we'll continue to reproduce "cultures of nowhere" wherever we go, and our ignorance will continue to wreak havoc on the people and species around us.

Rebuilding *genius loci*—like any form of restoring capital—is a long, long process. These days, it's rare for people to live in the same place for twenty years, let alone twenty generations. Nearly all of us in the Americas are relative newcomers, having arrived in the last few centuries either by force or drawn by the promise of a better life. But that shouldn't keep us from starting the process of building our own our *genius loci*. Every great journey starts with the first step, and by asking the right questions, we can make great strides in adapting ourselves to the place in which we reside. So pick a place that feels like home and stay there. Whether it's the place where you grew up, a place where your ancestors lived, or a new place entirely, dedicate yourself to becoming rooted in community there. Learn its history—geological, indigenous, and modern. Pay attention to the people who have a multigenerational history in the same place. Resist the urge to flee when the going gets tough or to wander around till you find the perfect community. Every community, after all, will have its challenges and opportunities—and every community has the opportunity to be made more whole.

FURTHER LEARNING

Sanders, Scott Russell. *Staying Put: Making a Home in a Restless World*. Boston: Beacon Press, 1993.

APPLYING THE PATTERN

Is there a place you call home? How long have you lived in your current location? Have you put down roots in the communities there? If not, what's stopping you? If so, have you found sources of *genius loci*? What knowledge or information do you already know about the place where you live and the communities in which you live? What have you learned about THE LONG GAME of your community— geological, indigenous, modern histories? What more would you like to learn?

11. THE EDGE OF CHANGE

The most valuable leverage points for change are usually found where our vision of the future overlaps with what's currently considered acceptable.

In ecology, the edges between two ecosystems are called *ecotones,* and they are dynamic places of chemical, material, and genetic exchange. The line of contact where waves lap up on a beach or a thicket of shrubs breaks into an open meadow functions like a crowded bazaar: species from both sides mingle with species that only exist on the line, and all of them form new alliances, intermingle, and swap everything from nutrients to parasites.

Human society is chock full of these ecotones, where the mingling of groups is at the leading edge of change. Think of frontier trading posts between two civilizations, urban neighborhoods on the cusp of gentrification, or the linguistic mash-ups of creole and pidgin languages.

As a SACRED ACTIVIST, one of the most important edges to pay attention to is the line between one's PERSONAL VISION and what's currently practical—the edge between the ideal and the possible. Stray too far ahead of the rest of your community, and you'll find yourself standing lonely in a field, isolated by your idealism. Settle for the easy way out, on the other hand, and you may end up lost in the jungle of misguided solutions, perpetuating injustice and exploitation under the pretense of positive change. But the sweet spot where the ideal and possible intersect is a powerful leverage point for change.

In political science, the range of ideas currently acceptable in public discourse is called the *Overton window,* after a twentieth-century Michigan think-tank leader named Joseph Overton. According to Overton's theory, it doesn't matter how much charisma you possess or how many lobbyists you have—if your idea falls outside the Overton window, it's dead on arrival. If you're an advocate of gun control, for example, you may believe in your heart that repealing open-carry laws is an important and necessary measure but also know that it falls outside the Overton window of what the legislature and voting public will accept. On the other hand, strengthening background checks is just within the Overton window, giving it a chance to succeed. Eventually, you may be able to open the Overton window enough to allow a discussion of open-carry laws—just not yet.

Overton windows are also a helpful tool for thinking about change at much smaller scales. Within any group, large or small, there is a set of ideas and behavior currently considered acceptable—which may or may not be in 100 percent agreement with your personal values. In HUMAN POLYCULTURES, this is represented by the dynamic tension between elders and radicals. In a REGENERATIVE ENTERPRISE, it is found in the negotiation between generating income and achieving the mission. In all cases, the key to maximum impact lies

THE EDGE OF CHANGE

IDEAL   POSSIBLE

personal vision: the range of ideas
the world you + acceptable within
want to create   your community

in knowing the Overton window for a given situation and working within it to enact your vision.

APPLYING THE PATTERN

Which elements of your PERSONAL VISION are within the Overton window of society as a whole? Of the community where you live? Of the organizations in which you work? Which elements are outside the Overton window? Which are on the edge? How might you engage your community in a productive way to move THE EDGE OF CHANGE?

12. MULTITUDES OF KNOWING

Scientific inquiry is a powerful framework for understanding our world. But it's only one of several such frameworks, all of which must be engaged and honored.

Sometimes a useful delusion is better than a useless truth.

—Colson Whitehead, *The Underground Railroad*

What does it mean to really know something? Do we need to experience something firsthand to label it as truth? And what are we to believe when our own observations contradict what the experts are telling us?

These are the big questions that philosophers sort into the realm of *epistemology:* the theory of knowledge. Like most realms of human experience, our systems of knowing have gone through many stages, each one closely tracking changes in our relationship with the world around us. For most of human history, our understanding of the world was shaped by information passed down orally from generation to generation. Knowledge was often encoded in myth and legend, or anthropomorphized with nature spirits. With the written word, knowledge was able to flow through generations in a more precise form, and early texts like the Code of Hammurabi and the Bible purported to contain absolute truth that was passed from the gods to humanity. Much later, with the Enlightenment and the advent of the scientific method, epistemology went through another phase change. Whereas religious epistemology called for placing faith in gods, prophets, and priests, the scientific approach posited a knowledge based on rigorous experimentation and individual verification. Truth was revealed through hypothesis and peer review.

In today's world, neither oral animism nor text-based religious faith are anywhere close to extinction. But in the West, it's the scientific way of knowing that has provided the dominant epistemological framework for the past couple hundred years. In general, our society accepts something is true only if scientists claim to have proven it. And the more sophisticated our scientific endeavors become, the theory goes, the more complete our understanding of the world will be.

What few of us dare acknowledge is that science is just as arbitrary and incomplete an epistemology as the modes that came before it. For one thing, the theoretical limits of scientific knowledge have been clear for nearly a century. In 1931, Austrian logician Kurt Gödel published a mind-bending paper logically proving that any form of logic we use to describe the world is inherently incomplete. And around the same time, Einstein's theory of relativity and the emerging field of quantum mechanics demonstrated that reality is necessarily subjective and impossible to entirely predict.

In addition to these internal paradoxes, cracks in the authority of scientific knowledge have begun to form from outside pressures. The incentive to produce original research has distracted scientists from verifying the results of their peers, and in fields as diverse as psychology and medicine, scientists are uncovering a "replicability crisis," with as many as half of all experiments producing different results when repeated.[14] What's more, the research questions themselves are often defined by those that provide the funding—increasingly, antimarket actors like oil or pharmaceutical corporations.

As these cracks become more and more pronounced, the temple of scientific authority has come under attack. Suspicious of scientific consensus, skeptics from all sides are now emboldened to draw their own conclusions about subjects as diverse as the 9/11 attacks, climate change, and even the shape of the earth. Wildly divergent worldviews now routinely coexist in our public discourse, egged on by the filter bubbles of social media, the deliberate obfuscations by corporations and government, and the clever framing of thought leaders.

In short, we've found ourselves in an epistemological crisis. The modern dominance of scientific truth is splintering into a postmodern mess of contingent truth, and the line between opinion and fact is becoming harder to parse. Like ice sheets shearing off into a turbulent sea, the structures of meaning upon which our shared story rests are cleaving apart, leaving us on our own separate, melting islands of reality.

But this great undoing of meaning doesn't have to be all that dire. In fact, it presents many unique opportunities—as long as we can internalize a few key lessons. First, we need to recognize that confining scientific inquiry to elites with advanced degrees is dangerous to a healthy society. Today, it's assumed that having a doctorate and university position are necessary prerequisites for practicing science. Yet there's no reason that someone with a high school education can't form a hypothesis, set up rigorous experiments, and learn from the results. Five hundred years ago, the Protestant Reformation democratized Christians' relationship with the divine by translating the Bible into vernacular languages and taking power back from the elite priesthood. We need a similar paradigm shift today—one that encourages all citizens to embrace scientific thinking as part and parcel of their everyday problem-solving skill set. The results might not push the boundaries of human knowledge, but that's not the point. Instead, embracing citizen science would empower our communities to refine their knowledge of what works in a specific place and under a specific set of conditions.

Second, we need to agree that science doesn't have a monopoly on truth. Within certain bounds, scientific knowledge is a very powerful tool. But ultimately, it's just that: a tool. Like every tool, it has limits to how it can be used, and it works best in combination with other tools that complement it. By documenting oral wisdom gleaned from a people that has lived in an ecosystem for millennia, for instance, the burgeoning field of traditional ecological knowledge is uncovering valuable knowledge in many domains that modern science is only beginning to investigate. And in many contexts, the embodied knowledge of experienced practitioners should be considered at least as valid as clinical evidence.

What Gödel and Einstein proved—and what poets, priests, and shamans have been saying all along—is that there are forms of truth that science is simply ill equipped to address. Science's reductionist lens, breaking each question into a series of discrete parts, is well-equipped to tell us the "what" and "where" of the world around us, but it has precious few answers for the "why." The slim volumes of Lao Tzu or Rumi offer insights into human nature every bit as valuable and profound as the accumulated data from thousands of peer-reviewed psychological studies. More can be learned about a landscape from an hour of conversation with an indigenous elder than from years of field research. Science can open a fire hose of information, but it leaves us with not a drop of wisdom. We need both to survive.

There are MULTITUDES OF KNOWING. Each one, in its own way, gives an important perspective on "truth." Each one has its own personality, its own strengths and weaknesses. The animist epistemology of our distant ancestors, the religious epistemology of the great religions, the scientific epistemology of industrial society—all offer valuable gifts that complement the others in ways we've yet to fully understand. As we seek to pick up the pieces from our present moment's epistemic fracturing, we are called to focus on connections rather than divisions, reweaving the tapestry of meaning into something more diverse—and therefore stronger—than any one way of knowing on its own.

APPLYING THE PATTERN

Can you remember a time when you've felt skeptical of something that was presented as fact? What about a time when you've been convinced of something that proved to be wrong? Which sources of information and wisdom do you tend to place the most stock in? Which do you place the least in? Which "ways of knowing" are most valuable in the communities where you live and work? What is one way you can expose yourself to ways of knowing you're not used to?

13. FEAR BURNS BRIGHT, HOPE BURNS LONG

Fear is a powerful catalyst to get us moving—but hope for a better future will keep us motivated much longer.

Hope has two beautiful daughters; their names are Anger and Courage. Anger at the way things are, and Courage to see that they do not remain as they are.

—Saint Augustine

The world at the beginning of the twenty-first century is a terrifying place. There are any number of situations that threaten to bring down society—catastrophic climate change, antibiotic-resistant bacteria, nuclear contamination, and peak oil, to name but a few. And even without considering these macro issues, most of us are facing everyday challenges to our personal sanity like an ever-worsening job market or the grinding microaggressions of racism and sexism. It's no wonder that many of the most important events of our young century have fear at their root. Since 9/11, fears of terrorism have created an environment of ubiquitous government surveillance at home and endless turmoil in the Middle East. The threat of economic collapse in 2008 led many Americans to brush up on their homesteading skills. And working-class whites' fears of being left behind in a rapidly changing America fueled Donald Trump's dramatic rise to the presidency in 2016.

These days, it's clearer than ever that fear is a powerful motivator for change. But as a day-to-day strategy, basing our decisions on fear is a recipe for depression and exhaustion. In fact, our current understanding of neurology is confirming just how irrational a fear-based mentality can be. Fear is one of the most primal emotions; it originates in our brain stem, the ancient neural structure that we share with birds and lizards. Whether provoked by a jungle predator or political rhetoric, fear sets off a series of physiological responses in our body collectively referred to as the *fight-or-flight response*. Our amygdala and hypothalamus react to the perceived threat by releasing adrenaline and cortisol. Our heart rate rises, our pupils dilate, and our digestion slows.

From an evolutionary perspective, these responses make sense; they make us hyperaware of an immediate threat and give us a momentary burst of energy to either confront that threat or escape it. Unfortunately, that mental state just doesn't cut it for the kind of innovative thinking we need to avoid twenty-first-century challenges. Avoiding a predator in the wild requires a burst of adrenaline and a keen focus on the present moment. But tackling issues like affordable housing or climate change requires observation, dialogue, foresight, reflection, and creativity—thought patterns that are all suppressed in the midst of a fight-or-flight response.

Today's problems, in other words, require a different catalyst entirely, one that originates not in our lizard brains, but in the neural pathways responsible for empathy and innovation. More often than not, that catalyst comes in the form of hope. Not the passive hope of wishing something will be okay, but an active hope, driven by a clear vision of a better world.

All of which isn't to say there's no place for fear in our lives. It remains a powerful catalyst to action, and in a genuine crisis, the fight-or-flight response can be a lifesaver. But in order to sustain action, anxiety about the negative must be complemented or supplanted by aspiration for the positive. Fear and hope, then, share a similar symbiosis that will be familiar to anybody who's started a campfire. Starting the fire requires something highly flammable—leaves, newspaper, and twigs. But paper and kindling won't sustain a fire. As any frustrated camper knows, the fire quickly runs out of stuff to burn and peters out. To keep a fire going, you need dense fuel like logs. Only with the combination of kindling and denser fuel can a fire be created and sustained.

In the midst of trying circumstances, nurturing hope can be like starting a fire in the rain. But once a vision for a different world catches on, it can be nearly impossible to extinguish.

FURTHER LEARNING

Macy, Joanna, and Molly Young Brown. *Coming Back to Life: Practices to Recon-nect Our Lives, Our World*. Gabriola Island, BC: New Society, 1998.

APPLYING THE PATTERN

What scares you about the world today—or about your community or yourself? When thinking about what scares you, what do you notice happening in your mind or body? How can you be intentional about defusing that response in your-self? And what gives you hope? When feeling hope, what happens in your mind and your body? In what situations is fear-based action the appropriate response and in which situations is hope or inspiration called for? When working with others, how could you shift the discourse from what we don't want to happen to what we do want to happen?

14. DESIGN TOOL: CREATIVE PROCESS

The art of healing communities is a creative act. As such, it follows the familiar rhythms of every creative discipline: setting goals, observing context, developing designs, putting designs into action, and learning from the results.

Design may have its greatest impact when it is taken out of the hands of designers and put into the hands of everyone.

—Tim Brown, CEO of IDEO

A musician composing a song to express frustration, awe, or heartbreak. An entrepreneur looking to earn a steady income while making the world a better place. An architect drafting blueprints for a house that looks beautiful, meets zoning and code regulations, and doesn't cost an arm and a leg to build. An organizer building trust among members of a community. An overwhelmed college graduate trying to find a meaningful career and work-life balance.

Each one of these people is engaged in an activity different from the others, requiring completely separate tools and skills. And yet all of them are engaged in creative acts. Each of these acts requires imagination to solve a challenge under a given set of real-world constraints. And each one can be seen as a design challenge. Thinking about it this way gives us a certain amount of systematic rigor while acknowledging the messy reality of the complex, unpredictable forces swirling around us.

In the mid-1960s, pioneering ecological designer Lawrence Halprin and his equally visionary choreographer wife, Anna, began to compare the similarities and differences in THE CREATIVE PROCESSes of their respective disciplines, and they realized that each one had a lot to learn from the other. Lawrence's process of tailoring a design to the ecosystem around it inspired Anna to choreograph works meant for specific outdoor public places, while the improvisatory nature of Anna's dance pieces led Lawrence to embrace a more open-ended dialogue between landscape designer and client. Eventually, the two solidified their insights into a system they called the RSVP cycles, which was published in book form in 1967.

The RSVP Cycles is long out of print, and its hippie-era philosophizing seems a little indulgent with half a century of hindsight. Yet the Halprins' fundamental insights about the nature of THE CREATIVE PROCESS continue to resonate. One of the book's key lessons is one of releasing control. Successful designs are rarely about the designer's grand vision; they are more the product of a process of harmonizing the needs of the various entities involved. In the case of a landscape design, the designer must find the sweet spot between the client's goals, the project budget, and ecological realities like climate, soil, and water availability. The analogous challenge in starting a REGENERATIVE ENTERPRISE is to use the time, money, and skills available to generate revenue while making an impact in restoring environmental or social health. In each case, the designer is more of a facilitator than a dictator, and the design process is one of dialogue with each of these forces.

Regardless of the design challenge, the unfolding of that dialogue proceeds in a somewhat predictable pattern. Across nearly every creative discipline, in fact, successful practitioners share a remarkable concordance about the steps to success and the order in which those steps need to take place. Depending on the discipline, one or more steps might be emphasized or minimized, and two steps might be combined into one. Nevertheless, enough of a coherent process has emerged that it's worth diving into step by step.

1. GOALS

What am I trying to accomplish?

As a first step, the designer develops a clear and articulate set of goals for the problem at hand. What exactly are you trying to achieve? How much time can you afford to take? How much money can you afford to spend? Who else do you want to involve?

· GOALS ·
what am I trying
to accomplish?

· OBSERVATION ·
what's going on?

· ANALYSIS ·
what does it
all mean?

· CONCEPT ·
what's the
big idea?

· DESIGN ·
how does the big idea
play out in more detail?

· IMPLEMENTATION ·
how will the design
become a reality?

· FEEDBACK ·
did it work as intended?

Spelling these things out might seem obvious at first. It's often the case, however, that the process of writing out our goals uncovers subtle motivations or priorities that become important later in the process. And if multiple people are involved, this step is also critical in getting everyone on the same page about what they're trying to achieve.

2. OBSERVATION

What's going on?

With the goals in place, the designer embarks on a process of long, careful observation of the situation and its context. Observation can be a left-brained process of rigorous, objective research or a right-brained process of engagement, participation, and Zen-like contemplation. Generally the designer employs some combination of these processes to get as well rounded a perspective as possible.

For the landscape designer, the observation process mean taking soil samples, inventorying existing species, researching applicable zoning laws, and watching the site change through the seasons. For the organizer, it might entail going to community meetings, interviewing leaders, reading about the community's history, and conducting surveys or workshops to gauge residents' desires. And for the entrepreneur, observation means conducting market research, analyzing the competitors, and looking for similar businesses in other cities. Even famous musicians have used observation of their fans as part of their songwriting process—in an interview with Dick Clark, soul singer Sam Cooke once remarked, "if you observe what's going on and try to figure out how people are thinking, I think you can always write something that people will understand."[15]

Regardless of the discipline, the point of this stage is to get a deep understanding of all the different factors that might influence the ultimate design.

3. ANALYSIS

What does it all mean?

While observation is about collecting data, analysis is about looking for a signal in the noise. Moving into analysis, the designer shifts roles from investigator to storyteller, synthesizing an abundance of information into a coherent narrative. Like a poet trimming every extraneous word to arrive at the essence of her message, the designer condenses all the information into a set of simpler and simpler patterns, looking for the most elegant pattern to explain what's going on.

Someone developing a design for his or her own PERSONAL VISION might use the analysis phase to make lists of what's working well in his or her life and what patterns could use some tweaking. An architect or landscape designer might end up with a handful of themes that a successful design must resolve around—stormwater drainage, gathering space, and privacy, for example. And for the designer of a social services program, analysis may entail distilling a series of "ingredients for success" from national best practices.

4. CONCEPT

What's the big idea?

The first half of THE CREATIVE PROCESS is an inhalation. During the slow, steady processes of observation and analysis, the designer takes in necessary and relevant information, sorting and shaping it into greater and greater fragments of meaning. The designer has immersed herself in the context of the design challenge, memorizing its contours, history, faces, and themes as if they were her own. The ground has been prepared for creation. The designer is ready to begin an exhalation: the process of creation.

How does design begin? At the most general level possible. As the permaculture principle counsels, good design proceeds from patterns to details, starting with a simple concept: a theme that encapsulates the overall solution to the problem. A concept is small enough to fit into one sentence, and ideally, it addresses most or all of the themes identified in the analysis phase.

"A passive-solar home built out of tires that harvests and recycles all its own water." "A social movement that publicizes and protests everyday examples of police brutality against people of color." "F, E minor, A 7th, D minor 7th." Each one of these examples is a revolutionary design—Earthships, the Black Lives Matter movement, and the Beatles' "Yesterday"—encapsulated in concept form. In each case, the concept alone is hardly enough for the design to succeed. But it forms the nucleus of inspiration, around which all the other aspects of the design can take hold.

Brilliant design concepts like these may seem obvious and easy in hindsight, but they rarely emerge without a struggle. Where do these concepts come from?

How does inspiration strike? More often than not, as it turns out, we come upon concepts during moments of rest. Research has shown that the best ideas of creative minds are likely to appear when the designer steps back from the project for a while and allows his mental chatter to subside. Pioneering neuroscientist Nancy Andreasen has spent years interviewing and studying the brains of well-regarded innovators in the arts and sciences and has found a clear commonality in their process of insight. In a 2014 *Atlantic* article, Andreasen explains, "almost all of my subjects confirmed that when eureka moments occur, they tend to be precipitated by long periods of preparation and incubation, and to strike when the mind is relaxed.... Many subjects mentioned lighting on ideas while showering, driving, or exercising. One described a more unusual regimen involving an afternoon nap."[16]

5. DESIGN

How does the big idea play out in more detail?

With the concept in hand, the designer is finally ready to engage in the process of detailed design, exploring the various implications and permutations of the concept and determining which ones are ideal for the context. Detailed design is what brings a business idea from a basic budget to a financial model sophisticated enough to secure a loan. It's what brings a building from an array of stacked forms into a set of construction drawings that account for every brick and wire. And it's what brings a social movement from a sweeping five-year strategy to week-by-week tactics. As legendary twentieth-century designer Charles Eames once put it, "The details are not the details. They make the design."

Be that as it may, detailed design is messy. A truly thorough design process explores all the potential options and eliminates those that are less than ideal. This phase necessarily entails many false starts, failed ideas, and moments of chaos. Along with observation, it's often the most time-consuming part of the design process, and it takes patience and skill to navigate successfully.

Incidentally, it's also the phase that many novice designers want to skip to right away. Because we're used to thinking in terms of discrete components, we're often tempted to start a design with the details and work backward from there. But tactics without strategy are dangerously untethered. Designing from details to patterns can lead to tunnel vision, with the designer fixated on a specific technique or element that may not actually be best suited to the context.

6. IMPLEMENTATION

How will the design become a reality?

THE CREATIVE PROCESS doesn't end with a finished design. In fact, it's only just beginning. With a design in hand, the next step is to bring it into the real world. Taking the leap from design to reality can be scary. The first five steps require skills that are largely intellectual, but implementation demands an orchestration of mind, heart, and muscle, often requiring long hours of practice and a sophisticated awareness of timing and craftsmanship.

This different set of skills and risks is why the roles of design and implementation are often separated in professional work. But if the designer separates himself too much from implementation, he poses the risk of creating designs that are unrealistic or fanciful. Stuck in his own head, he can lose touch with physical reality of design—the properties and constraints of materials, the messy politics of institutions, the fickle demands of customers. In architecture and landscape design, the growing trend of design-build firms reflects this understanding that the best designs often come from a single person being able to see a design through to completion.

Connection between the designer and implementer also allows for more fluidity between steps in the process. In *The RSVP Cycles,* Anna and Lawrence Halprin labeled the implementation stage the *performance* of a design and noted that performances can be "open" or "closed" to improvisation on the part of the performer. Closed projects must be implemented exactly as designed, or else the whole thing could fail. None of us would want to drive over a bridge that the contractors improvised, and most Western classical composers would throw a fit if the musicians playing their work went off the score. In open designs, meanwhile, implementation can be an act of co-creation. A plan for a garden might be tweaked in the field as the physicality of the landscape suggests other options. Open-source business models invite customers to participate in suggesting improvements to the product. And in jazz and Indian classical music, the soloist's improvisations are considered the primary measure of a song's greatness.

7. FEEDBACK

Did it work as intended?

Whether closed or open, the implementation of a design eventually winds down, and the plans are made manifest in reality. This brings the designer to a final and oft-overlooked step: learning from the process. Did the analysis provide an accurate summary of the design challenge? Did the vision and specific details of the design successfully solve that challenge? What were the unforeseen factors that required the original vision to be adjusted?

Many creative processes are iterative, with many rounds of design and implementation for the same landscape, business, or campaign. By taking stock of the inevitable missteps as well as the successes after each completed project, the designer can learn valuable lessons that can be applied to the next round. Feedback, in other words, is how designers learn. It's how they ascend the steps of mastery from good to great. And while many designers accept feedback casually and sporadically, a more structured process allows that learning to sink in deeper.

There are many ways to gain feedback. The designer can seek out a mentor to offer feedback based on his or her deeper set of experiences. He or she can debrief with clients, partners, and implementers to understand the process from their perspective. And he or she can seek more quantitative feedback, MEASURING SUCCESS through data.

FURTHER LEARNING

Aranya. *Permaculture Design: A Step-By-Step Guide.* East Meon, England: Permanent, 2012.

Halprin, Lawrence. *The RSVP Cycles: Creative Processes in the Human Environment.* New York: George Braziller, 1970.

15. DESIGN TOOL: SECTOR AND ZONE ANALYSES

Understanding concepts of scale and relative location are critical in designing successful social systems. Sector and zone analyses allow us to easily visualize these relationships, allowing us to make better-informed decisions.

A t its most elemental, the role of the designer is to pick the *right elements* and place them in the *right relationship* with one another. The florist chooses which flowers to put in a bouquet and how to arrange them. The architect conceptualizes a series of spaces and puts them together in a fashion that suits the needs of the building's users. The entrepreneur identifies a solution for a given population and then orchestrates the right arrangement of start-up funding, quality products, staff, marketing messages, and other elements necessary for the business to succeed.

In each case, the designer can be seen as a "systems curator" of sorts, arranging every element to support the others and setting up the system as a whole to thrive. This is simple enough if there are just a handful of elements, but as their number increases, the potential relationships between them (and the resulting complexity of the system) grows exponentially. As a result, systems designers have developed a number of tools for analyzing and synthesizing this information. Two of the most useful come from permaculture design and are paired together as SECTOR AND ZONE ANALYSES.

Sector analysis is concerned with the external energies and forces moving through a system. Our planet is buffeted by electromagnetic radiation, for instance, as well as the gravitational pull of the sun and other planets. Any particular landscape must negotiate the comings and goings of wind, precipitation, sunshine, and fire. And human groups of every size are situated within economic, political, and social trends that are largely beyond their control. Successful systems choose the right elements and relationships that allow them to captured beneficial energies and use them productively, while blocking other energies that might potentially be harmful.

By graphically charting these external energies and forces, sector analysis gives the designer a quick way of understanding their interactions and impact. In the context of permaculture landscape design, this means plotting natural forces like the path of the sun and prevailing winds, as well as human ones like foot traffic and areas of desired privacy.

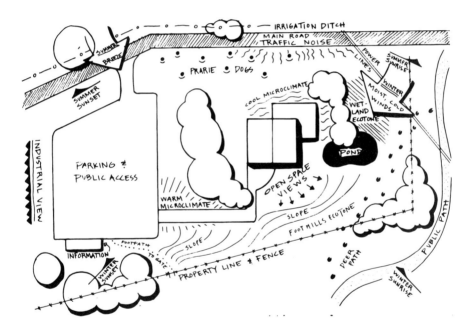

If sector analysis deals with external forces and elements, zone analysis is primarily concerned with internal ones—in particular, how those forces are arranged in relationship to the individual. Zone analysis starts with a simple premise: relationships that require more work and deliver a bigger yield should be placed closer to us, while ones that don't need as much of our involvement should be farther away. While it might sound obvious in theory, our lived experiences are full of counterexamples to this common-sense advice—a home at the other end of town from our workplace, or compost bins pushed to the far corner of our yards.

With zone analysis, the designer can address these issues at the beginning of THE CREATIVE PROCESS, prioritizing each element on a scale from 1 to 5, based on how frequently the user interacts with it. In a garden design, for example, we might assign the leafy greens that we harvest daily to zone 1, the tool shed that we access weekly to zone 2, and a patch of brambles to zone 4. Through zone analysis, the designer maximizes efficiency for the user by intelligently placing elements with an attention to maintenance and yield.

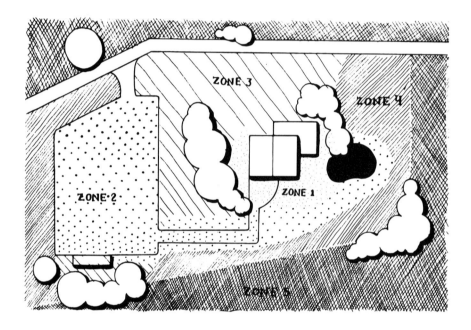

SECTOR AND ZONE ANALYSES emerged from permaculture landscape design and, as such, are traditionally employed in the design of physical spaces. But both tools are also a powerful ways of visualizing and understanding the complex forces at play in groups. The success of a social design for a SMALL BUSINESS or a campaign of NONVIOLENT STRUGGLE is always affected by external forces: news cycles, economic patterns, cultural attitudes and beliefs, and other institutions, to name a few. Sector analysis provides a way of identifying and categorizing these external forces, helping the designers understand how to either capture or deflect them to ensure success. Meanwhile, zone analysis helps us visualize the relevant RELATIONSHIP ZONES for an individual or organization, sorting out which connections are most important and therefore worth spending the most time nurturing.

In both cases, the design tools help us manage complexity, allowing us to more clearly discern things like gaps in support, stakeholders competing for the same resources, or a mismatch between a group's priorities and its skills. Whereas physical designs tend to have geographically grounded zone and sector analyses, placed over maps of the site, social design apply the same tools in a more abstract way—a prospect that can be both liberating and daunting. Here are a couple of examples of using ZONE AND SECTOR ANALYSIS in social systems design.

Zone 1 at the GrowHaus comprises our immediate neighbors in the community: the people for whom the organization was founded and the people whose voices we're most keen on empowering. Zone 2 represents other marginalized populations in the Denver area, and zone 3 is the group of well-intentioned Denverites that had the resources to pay full price for our services.

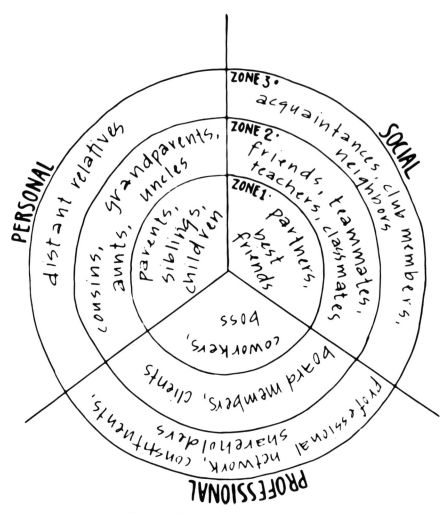

In this analysis for an individual—the concentric circles correspond to RELATIONSHIP ZONES, *while each sector represents a different area of the person's life.*

FURTHER LEARNING

Macnamara, Looby. *People and Permaculture: Caring and Designing for Ourselves, Each Other, and the Planet.* East Meon, England: Permanent, 2012.

16. DESIGN TOOL: NETWORK ANALYSIS

Social permaculture is ultimately an exercise in system design. Through network analysis, we can map the various elements of our social systems and see how they are connected.

Any form of design that involves living creatures—from restoring a riverbank to starting a reading group—is ultimately about system optimization. Systems come in all shapes and forms, but they all share an underlying architecture of nodes and links, elements and connections. Every system, in other words, is a network. And while most approaches to business and design are focused on the elements themselves, whole systems design recognizes that the relationships *between* those elements are of equal or greater importance to the network.

Over the last several decades, the evolving field of NETWORK ANALYSIS has led to any number of important insights about our world. Thanks to systems thinking, we can more precisely predict the diffusion of new ideas and technologies, the spread of infectious disease, and the way language evolves in a community.

Permaculture landscape designers routinely visualize these networks of nodes and links as way of optimizing relationships between trees, animals, humans, and structures like greenhouses and composting toilets. Similarly, designers of social systems can use NETWORK ANALYSIS to make better decisions about how groups work. NETWORK ANALYSIS can be used to discover key points of vulnerability in an organization, critical partnerships that need to be maintained, centers of power in a community, and interactions between horizontal and hierarchical decision-making structures.

NETWORK ANALYSIS starts by listing the key elements in a system—like people in a social circle, departments in an organization, or institutions in a community. With the list of elements in hand, the next step is creating a way for each element to be moved around and connected with the others. You could write each element out on a whiteboard, cut them out of paper, or use specialized mind-mapping software. Next, you can begin to draw relationships between the elements. Start with the obvious and important relationships and work down from there. Rearrange the elements as you go to make the diagram easier to read. And if the specific nature of the relationship is important, it can be helpful to label the connections.

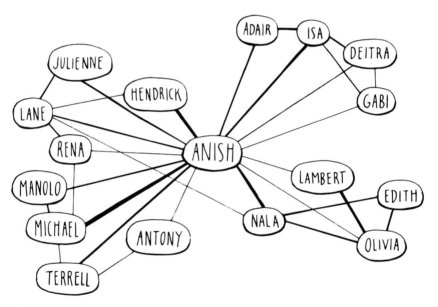

In this network diagram, Anish has mapped his sixteen closest friends and their connections to one another, with the thickness of the line representing the closeness of each relationship. The diagram reveals three distinct clusters of friends, with the cluster on the bottom right exhibiting a particular degree of closeness. Besides Anish, Nala and Michael emerge as particularly central nodes in the network.

Now that you've made a map of the network, you can start to look for key patterns and relationships. There are a few questions that might provide insight:

- *How dense is the network?* In network science, density is formally expressed as the ratio of actual links to the number of theoretically possible links.

Whether or not you actually calculate this ratio, take a look at how interconnected the network is. In general, more links leads to more stability and resilience. The more the people in a group all interact with one another, for example, the tighter the group is as a whole. On the other hand, too many connections in a larger network can put stress on our natural RELATIONSHIP ZONES, overwhelming our ability to process and maintain all those relationships.

- *How fragmented is the network?* The term *percolation* is used in NETWORK ANALYSIS to describe the fragmentation of a system into less-connected clusters. Most healthy communities percolate to a certain extent; institutions have chapters or departments to make work more efficient, while social circles sort themselves into cliques or CAUCUSES to give individuals a tighter sense of identity. But if the group becomes too fragmented, it can lose its coherence and momentum, eventually splintering apart.

- *What are the central elements?* Generally, after mapping a network, at least one element will emerge as a clear hub, with a disproportionate amount of other elements connected to it. In ecosystems, the species with these critical connections are called *keystone species* and are considered critical to the ecosystem's health. In human communities, these hubs represent the people or institutions with access to knowledge, power, and influence. These keystone elements are a natural part of optimizing any network, and they often, but not always, align with formal titles and other official recognitions of status. Again, however, ideal communities require a balance—the more everything depends on one or two people or institutions, the more opportunities there are for a system collapse, if those hubs are taken out.

- *How do things flow through the network?* How can a product proceed more efficiently from raw material to the store shelf? How does a team of organizers gather and analyze feedback from a community? A process map is a variation of a network diagram and is created to answer these sorts of questions. More than just specific relationships, process maps examine flows of things like materials, information, or money through a system. By mapping these flows, the designer can more easily identify points of waste, resiliency, redundancy, or unhelpful relationships.

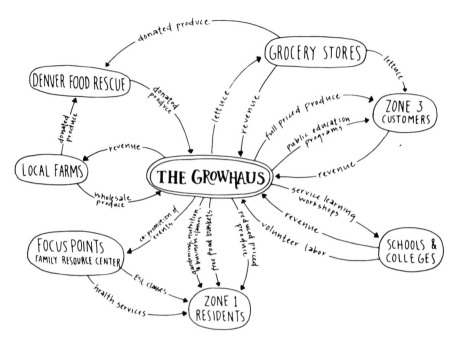

This process map shows the ecosystem of institutions, customers, and beneficiaries that the GrowHaus engages with. Each relationship is nurtured to be beneficial for both sides, and the system is made more dynamic by the many two-way feedback loops.

FURTHER LEARNING

Gopal, Srikanth "Srik," and Tiffany Clarke. "System Mapping: A Guide to Developing Actor Maps." http://www.fsg.org/tools-and-resources/system-mapping.

PART 2

Patterns of Justice and Resistance

If I transform the clay into a statue, I become a sculptor; if I transform the stones into a house, I become an architect; if I transform our society into something better for us all, I become a citizen.

—Augusto Boal, founder of Theatre of the Oppressed

To live in society is to participate in countless social systems. We work for companies and play in amateur sports leagues. We subscribe to insurance plans and form book clubs. We comment enthusiastically on internet forums and post vacation photos online. We pay taxes to local, state, and federal government, and we participate in Meetup groups, rallies, and nonprofits to counter aspects of those systems we don't like. We deposit our paychecks in a bank and withdraw money from our accounts to provide ourselves with housing, food, and entertainment. Every day, we navigate through a sea of overlapping groups of people, each one with its own implicit or explicit set of goals and rules.

Yet these social systems are rarely designed with thoughtfulness, love, or intention. Instead, they've evolved through some combination of circumstance, trial and error, and the inconsistent logic of the "free market." The result is that these systems can be short-lived, unjust, or unhealthy in any number of ways.

More than 90 percent of new businesses, for instance, fail within a couple years of opening. Most of our activity online, meanwhile, is dictated by executives and coders at a handful of big tech companies—companies whose interests aren't necessarily aligned with our own. Our monetary system, as ubiquitous to us as water is to a fish, systematically plunders natural systems and intact communities in order to concentrate wealth in the hands of the few.

In short, we've outsourced many of our vital life choices to technocrats, corporate executives, and elected officials—none of whom know as much as we do about our specific communities and the opportunities and challenges they face. If we're to manifest anything resembling the future sketched out in the first section of the book, we'll need to start making these decisions for ourselves—and that means creating the conditions for local, participatory, inclusive democratic institutions to thrive. We must have a thorough understanding of our past, and we must practice an ethic of caring for the people, plants, animals, and objects that surround us. We must recognize the life cycle of social movements, as well as the various strategies and tactics that propel them to success over the years. And we must be able to make use of activities that serve as social glue, leveraging them to bind our local communities closer and closer together. This section of the book covers each of these concerns and more, shifting from the broad philosophical patterns of the first section into the organizing principles for institutions, movements, and communities.

The first cluster of patterns investigates attitudes and practices necessary for effective and just social change. By probing the roots of our culture's dynamics of privilege and oppression, we can begin a process of DECOLONIZATION and develop new dynamics, ones that have justice at their core. By harnessing the ancient power of narrative, we can become experts at TELLING THE STORY in a way that catalyzes our work. By looking to our past for inspiration and closure, we become more whole, in a process some call SANKOFA. By cultivating practices of RITUAL AND CEREMONY, we can imbue our mundane acts with profound meaning, and by valuing maintenance equally with innovation, we can reclaim our atrophied skills of STEWARDSHIP, applying our sense of caring to the people, plants, animals, and objects around us.

The next set of patterns investigates the challenges and opportunities unique to the large communities that most of us live in. In an era when us-versus-them narratives are becoming ever more virulent, HUMANIZING THE OTHER invites us to seek common ground with those we see as "them." SLOW CITIES, meanwhile, outlines a vision for transforming our turbulent megacities into networks of autonomous villages. Finally, CITIZEN GOVERNANCE and INFRASTRUCTURE COMMONS suggest democratic alternatives for today's systems of decision making and property ownership, respectively.

Sometimes, significant change occurs through the incremental progress of collaboration with state and antimarket actors. In other cases, though, citizens must rise up to directly confront repressive institutions. CREATIVE DESTRUCTION calls our attention to society's phases of decay from which we generally tend to shift our gaze—and reminds us that they can be important opportunities for reinvention. NONVIOLENT STRUGGLE explores the history and theory behind campaigns of peaceful resistance, and the six patterns that follow elaborate on specific strategies for "waging peace." SOLIDARITY explains the importance and subtleties of acting in partnership with the disenfranchised, while ARTS OF RESISTANCE surveys the vital roles that theater, sculpture, song, and other media can play in social change. DISROBING THE EMPEROR shows the creative ways that activists can call attention to the hypocrisies of powerful people and institutions. COORDINATED NONCOMPLIANCE covers the efficacy and success factors for tactics like boycotts, divestment campaigns, and strikes. And as the dust settles on a period of turbulence, TRUTH AND RECONCILIATION provides a process of public reckoning for healing social wounds.

The final six patterns in the series cover specific techniques for bringing communities closer together—developing trust through BREAKING BREAD, releasing tension through LETTING LOOSE, witnessing each other's life transitions during RITES OF PASSAGE, engaging in activities of collective labor called GADUGI, working through shared hardship to gain INTIMACY THROUGH ADVERSITY, and sharing our vulnerabilities and sorrows through PRACTICING GRIEF.

17. DECOLONIZATION

Our society will never heal until we identify and transform the internal, interpersonal, institutional, and ideological structures that systematically marginalize members of our culture.

F or millennia, human society has been divided along lines of race, class, gender, sexual orientation, age, body type, and a host of other factors. Despite brave and powerful efforts to expose these injustices and reverse them, they continue to express themselves in all kinds of subtle (and not-so-subtle) ways. They are so often ingrained in our behavior that they can lead to self-reinforcing patterns of oppression—patterns that can be hard to break without a lot of time and care.

Colonization is a consequence of empire—the involuntary (and often violent) transfer of resources from one people to another. For all their remarkable achievements, empires function ecologically like parasites, drawing upon a vast array of resources to nourish themselves, without giving back. The Romans, Chinese, Mongols, Arabs, and Aztecs all followed a similar pattern, building massive public works through the enslavement of millions, while feeding themselves through heavy taxes on the harvests of those who remained free.

The logic of empire is not confined to one people, but Europeans have made a particularly fierce go of it over the last several centuries. Between 1400 and 1650, Europe went from a global backwater to the world's most powerful region, due in large part to the plundering of American resources and the enslavement of Africans. Indeed, the "New World" as we know it today was made possible only by stolen land and slave labor. And while the egregious sins of conquistadors and plantation owners have long since been disavowed, the ensuing generations of liberal humanism have not ended the exploitation of human and natural capital; they have only made it more subtle. In the United States today, the hub of a global antimarket empire, the ramifications of four centuries of slavery remain all too real. Through the compounded effects of discriminatory practices in housing, policing, justice, hiring, education, and more, blacks remain a de facto underclass, prevented from accessing equal resources. Meanwhile, we've turned our backs on the deep Latin American heritage of the western half of our country in favor of xenophobic outcry involving walls and deportation.

But the dynamics of domination aren't as simple as black and white. Even as race continues to influence power dynamics in the United States, many other factors conspire to hold some back while giving others an unearned advantage. From the bedroom to the boardroom, for instance, outdated gender roles prevent women from sharing power and prosperity equally with men. In our staunchly capitalistic society, the chasm between economic classes is growing deeper by the day. And in an escalating spiral of mutual scorn, fears of Islamic terrorism are exacerbating hatred toward Muslims, which provoke Islamic terrorists to strike more and more frequently. In short, the imperial behavior of America's tangled past has led us to a present that, whether we choose to acknowledge it or not, remains full of knots. Relentlessly optimistic and future-oriented as we are, we've avoided the task of examining these knots—much less disentangling them. Yet we'll never be able to achieve mutual trust and SOLIDARITY until we begin the hard, slow process of doing just that.

This is the premise of DECOLONIZATION. Less a movement than a mindset, DECOLONIZATION acknowledges that these patterns of exploitation are interconnected, all of them stemming from the same mentality of empire. It aims to redistribute financial, cultural, and material capital more equitably, not merely out of a sense of ethical obligation, but out of a recognition that a diverse world is a strong world. At the scale of an entire culture, DECOLONIZATION has many avenues for proactive change—through the NONVIOLENT STRUGGLE of social movements; through the brief, roving spotlight of the national news cycle; and through the cold calculations of policy debate.

But just as important as these society-wide narratives are the ones we create at more intimate scales. DECOLONIZATION invites us to think critically about the people we choose to socialize with, the assumptions we hold about dating and romantic partnership, and the lengths we go to accommodate others. Identifying and dismantling empire's many tendrils can sometimes feel overwhelming. The process of decolonizing one's own mind happens slowly over time, in a process that can be compared to Elisabeth Kübler-Ross's famous stages of grief. Those that benefit from the inequities of colonization—the white, the male, the straight, the middle-class—tend to start with denial that these inequities exist at all. Like a fish asked to perceive the water it swims in, it's hard for us to perceive advantages we've carried our whole lives, and instead we assume that those advantages are just how the world works. Once we're confronted with a contrasting narrative, the natural reaction is one of defensiveness or even anger. How dare someone accuse us of racism! But slowly, as the reality of empire's injustice sinks in, anger segues to guilt, as we look back at all the ways we've been complicit.

It's all too easy to get lost in any one of these stages; indeed, there are entire subcultures that feed off each one. But only once we shed each of these successive skins can we accept the reality of DECOLONIZATION and approach it from a place of responsibility. Once there, we can engage in personal and cultural processes of TRUTH AND RECONCILIATION, reckoning with the brutalities of the recent and distant past. We can practice HUMANIZING THE OTHER, reaching out to those unlike us with a sense of compassion and yearning for common connection. And we can demonstrate that our desire for change is more than theoretical by committing to ACTIONS, NOT INTENTIONS.

The vital promise of DECOLONIZATION is that *Homo sapiens* is not doomed to be a parasitic species. While violence and competition may well be necessary facets of human existence, conquest and forced assimilation are not. The empires that use them are only one form of human organization—and an unsustainable one at that. In THE LONG GAME of empire, the dynamics of exploitation inevitably undermine the empire's own base of natural and human capital, causing both oppressed and oppressor to lose.

In contrast, DECOLONIZATION reminds us that—no matter how assimilated we might be—each one of us has roots in a culture untainted by domination. By rediscovering and recontextualizing those roots, we can work together to make a more perfect society, one that doesn't have exploitation at its core. The centuries-old knots of racism, sexism, and all the rest may not become untangled in one generation, but that doesn't mean that it can't be done. From the agricultural revolution to the spread of monotheism to the Enlightenment, our world has been reshaped time and time again by successive waves of new stories. This time, let's weave together a story that includes and supports us all.

FURTHER LEARNING

Dunbar-Ortiz, Roxanne. *An Indigenous Peoples' History of the United States.* Boston: Beacon Press, 2014.

APPLYING THE PATTERN

What is the history of colonization in your community? How has colonization shaped your community—the physical space as well as the invisible structures? What groups or individuals are working to decolonize your community? What is your place in that work? Do you have privileges to acknowledge and leverage? How would decolonized inner, physical, and social spaces look and feel?

18. TELLING THE STORY

Unlock the age-old power of narratives to understand and share your thoughts about the world around you.

The truth does not reveal itself by virtue of being the truth: it must be told, and told well.

—Stephen Duncombe

How many parts per million of carbon dioxide in the atmosphere is the highest acceptable level to maintain a stable climate? How many square feet of thermal mass do we need to heat our home passively on the winter solstice? How much funding do we need to make our program a success? In challenges large and small, getting the numbers right is critical to our success in designing a regenerative, resilient future.

But while facts and figures help us figure out the details, they're rarely what actually motivates us to change our behavior. To the contrary, statistics can end up creating what media theorist Douglas Schuler calls a "mystifying fog that stifles effective intervention."[17] And despite their supposed solidity, numbers can be just as easily manipulated as words to suit a given agenda.

No, the pathway to meaningful social change isn't through our heads—it's through our hearts. Humans are meaning-makers; we have a knack for finding patterns amid the chaos and complexity of our lives and for charging even the most mundane details with currents of emotional significance. Story is an essential part of being human, and it acts as the foundation of our identities as individuals and entire cultures. It follows, then, that changing our stories is one of the most powerful ways we can change society. So powerful, in fact, that renowned systems theorist Donella Meadows called "the power to transcend paradigms" the most effective way to intervene in a system.[18]

No matter what the future holds for our species, there's no doubt that the stories we tell ourselves will play a key role in how it unfolds. In which case, the question becomes: whose stories will we be listening to, and what tales will they be telling? In many cases, the stories of our culture are handed down to us by those in power, and—surprise, surprise!—they tend to favor the agenda of the storyteller. For centuries, the Catholic Church kept the masses of Europe in check through fear-based narratives of original sin, penance, and eternal damnation. Beginning in the late Middle Ages, the emerging economic order of anti-markets and centrally issued currencies reinforced winner-takes-all stories of competition for scarce resources. And over the course of the twentieth century, the advertising industry perfected its art of telling stories that encouraged conspicuous consumption.

What all of these entities understood was that the narratives that have the power to change history have little to do with how *truthful* they are and everything to do with how *meaningful* they are. We are drawn to stories that stir our emotions, that connect us to larger narratives of triumph—regardless of whether those stories are rooted in science, logic, or virtuous intentions. Today, our daily life is inundated with cynical illustrations of this principle. We're soothed into complacency about climate change through utopian visions of high-tech leisure. We're distracted from the systemic flaws in our political structures through horse-race polling and feedback loops of punditry. Our movies and television shows cajole us into lusting after attention and power—and when we don't receive it, we're chided with narratives of shame and doubt that have colonized our very minds.

Counter-narratives abound, of course. The elites themselves hardly agree on a single narrative, and the growing democratization of media is slowly shifting the power of storytelling into the citizens' hands. But with that power comes the responsibility of telling stories that are both truthful *and* meaningful. If each one of us is now a storyteller, we'd better get good at storytelling.

Fortunately, we can stand on the shoulders of giants; expressing knowledge through story is a tradition far older than the written word. In the Western world, theorists like Joseph Campbell and George Lakoff have drawn connections between stories across divergent cultures and eras and have demonstrated their power to shape our worldviews. Since 2002, the Center for Story-Based Strategy has been working with social movements to help them apply the lessons of a good narrative to their work. Through trainings and consulting, they help changemakers to identify the key conflicts, characters, and unstated assumptions of their situation and to use those elements to draw out narratives of meaning that imbue their work with more emotional resonance.

Groups like CSS are proving the untapped potential of storytelling to catalyze social movements. Meanwhile, we each have a similar opportunity to transform the stories within our own heads.

KEY QUESTIONS FOR TELLING POWERFUL STORIES THAT HEAL

From *Harnessing the Power of Narrative for Social Change* by the Center for Story-Based Strategy

The Conflict: What is the problem we are addressing? How is it framed? What aspects are emphasized and what is avoided? How can we reframe to highlight our values and solutions?

The Characters: Who are the characters in the story? Do impacted communities get to speak for themselves? Who are cast as villains, victims, and heroes?

Show, Don't Tell: What is the imagery of the story—what pictures linger in our minds? How does it engage our senses? Is there a potent metaphor that describes the issue?

Foreshadowing: What is our resolution to the conflict? What vision are we offering? How do make the future we desire seem inevitable?

Assumptions: What must be believed in order to believe the story is "true"? Does our opponent's story have unstated assumptions we can expose and challenge? What assumptions and core values do we share that unite our communities around a common vision?

FURTHER LEARNING

Campbell, Joseph. *The Hero with a Thousand Faces*. Novato, CA: New World Library, 2008.

Dillard, Annie. *Living By Fiction*. New York: HarperPerennial, 2000.

Lakoff, George, and Mark Johnson. *Metaphors We Live By*. Chicago: University of Chicago Press, 1980.

APPLYING THE PATTERN

What stories inform your life? Your community's life? Who is telling them most powerfully? Whose stories are being quieted? Practice writing out your story or the story of your organization or community, answering the questions in the sidebar above.

19. SANKOFA

In order to design a thriving future, we each must reach into the past. Take time to understand the good and not-so-good aspects of your own heritage, and commit to honoring it on your own terms.

Our greatest responsibility is to be good ancestors.

—Jonas Salk

Each one of us has a heritage, no matter how disconnected from it we are. Our bloodstreams pulse with unique epigenetic echoes of recipes, bedtime stories, and turns of phrase uttered by our ancestors' ancestors. These patterns remain with us as individuals, families, and entire cultures, shaping our understanding of the world around us and of our own role within it. These pasts are afforded little value, however, in today's forward-looking world. The homogenizing influence of antimarkets, our ever-increasing mobility, and the complicated hybrid identities created by the mixing of cultures all conspire to make our heirloom cultures seem outdated.

Meanwhile, there's another reason that we might avoid embracing our past—it's not always pretty. Our nation's history is riddled with phases of forced migration, slavery, even genocide, and nearly all of us have ancestors who participated in them, either as victims or perpetrators. Our culture encourages us to disregard these historical injustices the same way we throw trash in a landfill, shoving them out of our minds and hoping that they will go away. But that only lets our historical wounds fester under the surface, returning decades or generations later in even more toxic form.

Not surprisingly, many other cultures take a different approach. In the Twi language of Ghana, the word *sankofa*—meaning "go back and get it"—represents the value of actively looking back to the past to give us strength moving forward.

SANKOFA (and its equivalent memes in other cultures) invites us to treat our pasts like compost, not garbage. By continuously revisiting the past, exploring it from many angles, turning it over and over in our minds, we can turn even the most bitter memories into sources of inspiration and nourishment. Whereas revisionist history aims to paint over our sordid past with a glossy sheen, SAN-KOFA is more like alchemy, encouraging us to get our hands dirty as a means of transformation.

This act of historical composting is more than a mere exercise in curiosity—it has real implications for our future. Learning about the struggles and triumphs of our ancestors provides a helpful reflection on our own, helping us to understand that our present situation may have some precedent after all. Perceiving THE LONG GAME of our distant past allows us to ground ourselves in a greater narrative, one that lasts beyond our current job or political climate. And understanding the identities of those who came before gives us the tools to begin crafting new identities.

Of course, many lessons of the past might not directly translate to our present circumstances. Yesterday's sincere rituals may look naive or insensitive today. Traditional foods may need to be adjusted to fit new homelands (or a changing climate). The point isn't to force the culture of one time and place into the context of another. But by exploring the deep-rooted cultural identities of our past, we draw inspiration to root ourselves where we are, in turn becoming good ancestors for our own descendants.

APPLYING THE PATTERN

What do your first and last names mean? How did you come to receive them? How well do you know the stories and cultures of your ancestors? Are there elders in your family or community whom you can learn from? What are the tales, clothes, foods, and rituals that make your heritage unique? Which aspects may have relevance to your life today? Which ones no longer serve you? What wounds exist under the histories of yourself, your ancestors, or your communities?

20. RITUAL AND CEREMONY

Naming an action—and repeating it on a regular basis— affords it a unique power in our consciousness. Use this power to encode healthy patterns and discourage unhealthy ones.

Ritual is necessary for us to know anything.

—Ken Kesey

Quick—what are the first images that come to mind when you hear the words *ritual* and *ceremony?* Hazy memories of a childhood church service? A wedding or funeral? Or perhaps a New Age circle complete with bare feet and crystals? In a society where the values of science and secularism are paramount, these words often have a ring of superstition and anachronism. Rituals, after all, are mere superstitions, right? Haven't we moved past that?

Well, not quite. From an anthropological perspective, even the most ardent rationalists perform rituals and ceremonies as part of daily life. Handshakes, birthday candles, and marriage proposals are all examples of everyday actions that fit the anthropological definition of a ritual. Regardless of whether they're identified as such, these acts are a fundamental part of every community's cultural capital and shared identity. As cultural anthropologist Kevin Carrico puts it, "Ritual is arguably a universal feature of human social existence: just as one cannot envision a society without language or exchange, one would be equally hard-pressed to imagine a society without ritual."[19]

If rituals are so commonplace, how are we to identify it? The question is surprisingly challenging to answer. Depending on the cultural context and resources at hand, rituals and ceremonies can take an unimaginable diversity of forms. Nevertheless, anthropologists tend to agree on three patterns that all rituals appear to follow.

- *Rituals have rules.* There are typically instructions for who performs the rituals, when they are performed, what preparation is necessary, and the like. These rules may be explicit or unspoken, and they may vary significantly from place to place. Regardless, rules are essential to give rituals a consistent, coherent identity. The annual Jewish ceremony of Seder, observed every year at Passover, is an elaborate ritual meal with a series of fifteen distinct steps. While Jews all over the world celebrate the same steps in the same order on the same night, every community and family gives the rules their own spin, hastening some steps while spending more time on others.

- *Rituals have symbolism.* Though rituals sometimes lapse into perfunctory repetition, the most resonant rituals have a meaning beyond their superficial appearance. Most Seder ceremonies, for instance, include a plate that holds a boiled egg, horseradish, a roasted lamb shank, and several other foods in the center of the table. Each one of these foods contains a different meaning in the context of the Seder—the egg represents the coming of spring, while the horseradish reminds participants of the bitter tears of slavery.

- *Rituals are performed.* They demand our full attention while we're engaged in them, and they often take place in a group context. Most Seders have a leader or facilitator, a variety of participants, and often a few non-Jewish guests.

From a rational perspective, rituals and ceremonies such as the Seder can seem silly or superstitious. There's no practical reason to spend so much time cooking and cleaning to prepare for a single meal and then performing all fifteen steps of the ritual. There's no money to be gained, no glory to be earned. And yet, the Seder continues to be held in communities around the globe, thousands of years after it originally began.

What compels us to spend so much time and energy on activities that appear so frivolous? For starters, rituals are one of the best tools for weaving the fabric of INTERDEPENDENT COMMUNITY. Every time a ritual takes place, participants are subconsciously reaffirming and strengthening their shared sense of identity. Rituals can help assure us that we're not alone in our beliefs, giving us courage in the face of adversity. Rituals also remind us of our humanity. When most of our energy is spent on the tedious and prosaic—driving our kids to school, pulling weeds, sitting in meetings—rituals serve as a counterweight to the mundane. They remind us that we are not machines, that our actions have more than utilitarian value. And rituals can serve as important markers of the passage of time, nudging us to step back and place our stories in the context of THE LONG GAME.

Armed with this anthropological understanding of the functions and importance of RITUAL AND CEREMONY, we changemakers have the opportunity to design rituals to strengthen our own work. No matter a group's size, culture, or political orientation, there is always an opportunity to adapt the principles of rules, symbolism, and performance to honor and catalyze its work. Even the simple practice of starting or ending a gathering with a short ceremony can have a profound impact—opening rituals establish a sense of purpose and clear our minds of distractions, while closing rituals can leave participants with a sense of excitement. Successful rituals in contemporary activist movements range from the white "ghost bikes" commemorating slain cyclists to Occupy's call-and-response chants to the eye-opening tactics used in Theatre of the Oppressed.

For over three decades, the activist and writer Starhawk has been harnessing the power of ritual to further social change, leading ceremonies both spiritual and secular for groups throughout the globe. Starting with her book *The Spiral Dance,* she has articulated a three-step pattern for designing successful RITUAL AND CEREMONY.

Create or enter a sacred space. The start of a successful ritual, according to Starhawk, requires getting in the proper frame of mind by creating or entering a sacred space. By burning a smudge stick, observing a moment of silence, or entering into the grand architecture of a cathedral, we signal to ourselves and others that we've left our everyday realities and entered into a ceremonial mindset. In the familiar North American birthday ritual, for instance, we observe this first step by lighting candles.

Mark a shift or change. Once participants have entered the sacred space, the ritual fulfills its core purpose of marking a shift or change—the completion of a challenging task or a rite of passage, such as a wedding. During this stage in the ceremony, we direct our focus toward the person or group of people under-going the shift, who will often perform a set of actions to mark it. For birthday ceremonies, these steps are marked, respectively, by the singing of "Happy Birthday" and the celebrant blowing out the candles. In more elaborate rit-uals, this stage is often heightened by prayer, chanting, dancing, or other activities that allow participants to "burst beyond the limits of the socially conditioned mind."[2]

Affirm the change. Rituals resolve with an affirmation of the change and return to the everyday world. Whether formally or informally, we acknowledge the transforma-tion that just occurred and reflect on its mean-ing—generally in a celebratory way. Often, this entails BREAKING BREAD, LETTING LOOSE, or other activities that build social capital. The ending of our birthday rituals embody both of these, with cake and a party.

FURTHER LEARNING

Starhawk. *The Spiral Dance: A Rebirth of the Ancient Religion of the Goddess.* New York: HarperCollins, 1979.

APPLYING THE PATTERN

What rituals do you engage in, as an individual or within your groups and community? Why do you engage in them? Are there shifts or changes within your community that would benefit from associating with a ritual? What images or symbols have resonance in your community or groups?

21. STEWARDSHIP

Take responsibility for your own impact on the world by taking care of the things around you.

Taking care of yourself and your family is not selfish. It means that someone else doesn't have to take care of you. You should work to become strong enough that your presence adds, not subtracts.

—Stephen Gaskin

The man who can keep a fire in a stove or on a hearth is not only more durable, but wiser, closer to the meaning of fire, than the man who can only work a thermostat.

—Wendell Berry

I need to make a confession: I'm a novelty addict. I get tired of my clothes after a few years of wearing them. I'm always on the lookout for new music to listen to, despite having a library of thousands of albums. I constantly crave new fruits and veggies to grow and new ways to prepare the ones I'm familiar with. If there's any solace in my addiction, it's that I'm hardly alone. In fact, novelty has become essential to our current economic order—when the world's affluent already have access to everything they could possibly need, the imperative becomes selling them stuff they *don't* need. Our education system is pushed from one hollow innovation to another, tossing teachers and students about like ships in a storm. Even activists for a better world are compelled by the allure of novelty toward uncertain ends, diluting and distracting their efforts by taking on new projects before the current ones have run their course.

In our obsession with the new and the next, we've forgotten that *innovation* is not the same thing as *progress*. Most of the conceptual seeds we need to restore dignity, balance, and justice to our society are already present in some form or another—often right under our noses. But in order for those seeds to thrive and bear fruit, they require dedication, patience, and a community of supporting factors. In short, they demand an ethic of STEWARDSHIP.

In all but the past dozen or so generations, the importance of long-term maintenance and preservation to a healthy society was self-evident. No people could last for more than a generation or two without acting as stewards of land, buildings, tools, clothes, and stories alike. This attitude was embedded in laws and sacred texts the world over, from the Judeo-Christian dictum to "not pollute the land where you are" (Numbers 35:33) to the famous Iroquois mandate to think about the impacts of our decisions seven generations in the future. But as fossil fuels and industrialization made new goods ever more available, the STEWARDSHIP ethic began to seem quaint and boring. One by one, the routine tasks that connected us with the world around us were replaced with products and services that promised less work. Why pull weeds when we can spray chemicals? Why pay attention to the health of our watershed when we get clean water from the tap regardless? Why fix Last Year's Model when we can buy a Brand New Version™—one that comes in a Shiny New Color to boot?

Lee Vinsel and Andrew Russell, researchers at the Stevens Institute of Technology in Hoboken, New Jersey, have mounted an effort to shift that story. They'd like to steer our focus away from innovators and toward "maintainers"—the unsung heroes that actually keep our society functioning on a day-to-day basis. In a widely circulated 2016 essay in *Aeon* magazine, Vinsel and Russell argue that fetishizing the new takes the spotlight away from the real and important work of maintaining the things that are working just fine. "The peddlers of innovation," they write, "radically overvalue innovation.... Maintenance and repair, the building of infrastructures, the mundane labour that goes into sustaining functioning and efficient infrastructures, simply has more impact on people's daily lives than the vast majority of technological innovations."[21]

As Vinsel and Russell astutely point out, our emphasis on innovation over STEWARDSHIP has left us increasingly untethered from the material world, drifting farther and farther away from the embodied knowledge of human and natural systems alike. Novelty makes us all dilettantes, knowing the surface details of everything—and the lived-in truth of nothing. Two and a half millennia ago, Aristotle denounced just such a state of affairs in his treatise *On Generation and Corruption:*

"those who dwell in intimate association with nature and its phenomena are more able to lay down principles such as to admit of a wide and coherent development; while those whom devotion to abstract discussions has rendered unobservant of facts are too ready to dogmatize on the basis of a few observations."

Our novelty addictions don't just erode our own character; when we shirk our duties of STEWARDSHIP, we're often perpetuating injustice as well. After all, *someone* has to do all the maintaining that we've chosen not to. While society's innovators skew white, male, and educated, the work of maintenance tends to fall to marginalized groups like women, racial minorities, and those without college degrees.

In short, we've forgotten the dignity of STEWARDSHIP. But if we can manage to break our innovation addictions, if we restore honor to the mundane work of taking care, an entirely different set of priorities emerges for our work as SACRED ACTIVISTS. Rather than valuing only those who blaze new paths, we can recognize the equal, subtle worth of keeping those paths clean and well lit. Rather than aiming to disrupt today's dysfunctional systems with even more ambitious ones, we can seek guidance from yesterday's systems, which long provided abundance for all.

FURTHER LEARNING

Crawford, Matthew. *Shop Class As Soulcraft: An Inquiry into the Value of Work.* New York: Penguin, 2009.

APPLYING THE PATTERN

What is your impact on the world? Think in terms of how you put food on your table, dollars in your bank account, activities in your life—which resources are you stewarding? How can you be a better steward of them? What skills or people could help you? Are there maintenance activities that deserve more time and attention in your life? Who are some of the maintainers who help you do your work? What could you do to honor the maintainers in your life?

22. HUMANIZING THE OTHER

Minimize antagonistic us-versus-them thinking and instead seek to identify common ground between seemingly opposed communities.

When we go inward and our heart is open, we will connect with the heart, and the heart will compel us to go outward and connect with others.

—James Doty

In 2013, I spent two weeks with permaculture practitioners from across the globe at the thirteenth International Permaculture Convergence in Havana, Cuba. Over cafeteria meals of rice and beans, I met inspiring souls from Africa, Europe, and South America who were applying their permaculture skills with great success and under unimaginably different circumstances. "All these folks aren't so different from me, after all," I thought. "Perhaps there really is something to the concept of a 'global nation,'"

After the convergence, I took a pit stop in West Palm Beach, Florida, for my grandmother's eightieth birthday celebration. Only a few hundred miles separated the ramshackle permaculture summit from the gated communities of the Miami suburbs, but as soon as I got off the plane, I felt like I'd stepped into a different world. This was a place of $100-dollar dinners and manicured golf courses, of strict dress codes and chauffeured rides in black sedans.

My first reaction was dread—and my second was scorn. After the revolutionary simplicity of the convergence, being in this land of decadent sprawl felt like a slap in the face, the epitome of all that the convergence in Cuba was meant to overturn. All around me, I saw the signs of a corrupt and dying empire: extravagant wealth, underpaid migrant labor, and toxic pesticides, all planted squarely in the path of the rising ocean.

Trying to be polite, I kept these thoughts to myself and joined the festivities as gamely as I could, and later I went for a run around a nearby golf course to clear my head. As the endorphins pulsed through my veins, I saw clearly what my brain had been preventing me from internalizing: like it or not, this landscape was every bit as human as the one I'd just left. As much as I disapproved of it, I couldn't deny that I *understood* it far better than the landscapes from which my compatriots came. My judgment was helping no one. Instead, it was time to meet my family halfway and try to be of service.

As I experienced so vividly in those few weeks, it can be much easier to get along with like-minded people on the other side of the globe than it can with members of your own family. But at a certain level, we all want the same things— peace, security, and opportunity for our friends and loved ones. Humans have a tendency to blame society's problems on other groups. "If only," we lament, "we could convince these wealthy golfers to understand how wasteful they are." "If only we could get those liberals to understand the sanctity of all life." If only *they* would change, *we* would all be better off.

To be sure, it's important to acknowledge our differences. And, in certain cases, direct confrontation is indeed the only clear strategy for creating change. But all too often, our vehement opposition to something only steels the resolve of those that favor it. Our us-and-them thinking becomes counterproductive, causing each side to dig in their heels and making compromise seem more remote.

A growing body of research is showing that focusing on our *commonalities* is a surer path toward lasting change. Social psychologists have shown that having just one friend from a so-called out-group can reduce our prejudice and unconscious biases.[22] Meanwhile, neuroscientists like James Doty have observed that practicing compassion for others actually shrinks the size of our amygdala—the part of the brain where our "fight-or-flight" response originates.[23]

These researchers are pointing the way to an entirely different approach to social change from the protest and demonstration. Jonathan Matthew Smucker, a sociologist and grassroots trainer with Beautiful Trouble, speaks of "narrative insurgency": "Narrative insurgents do not reject problematic narratives wholesale, but distinguish between those components that are allied, hostile or neutral to their cause. They embrace as much of a cultural narrative as possible—the allied and neutral components—and encourage the further development of the allied components, using these as the foundations for their organizing efforts with and within the given community."[24]

In other words, they seek out areas of commonality to build on, rather than areas of difference to attack. Here in the United States, for instance, it's becoming clear that populist factions on both sides of the political spectrum have as much in common with each other as either one does with the mainstream of its party. Both stand opposed to monopolistic forces that they feel have gotten too large and self-serving. Both are skeptical of the motives and outcomes of the United States' military interventions abroad. And both are concerned about the impact of policies like free trade on local jobs. At present, each side has different solutions to these problems; reformers on the right tend to target the federal government, while those on the left are more likely to point their fingers at corporations. But an agenda of localized economies could conceivably unite them both. In an era of global societal crisis, there is no "them," there is only "us"—one species, which will sink or swim together. Which fate we choose rests on how well we are able to overcome our differences and solve our challenges as an integrated whole.

APPLYING THE PATTERN

Who are your "others"? To whom are you an other? What things do you have in common with each other or with each other's goals? How can you overcome barriers between you and your others and engage with them in meaningful ways (such as BREAKING BREAD)?

23. SLOW CITIES

Contemporary cities are parasitic systems, exploiting their hinterlands and driving their residents crazy. By retrofitting our urban areas into clusters of close-knit, self-determining, self-sustaining villages, cities can deliver on their true potential.

In the grand sweep of history, small, interconnected villages may prove to be the most resilient pattern of settlement. But here and now, the metropolis is the definitive social arrangement of our era. With their grandiose aspirations, their obsession with speed and novelty, and their sink-or-swim bustle, cities reflect all the hallmarks of the times we live in. It's no wonder—cities are epicenters of innovation and have been the seats of cultural, financial, and political power for millennia. It's hardly an exaggeration to say that urban centers are the key to our success as a global culture. But at the same time, cities present a number of confounding paradoxes as we attempt to create a more equitable and regenerative society.

For one thing, cities appear to flout the laws of biology. That may not at first seem like a meaningful statement. After all, cities are mostly made of concrete, glass, asphalt, and steel—decidedly un-biological materials. But in many ways, cities have remarkable parallels with organisms. They perform many of the same essential functions of moving around materials, digesting inputs, excreting outputs, communicating between parts, and the like, and do so in remarkably similar ways. So in a sense, cities can be said to have a metabolism.

In the animal kingdom, metabolism tends to slow down with mass—an elephant has a far slower heart rate and gestation period than a mouse. But Geoffrey West and his colleagues at the Santa Fe Institute have found that cities are just the opposite—the bigger they get, the faster the activity within. This results in a feedback loop, whereby growth in a city's activity encourages more growth. In order to maintain that growth, cities are compelled to feed like a parasite off their environs, draining people, materials, and money from the surrounding countryside. In order to compete with other cities, meanwhile, they are forced into an arms race of innovation, and they do so at an ever-faster pace in order to avoid collapse.[25]

Meanwhile, the very scale of cities affects the people that dwell in them in important ways. In any community with more than 1,500 individuals, it becomes impossible to know everyone else. Most of the people around us are strangers, and our default attitude becomes one of wariness or suspicion rather than friendliness.

In our attempts to create order out of the chaos of the city, city-dwellers bind themselves to loose subnetworks in the zones of reciprocity (50–150 people) and recognition (150–1,500 people), each overlapping in geography and membership (see RELATIONSHIP ZONES). These networks form the communities that shape our identity: the salsa-dancing scene, the group of parents at an elementary school, the company cohorts.

For much of the past few centuries, this patchwork of networks and communities stuck together, creating enclaves that endured for generations. But with the ever-quickening churn of urban metabolism, the bonds of INTERDEPENDENT COMMUNITY began to snap under the pressures like individual ambition, economic stagnation, and gentrification. Today, urban enclaves scarcely get the opportunity to form before they begin to crumble. In his seminal 2001 book *Bowling Alone*, political scientist Robert Putnam observed that living in a twenty-first-century urban center is positively correlated with a decline in social capital: "The resident of a major metropolitan area, either in the central city or in a suburb, is significantly less likely to attend public meetings, to be active in community organizations, to attend church, to sign a petition, to volunteer, to attend club meetings, to work on community projects, or even to visit friends. Metropolitans are less engaged because of where they are, not who they are."[26]

Of course, none of this is to suggest that we abandon the urban endeavor altogether. As mentioned above, cities are remarkable generators of novel ideas and cultural artifacts, and on the issue of sustainability, there's a compelling case to be made for packing ourselves into dense urban habitats. Instead, we merely have to redesign the way cities interact with their resource base and inhabitants.

First, we need to slow down the urban metabolism. That means everything from lowering speed limits to incentivizing adaptive reuse over scrap-and-start-over development. It means closing the loop on resource flows, looking for ways in which cities can generate their own power and grow much of their own food nearby. And it means ensuring that important goods and services are within walking distance of every home.

Second, we've got to design the right conditions for city-dwellers to create their own INTERDEPENDENT COMMUNITIES. Place-making and related activities that alter the physical design of our neighborhoods can encourage chance interactions. INFRASTRUCTURE COMMONS can prevent forced displacement, keeping residents around long enough to develop roots. And CITIZEN GOVERNANCE and other forms of SUBSIDIARITY can cede control of budgets, zoning, and other decisions to those most affected by them.

Ultimately, cities should work for people—not the other way around. By embracing the idea of the slow city, we can reclaim control of the urban organism for the benefit of us all.

FURTHER LEARNING

Jacobs, Jane. *The Life and Death of Great American Cities.* New York: Vintage Books, 1992.

APPLYING THE PATTERN

Look at the community in which you live—how would you characterize its pace? How strong is the social capital? In what ways does the physical environment contribute or detract from the strength of the social capital? In what ways do you think your community can or should slow down? How could you use a NETWORK ANALYSIS to gain insight into your community?

24. CITIZEN GOVERNANCE

Members of the general public are rarely involved a truly meaningful way in making key decisions about their community. Involving citizens in each STREAM OF ENGAGEMENT is a critical part of COMMONING our society.

What is needed is for every person to feel at home in the place of his local government with his ideas and complaints.

—Christopher Alexander

For many years, I worked in an immigrant community in north Denver that was split in two by an interstate highway. Choked with traffic and literally falling apart, the viaduct was in need of replacement, and Colorado's Department of Transportation was keen on upgrading the aging infrastructure. As part of their redesign process, CDOT scheduled a series of federally mandated community-input sessions. But like a scowling teen forced into community service, the agency's distaste for public input could barely be concealed. Meetings were scheduled at inconvenient times with little notice. Spanish translation was spotty, and even the English-speaking residents had a hard time understanding all the bureaucratic jargon.

Those residents who were able to participate were loud and clear: they wanted the highway out of their community. They were tired of having their neighborhood split into by a concrete monstrosity and tired of suffering from the highest air pollution levels in the state and corresponding rates of asthma. These complaints may have seemed like pipe dreams if it weren't for the fact that a viable alternative actually existed—two existing highways a few miles to the north. Yet CDOT refused to even consider the community's pleas, using oversimplified and outdated traffic models to justify their claim that tearing down the highway was simply not an option.

Unfortunately, this experience was hardly unique. Communities have little say in the most important decisions about their neighborhoods. And more often than not, the changes that take place are designed to maximize profit at the expense of natural, social, and cultural capital. Neighborhoods are zoned to encourage gentrification. Corporations are lured in with tax breaks worth tens of millions of dollars. Prime farmland and natural habitats are destroyed for new development. Public school reforms do little to improve educational outcomes, while stretching teachers' time farther and farther.

Many of these efforts do make attempts at public input. Some of them are sincere, while some of them, like CDOT's, are clearly perfunctory. But even the best public processes tend to treat residents as just another stakeholder—and when push comes to shove, the actual decision makers can choose to heed local desires or ignore them. With this state of affairs, it's no wonder that so many people feel cynical and apathetic about civic engagement.

What would our communities look like if everyday citizens played a more fundamental role in the decision-making process? This is the question behind the idea of CITIZEN GOVERNANCE. Drawing directly from the patterns of COM-MONING and SUBSIDIARITY, efforts at CITIZEN GOVERNANCE aim far higher than a tired public-input process. They seek to transform towns and cities into "participatory landscapes"—areas where the general public is engaged in shaping the physical and invisible fabric of their communities.

The City Repair movement, based in Portland, Oregon, is a shining example of the possibilities for such an approach. Initiated by architect Mark Lakeman and his neighbors, City Repair empowers everyday citizens to create infrastructure that enlivens the public right-of-way: intersection murals, little free libraries, sidewalk tea stalls, avant-garde bus stops, and more. In the two decades they've been at it, City Repair has accomplished projects at more than two hundred sites throughout the city, enlivening neighborhood after neighborhood in the process.

Meanwhile, more and more cities are putting budgetary decisions in the hands of citizens. Participatory Budgeting, as it's called, began in Porto Alegre, Brazil, in the 1980s, and today is used by hundreds of cities the world over. Every year, for example, Boston selects a cohort of teens and young adults to choose how to spend $1 million in city tax dollars. New York City's program engages over fifty thousand residents in determining the allocation of $32 million dollars in capital projects. And Minneapolis's Neighborhood Revitalization Program has committed over $300 million since 1991 through a resident-led process. As compared to the typical budgetary procedures, programs like these have been shown to increase civic participation and distribute resources to the communities that need them most.[27]

By allowing the people to make some of the decisions for municipal spending, participatory budgeting goes a long way toward CITIZEN GOVERNANCE. Even so, local officials are still the ones spending the money. Even more radical are initiatives in which local governments step back and let the people solve as many of their own problems as they can. Recently, several European cities have begun to pursue such arrangements, creating legal frameworks for municipal government to partner with grassroots citizen groups to solve urban problems. Since passing its "Regulation for Care and Regeneration of Urban Commons" in 2014, the Italian city of Bologna has seen more than one hundred citizen-driven projects take advantage of the legislation, ranging from a volunteer-run boutique distributing used clothes to the needy to community bulletin boards and graffiti removal.

Of course, acts of CITIZEN GOVERNANCE aren't always practical. For one thing, municipal governments may be resistant to putting so much power in the hands of the people. Many citizens may lack the knowledge, interest, or time to engage fully in the process. And in particularly complicated or contentious situations, the greater good might actually be compromised by full public

IAPP'S SPECTRUM OF PARTICIPATION

Inform. The public is kept aware about government activity.

- Examples: newsletters, crime reports, official social media accounts.

Consult. Public feedback is sought on a predetermined set of alternatives.

- Examples: charrettes, town meetings, referenda.

Involve. Institutions work directly with public throughout the process.

- Examples: community advisory boards.

Collaborate. The public is engaged as key partners in design and implementation. Agencies seek to involve the maximum amount of citizens possible.

- Examples: participatory budgeting, community benefits agreements.

Empower. The public has final decision-making powers.

- Examples: City Repair, COMMONING ordinances.

participation. But even without giving citizens full control, there are many ways to move THE EDGE OF CHANGE farther toward CITIZEN GOVERNANCE. The International Association for Public Participation's "Spectrum of Participation" highlights five ways the public can be engaged in civic processes, depending on the context and resources at hand.

No matter where an initiative falls in the spectrum of participation, any effort at CITIZEN GOVERNANCE must address certain design considerations:

- *How many citizens will be involved, and how will they be selected?* Even the most homogeneous communities have diversity in perspectives, ages, and many other variables. In many cases, the most valuable voices are those that are hardest to find. Designers of CITIZEN GOVERNANCE initiatives must therefore think carefully about THE RIGHT SIZE of the group of participants and how they will represent as much of the community as possible.

- *How will institutions hold themselves accountable to incorporating citizen input?* Too many efforts at community feedback resort to placating or tokenizing resident voices and making minor changes—at best—to the business-as-usual scenario. Rather than strengthening community connections, this attitude reinforces attitudes of mistrust and cynicism. To avoid this cycle, CITIZEN GOVERNANCE efforts must design mechanisms to incorporate feedback in a genuine manner and to communicate these mechanisms frequently and transparently.

- *How will citizens be incentivized to participate?* Many folks are too busy putting food on the table and taking care of their kids to spend time thinking about abstract concepts of community change. If the goal of CITIZEN GOVERNANCE is to engage all perspectives in a community, these folks might need incentives to participate that relate to their day to-day needs. Free food, gift cards, and public transit vouchers are just some of the tangible rewards that might entice participants to show up.

- *How will engagement be structured in a way that acknowledges the norms and values of the people being engaged?* Each community has its own unique culture of communication. The most successful efforts at CITIZEN GOVERNANCE adapt to that culture, rather than asking participants to adapt to that of the hosts. Andrea J. Nightingale, a commons researcher, notes an example of this cultural disconnect in an essay on Scottish Fishermen: "Men who are used to coping with dangerous and physically demanding environments find it literally uncomfortable, physically and subjectively, to situate their bodies in a meeting room." When meetings are held indoors, "the exercise of power changes in profound ways and they end up being in a more defensive position relative to their occupational identity."[28] To avoid these defensive positions, be sure to host meetings in spaces that feel safe to participants, during times that are convenient to them, and use facilitators that they can relate to.

- *How will participants acquire the knowledge necessary to make informed decisions?* Choices affecting an entire community are necessarily complex, and no single person—bureaucrat or resident—is likely to understand all of the variables. As such, CITIZEN GOVERNANCE projects must carefully consider the STREAMS OF ENGAGEMENT and include ample time for exploration and assessment, in addition to visioning, editing, and conflict resolution. It should go without saying that this learning time should be seen as a two-way street, with experts learning from residents, residents learning from experts, and both learning new information together.

FURTHER LEARNING

Green, Mike. *When People Care Enough to Act: ABCD in Action.* With Henry Moore and John O'Brien. Toronto: Inclusion Press, 2007.

APPLYING THE PATTERN

For individuals—what is your local governing body (city council, county commission, and so forth)? Have you attended any public meetings? If not, when do the meetings take place, and what issues on the agendas do you see as affecting you and your community the most? If so, did you provide input? How was it received? What would make your local governing body more accountable to you and other citizens?

For organizations—how does your organization seek input from members of the community? How can your organization involve the public more?

25. INFRASTRUCTURE COMMONS

Tools and infrastructure can be some of the most durable forms of community wealth—but only if they are developed and maintained with equity and sustainability in mind.

The quality of owning freezes you forever into "I," and cuts you off forever from the "we."

—John Steinbeck, *The Grapes of Wrath*

It's no secret that our current systems of infrastructure are unsustainable. Designed and built with a mindset of infinite material abundance, our buildings, transportation systems, and communications networks are beginning to show signs of wear as we enter an era of resource limits. Fortunately, the past fifty years have seen intrepid engineers, architects, and other visionaries prove a wealth of strategies for designing, building, and maintaining our material capital in a better way. Initiatives like the natural-building movement, the Biomimicry Institute, the Living Building Challenge, cradle-to-cradle manufacturing, and green chemistry have all brought a realistic vision of regenerative infrastructure into sharp relief, showing in vivid detail how such a society might look and feel.

But while the technical solutions have been available—in some cases, for decades—they've largely languished at the fringes of mainstream acceptance. With the notable exception of wind and solar energy, regenerative infrastructure remains confined to one-off examples and niche markets. Why? To a certain extent, the need is not yet pronounced enough to motivate us to act. Building out regenerative infrastructure systems also requires retraining millions of designers and installers—no small feat. But perhaps most important barrier is capital. Compared to its unsustainable counterparts, regenerative infrastructure tends to require more labor to create and materials that cost more. In a society where big decisions come down to returns on financial capital, it loses out.

To truly transform our relationship with material capital, we must consider not just the *forms* it takes but also the *processes* by which it gets created and maintained. You don't have to look hard at how these processes work to see that they're entwined in the same antimarket forces that are eroding all other forms of capital today. We make use of material capital every time we travel a highway, make a phone call, or turn on the tap—but few of us *create* material capital, and even fewer *own* it. Indeed, the elite ownership of material capital in the form of real estate is one of the main driving forces behind the exponential inequalities of our age. Every time we pay rent, we are participating in a great channeling of wealth from those who are just scraping by to those who already own it.

The uneven control of material capital is how thousands of homeless people can desperately stalk the streets while equal numbers of second homes sit vacant. It's how so-called sharing economy platforms like Uber and Airbnb can democratize the services performed by taxis and hotels, while concentrating wealth even more efficiently than their corporate predecessors. And it's how Americans end up wasting millions of tons of food each year while millions of its people go hungry.

A truly regenerative infrastructure must be decoupled from the massive government and antimarket forces that currently finance and maintain it. And in their place, we must design social structures that make the *owners* of material capital the same people as its *creators* and, to a lesser extent, its *users*. Once again, however, the solutions already exist.

Among the most elemental forms of material capital are the tools used to make other forms material capital—wheelbarrows, power drills, soldering guns, and the like. In dozens of communities across the country, these tools are entering the commons in the form of tool libraries, community-owned institutions that lend tools to members who pay a small annual fee. More ambitiously, projects like Marcin Jakubowski's Open Source Ecology are aiming to create a whole set of self-replicating tools using open-source technology.

At least as important as tool commons are land and building commons. While groups like tenants' rights organizations can be seen as a necessary bulwark against the abuses of property owners, a number of initiatives are going much further, reimagining the structures that make exploitation of renters possible in the first place. Perhaps the most successful is the Landless Worker's Movement in Brazil, a NURTURED NETWORK that, since 1984, has put increasing political pressure on the state government to reverse Brazil's ongoing concentration of land ownership. Through nonviolent actions like occupations and marches, the movement has successfully resettled over 370,000 peasants onto land they now own.[29] A small fraction of the work that is needed, but a significant step in the right direction.

Another case study comes in the British community of Letchworth, where an experiment in community ownership has been playing out for over a century. Since 1903, Letchworth's four thousand acres of land have been owned by the community as a whole, while the homes built on them are owned by individual families. The community generates income by leasing homes and businesses, which is then used to fund public services such as schools and hospitals.[3]

In the United States, a number of innovative organizational models are emerging to provide community-owned housing, retail services, electricity, and open space. Community land trusts such as Charm City in Baltimore and TRUST South LA are buying abandoned homes to fix up for low-income homeowners and vacant lots to transform into public commons. Cooperatives like the Renaissance Community Co-op in Greensboro, North Carolina, and the Westwood Food Co-op in Denver are building democratically owned grocery stores in food deserts from the ground up. Real estate investment cooperatives from New York City to Detroit are establishing mechanisms for investors to fund property acquisitions and renovations to fill critical gaps that the antimarket won't provide. And in the realm of electrical power, a number of municipal and cooperative utilities are disrupting the oligarchic practices of for-profit utility companies, placing the sources and profits of electricity generation in the hands of those consuming it.

While the hard technologies of regenerative infrastructure are nearing maturity, the invisible structures of INFRASTRUCTURE COMMONS are still nascent. As of yet, none has fully succeeded in DETHRONING THE ANTIMARKETS from their role as lords of our infrastructure, but little by little, communities are figuring out how to gain control of their infrastructure, opening the doors for a vastly more creative and equitable future.

FURTHER LEARNING

City Repair. *City Repair's Placemaking Guidebook—Creative Community Building in the Public Right of Way.* N.p.: Lulu, 2011.

APPLYING THE PATTERN

What material capital in your community is in the commons? What opportunities are there in your community to return infrastructure and community capital to the commons? What things do you own that could be shared? What are you planning to buy that you could share instead? What are some basic common needs—such as housing, healthy food, and green spaces—that are not being adequately provided for in your community by existing forces of government and corporate power? What would a commons approach to developing, obtaining, or distributing such resources look like? Is there a void of power, or would you need to wrest power from existing authorities to accomplish your aims?

26. CREATIVE DESTRUCTION

Things fall apart. Be mindful of the inevitability of change, and aim to ally yourself with the forces of disturbance.

Difficulty is what wakes up the genius.

—Nassim Nicholas Taleb, *Antifragile:*
Things That Gain from Disorder

Most of the time, ecosystems show a remarkable stability in the face of nature's harsh conditions. During challenging situations—a dry spell or a cold, dark winter—the dense web of relationships between species keeps the system hanging together until the conditions become more favorable. Most of the time. Every once in awhile, however, that web of interconnections is ripped to shreds by more dramatic events. Forest fires, earthquakes, floods, and disease outbreaks wreak their own kinds of havoc, driving some creatures out and leaving empty niches in their wake. In ecology, events like these are called *disturbances*.

For an individual organism, disturbance is often deadly, and being individuals ourselves, we tend to think of disturbance as something to be avoided. But from the perspective of the system itself, these disasters are a feature, not a bug. In THE LONG GAME, most ecosystems actually need disturbance to maintain long-term health. In the mountain forests of the American West, for instance, many species of conifer require the heat of a forest fire for their seeds to germinate, and their soils rely on the jolt of fertility supplied by the burn. What's more, the empty spaces created by disturbance events also allow for the web of life to be rewoven in novel ways, creating new connections between species and accelerating the pace of evolution. Paleontologist Stephen Jay Gould coined the memorable phrase *punctuated equilibrium* to describe his theory that these shakeups are actually responsible for most evolutionary change.

As in ecology, so too in the human realm. Throughout history, instances of civilizational disturbance have been profound events, shaking up the arrangements of what we consider normal like a snow globe. Five hundred years ago, nascent European antimarkets unleashed a global disturbance event, exploiting the Western Hemisphere's vast reserves of natural capital while decimating local populations through disease and slavery. Four hundred years later, the disturbance of World War I marked the beginning of the end for the European colonial endeavor and the start of a century of American global hegemony.

While global disturbances like these make the history books, smaller examples are happening all the time on more humble scales. Natural disasters or local civil wars shake up the established order of specific regions. Layoffs, lawsuits, bankruptcies, and buyouts are all forms of disturbance at the institutional level. Disturbance rears its ugly head on an interpersonal level through family feuds, romantic breakups, and the death of loved ones, while individuals experience it as times of acute illness, addiction, or existential crisis.

No matter the scale, these are times of profound challenge and distress for those experiencing them. But, as the saying goes, what doesn't kill you makes you stronger—as long as the disturbance leaves some part of the affected system intact, it will be a vital leverage point for positive transformation. Precisely *because* disturbance is a time when everything is up for grabs, it provides opportunities for new ways of thinking and acting to take root. Just as new species and relationships emerge from ecological disturbance, hitting rock bottom can inspire a desperate person to start a new life path. A bankruptcy can lead to a new business model. A natural disaster can strengthen social capital, creating INTIMACY THROUGH ADVERSITY. And disturbances at the scale of civilizations can point our society in profoundly exciting new directions.

This pattern of creation-via-destruction has long been central to paradigms in eastern Asia. The Hindu gods Shiva and Kali are both considered agents of creative destruction. Taoism's fundamental premise is that change is inevitable, and Taoist philosophers have spent millennia examining the best ways to respond to change. Slowly, the scientific worldview is beginning to catch up, as well. From Darwin's seminal writings 150 years ago to David Holmgren's permaculture principle "creatively use and respond to change," adaptability in the face of disturbance has increasingly been recognized as a critical component of healthy systems. One of the most vivid contemporary depictions of creative destruction comes from Nassim Nicholas Taleb, who coined the term *antifragile* to describe people, organizations, and other systems that actually benefit from chaos.

In today's increasingly chaotic world, the concept of antifragility seems more pertinent than ever. How can our movements and organizations take after Shiva and learn to thrive in the face of ecological and social disturbance? How can we make our personal lives antifragile without becoming cold and callous? No matter the scale, managing disturbance is a delicate balancing act. The line between CREATIVE DESTRUCTION and plain old destructive destruction is a tightrope, and the ground a long way down. Philosophers have been pondering that tightrope for many generations—and ecosystems have been walking it for many times longer. Together, their insights point to a few key attitudes to keep in mind.

WELCOME DISTURBANCE

If you realise that all things change,
there is nothing you will try to hold onto.
If you aren't afraid of dying,
there is nothing you can't achieve.[31]

The most destructive disturbances can often be avoided by learning to live with frequent smaller ones. Our mismanagement of the fire-adapted western forests mentioned above is a case in point. For the last 150 years, we've been so successful at keeping fire at bay that the trees are now far denser than they've ever been. Now, when a fire does start, the abundance of fuel leads to infernos that are much too long and hot for the trees to recover from. In nearly every discipline, analogous situations abound. From our use of antibiotics and pesticides to our eagerness to pave over storm-water basins, we've unwittingly created the conditions for lethal destruction by trying to dodge minor disturbances. If we're to minimize long-term damage, we must learn to accept disturbance as a fact of life.

HAVE A PLAN

Prevent trouble before it arises.
Put things in order before they exist.

What's the biggest threat to geopolitical stability? What's plan B if I get laid off? What should I do if I get stuck in a storm on a backcountry hike? The people most likely to benefit from CREATIVE DESTRUCTION are the ones who see it coming and have solutions on hand. We can hope to avoid destructive situations, but our hopes shouldn't blind us to the threats around us. Pursuing Wilderness First Responder training, creating a firebreak on a wooded property, and planning our RIGHT LIVELIHOOD around a polyculture of incomes are just a few examples of planning for disturbance.

STAY OPTIMISTIC

Therefore the Master remains
serene in the midst of sorrow.
Evil cannot enter his heart.

In times of disturbance, there are many factors beyond our influence. But the biggest single factor we can control is our attitude. Our ability to survive and thrive in the face of destruction is dramatically influenced by the way we frame external events to ourselves and others around us. In short, it's about TELLING THE STORY that will allow us to maintain inspiration and hope in the face of trying circumstances.

MINIMIZE RISK

Confront the difficult
while it is still easy;
accomplish the great task
by a series of small acts.

Some parts of a system are more vulnerable to shock than others. People who prepare themselves for CREATIVE DESTRUCTION are experts at recognizing the weakest link in the chain, and taking the necessary steps to strengthen or eliminate it. Is your SMALL BUSINESS relying too much on the whims of a single customer? Spread the risk by seeking out other markets to sell to. Worried about a political action leading to arrests? Take extra care to train everyone involved in the principles of NONVIOLENT STRUGGLE—and have a bail fund set aside, just in case. Finding your personal goals stymied by bad habits? Use Looby Macnamara's concept of SPIRALS OF ABUNDANCE to identify the roots of your unhealthy behavior and turn them around.

STICK AROUND LONG ENOUGH TO STICK AROUND

Do you have the patience to wait
till your mud settles and the water is clear?
Can you remain unmoving
till the right action arises by itself?

Humans have a tendency to cling to what's familiar. We go out of our way to preserve those things we're used to. For nonperishable things like ideas, practices, or institutions, this can lead to something called the *Lindy Effect*, which states that the mortality rate of memes actually decreases with time. The longer something's been around, in other words, the more likely it is to stick around even longer. In practice, this means that if our efforts can help us make it out of the phase of novelty and become part of the new normal, they will have a much higher chance of surviving unexpected circumstances.

FURTHER LEARNING

Greene, Graham. "The Destructors." In *Twenty-One Stories*. London: Penguin, 1993.

Lao Tzu. *Tao Te Ching*. Translated by Stephen Mitchell. London: Francis Lincoln, 2009.

Taleb, Nassim Nicholas. *Antifragile: Things That Gain from Disorder*. New York: Random House, 2014.

APPLYING THE PATTERN

What potential disturbances face your community? You can use SECTOR AND ZONE ANALYSES to identify potential vectors of disturbance at the personal, interpersonal, institutional, and regional levels in your life. In facing these vulnerabilities, what opportunities do you see for CREATIVE DESTRUCTION? Who or what are the forces for CREATIVE DESTRUCTION in your community? How could you initiate or leverage disturbances at each of these scales to grow more resilient?

27. NONViOLENT STRUGGLE

When policy and law fail to deliver justice, the patient, creative, and dedicated efforts of nonviolent groups can bring about unprecedented transformation.

A crowd whose discontent has risen no higher than the level of slogans is only a crowd. But a crowd that understands the reasons for its discontent and knows the remedies is a vital community, and it will have to be reckoned with.

—Wendell Berry

A society modeled on nature is one that seeks, by default, to collaborate. The abundance and longevity of natural systems is due in large part to countless mutually beneficial relationships between organisms, some of them quite unexpected. As we humans seek to expand THE EDGE OF CHANGE, a good deal of our progress is likely to happen by transforming relationships of enmity into ones of partnership.

Sometimes, however, partnership simply isn't an option. All too often, our liberatory efforts are about escaping violence and repression—conditions that don't exactly respond well to collaboration or bargaining. Even in less extreme cases, our aims are frequently diametrically opposed to those in power. The principle of SUBSIDIARITY, for instance, is about weakening the control of the central state, while acts of COMMONING are explicitly designed to loosen the grip of antimarkets. Sometimes we have no choice but to confront these institutions directly to bring about the change demanded by the people.

These confrontations, in which courageous citizens challenge tyrants and colonizers and demand their freedom, have been happening since long before recorded history. Many of these struggles failed tragically, with countless lives and stories alike lost in the sea of historical forgetting. Of the ones that succeeded, meanwhile, many did so when the people took up arms, only to become the very despots they had despised years earlier. As effective as it may be in achieving short-term victory, violence has a way of blurring the line between good guys and bad guys, bringing all sides down in a spiral of erosion.

A small but growing number of resistance campaigns, however, have found another way out: nonviolence. The modern nonviolent movement is generally considered to have begun in the 1920s with Mahatma Gandhi's remarkably successful campaigns to gain India's independence from British colonial rule. Gandhi articulated a doctrine he called *satyagraha*, "insistence on truth": a commitment to big-t Truth that focused as much on the means of resistance as the ends and that aimed to convert the opposition instead of overpower it. Nearly a century later, revolutionaries from Tunisia to Ukraine continue to employ many of Gandhi's techniques, along with other methods gained along the way.

Perhaps incredibly, it appears to work. In 2007, researchers Maria J. Stephan and Erica Chenoweth set out to systematically explore the relative success of violent and nonviolent campaigns against state governments throughout the twentieth century. They found that nonviolent efforts were about *twice* as likely to succeed as armed ones.[32] Their analysis posits that this remarkable gap largely comes down to public perception. Internal and international stakeholders alike are more likely to sympathize with nonviolent campaigns than violent ones, seeing them as less extreme, and this increases the pressure on the state to back down.

Of course, nonviolent struggle isn't just about endeavors as epic as toppling dictators. Contemporary campaigns are racking up wins in favor of criminal justice reform and against oil pipelines and sexual assault policies on college campuses. Regardless of their aim, successful nonviolent campaigns require just as much strategy and hard work as any other political movement. The critical difference is that they use tools that are creative rather than destructive.

A key strategy of successful nonviolent struggle is setting up strategic confrontations aimed at DISROBING THE EMPEROR. In these "dilemma situations," authorities are forced to choose between backing down or taking their repression to patently absurd lengths, thereby calling into question their very legitimacy. In August 2016, students at the University of Texas at Austin set up just such a dilemma situation to protest a new law allowing gun owners to carry firearms on campus. They openly brandished dildos, which was against university policy, to display a ridiculous contrast with the legal guns.

ARTS OF RESISTANCE, meanwhile, can create a unified brand for a nonviolent struggle. From the spirituals sung during the civil rights movement to contemporary hashtag- and meme-based organizing, creative expression plays a central role during times of nonviolent struggle by countering the fear of confronting powerful interests.

But perhaps most important is building a solid grassroots base of support. The images most associated with nonviolent resistance are the grand marches and protests, but these transformative moments can succeed only after countless hours of strategic and tactical organizing, conducting POWER ANALYSES, forming coalitions, TELLING THE STORY, and slowly building LEADERSHIP FROM WITHIN. As Srdja Popovic puts it, "The big rally isn't the spark that launches the movement. It's the victory lap."[33]

Even with all these factors in place, the chance of a nonviolent movement succeeding, according to Stephan and Chenoweth, is only slightly greater than fifty-fifty. Nevertheless, with enough dedication, the right HUMAN POLYCULTURE, and a careful strategy, nonviolent struggle is capable of accomplishing what may at first seem impossible.

FURTHER LEARNING

Chenoweth, Erica, and Maria J. Stephan. *Why Civil Resistance Works: The Strategic Logic of Nonviolent Conflict.* New York: Columbia University Press, 2012.
Popovic, Srdja. *Blueprint for Revolution: How to Use Rice Pudding, Lego Men, and Other Nonviolent Techniques to Galvanize Communities, Overthrow Dictators, or Simply Change the World.* New York: Spiegel and Grau, 2015.

APPLYING THE PATTERN

What parts of your PERSONAL VISION cannot be solved through traditional channels of policy change or economic transformation? What NONVIOLENT STRUGGLES are you familiar with? How did you find out about them? How did you feel about them? What NONVIOLENT STRUGGLES are happening now in your community? Are there ways to lend your skills in support of them? What principles of NONVIOLENT STRUGGLE can you use in the work you're currently doing or in your community?

28. SOLIDARITY

No matter our position in society, the chances are that there's someone in our community who has less access to opportunity than we do. Allyship and solidarity acknowledge our obligations to those people—and offer the opportunity for our entire community to be made more whole.

Washing one's hands of the conflict between the powerful and the powerless means to side with the powerful, not to be neutral.

—Paulo Freire

If you have come here to help me, you are wasting your time. But if you have come because your liberation is bound up with mine, then let us work together.

—Aboriginal activist group, Queensland, 1970s

Why care about the downtrodden? More than a century of liberal humanism has taught us that the well-being of the marginalized is a moral issue, but the lessons of ecosystem dynamics demonstrate that it's a practical one as well. If ecology has anything to teach us about human communities, it's the importance of looking after the health of *every* member of a community—not only those who are directly connected to us. Destroying a pollinator's habitat can result in trees thirty miles away failing to reproduce. Contaminants absorbed at the bottom of the food chain can quickly work their way up to the top predator, becoming more and more concentrated as they go. The system is only as durable as its weakest link.

Our human communities are no different; chronic stress in one part of society taxes the system as a whole. Unlivable wages necessitate the creation of expensive (and often inefficient) social programs to provide a safety net. Pollution in one community leads to higher cancer rates, which raise insurance premiums for everyone. Mass incarceration crystallizes attitudes of distrust and apathy, creating a spiral of criminal behavior and further arrests.

In Catholic philosophy, SOLIDARITY was conceived of as the equal and opposing force to SUBSIDIARITY. While the doctrine of SUBSIDIARITY says that decisions should be made at the smallest practical scale, SOLIDARITY reminds us that groups within society have obligations to one another to ensure their mutual well-being. Like SUBSIDIARITY, SOLIDARITY was a key value of progressive movements throughout the late nineteenth and early twentieth centuries. In recent years, the concept has reemerged under the banner of "allyship," the obligations of the privileged to remove injustice. The Multicultural Resource Center at Oberlin College defines an ally as "a member of the 'dominant' or 'majority' group who questions or rejects the dominant ideology and works against oppression through support of, and as an advocate, with or for, the oppressed population."[34]

Over the last several years, dozens of committed and thoughtful allies have documented their journeys and lessons, and a number of common themes have emerged:

- *Understand and recognize privilege.* Conditions of inequality tend to be much more obvious when viewed from below. Men rarely have to think about sexism, for example, while for white people the specter of racism is more intellectual than visceral. Many of us have lived our entire lives without having to contemplate the daily challenges encountered by our neighbors. The first step in SOLIDARITY is acknowledging privilege—a process that takes intention and effort. While we cannot understand the lived experiences of groups other than our own, by maintaining a curious and open mind, we can begin the process of mutual understanding.

- *Don't consider yourself a savior.* Those of us with privilege are used to being the center of attention. We're the first to raise our hands in class and the first to be called on. We're consulted for advice and asked to give public talks. Over time, these actions reinforce our self-perception as being the ones that everyone else gathers around. But when it comes to allyship and SOLIDARITY, this mentality reinforces the very dynamics we're trying to undo. As student antiracist organizer Chris Dixon puts it, "we absolutely should not be 'getting' people of color to join 'our' organizations. This is not just superficial; it's tokenistic, insulting, and counterproductive."[35] Instead, it's up to allies to cultivate the self-awareness and humility to put themselves in roles of support rather than dominance.

- *Acknowledge your guilt—and compost it.* It's natural to feel guilty or ashamed for all the ways you and your ancestors have taken advantage of others. But as JLove Calderón and Marcella Hall explain, focusing too much on that guilt "centers the story/process/group back on the privileged person—which is typically the opposite of what would be liberating for the group."[36] Instead, we can heed the advice of SANKOFA, striving to transcend our feelings of guilt and shame and approaching our work with a sense of responsibility and open-mindedness to change. After all, it's not our whiteness, maleness, or class privilege that defines who we are—it's how we *respond* to those facts of our identity that shapes our destinies.

- *Earn trust.* SOLIDARITY happens through consent, not imposition. Meaningful allyship must be grounded in trust, which, given the circumstances of engagement, can take a long time to form. I had the opportunity to learn firsthand what it takes to earn trust during my time at the GrowHaus. From the beginning, we'd envisioned an organization led by the Latino immigrants who lived in our community. Yet no one in our founding team came from that background, and our initial efforts at outreach and feedback were met with indifference and polite skepticism. It took a full three years of continuously listening, building relationships, and learning the subtle dynamics of the neighborhood before residents took us seriously. Eventually, more and more community members stepped into leadership roles, and the organization took on the community-driven structure we'd always wanted. But it was only through humility, patience, and a willingness to engage in authentic listening that we were able to get there.

- *Educate yourself.* At some point in the past, nearly all of our ancestors lived in small, humble communities rooted in the rhythms of a specific place. What was our family's path from these INTERDEPENDENT COMMUNITIES to our current place in society? When did they struggle, and when were they in positions of relative strength? What was their relationship with neighbors unlike them? The answers may not always be pretty. But the more we learn about our own family's negotiations with privilege and oppression over the centuries, the better equipped we'll be to understand how we got where we are.

It's equally important, meanwhile, for us to explore the histories of the communities we currently live in—particularly the oft-untold stories of marginalized communities. What policies and people accelerated injustice? Who were the unsung heroines that spoke truth to power? My hometown, Denver, was dominated by the KKK in the 1920s and was ground zero for the national Chicano movement forty years later—but I wouldn't have known any of that history if I hadn't started digging.

- *Be willing to make mistakes and to learn from them.* Mistakes are an unavoidable part of allyship and SOLIDARITY. Given that so many of our cultural norms guide us back toward patterns of exploitation, a few stumbles on the road to DECOLONIZATION are expected and perfectly okay— as long as we're committed to learning from them. Don't be surprised if you become the subject of CALLING OUT, CALLING IN, and resist the kneejerk reaction of defensiveness when you are. Showing Up for Racial Justice (SURJ)—a national network of local groups committed to white allyship—has designed systems of feedback and accountability built into their very organizational structure. In order to ensure that members are acting the spirit of allyship and SOLIDARITY, every SURJ member in a leadership role is asked to check in with an "accountability group" on a regular basis. The organization as a whole, meanwhile, has an accountability council led by people of color.

- *Emphasize action, not intention.* Most of us genuinely want to see a world where the wounds of our past are healed, where all members of society are able to express their fullest potential. But good intentions are seldom enough to catalyze change. Unless we seek to back up our intentions with proactive behavior, we'll remain passive witnesses to injustice. That means putting our money where our mouth is and sharing access to resources with people who have historically been shut out of the levers of power.

These tips are a starting point, but they're not comprehensive. Much like our acts of ecological STEWARDSHIP, our acts of SOLIDARITY will never feel complete or perfect. But making the effort is extremely valuable. If we progressively challenge our personal and collective EDGES OF CHANGE, our models for change will become wiser and more inclusive as a result.

FURTHER LEARNING

Calderón, JLove. *Occupying Privilege: Conversations on Race, Love, and Liberation.* Brooklyn, NY: Love-N-Liberation Press, 2012.

Freire, Paulo. *Pedagogy of the Oppressed.* New York: Bloomsbury, 2000.

APPLYING THE PATTERN

Have you begun the journey of acknowledging your privileges? How does it feel to acknowledge your privileges? Are there ways you can use those privileges in allyship and SOLIDARITY with others in your community? Look at the list above— how can you be a better ally to those with fewer privileges than you? How can you encourage those with more privileges than you to become allies?

29. ARTS OF RESISTANCE

In the face of injustice and fear, creative expression has a unique power to inspire, unite, and educate.

Art should comfort the disturbed, and disturb the comfortable.

—Cesar A. Cruz

Since humans first scrawled on the walls of caves and tamed their grunts into song, art has served as a vehicle for social change. If policy is the tool of the mind and armed conflict the tool of the vengeful body, art is the tool of the heart, tapping into the reserves of compassion, outrage, and inspiration that appear to be bottomless. When wielded skillfully, art can motivate everyday citizens to act, even where facts and rhetoric have already failed.

One of the most natural forms of public art is song. It doesn't take any special equipment or training to join in a group chorus—but the right words and melody, deployed at the right time, can inspire crowds of thousands. In the United States, protest songs have long played a critical role in African American liberation movements, from chain-gang chants to the spirituals of the civil rights era to contemporary Black Lives Matter anthems by Beyoncé and Kendrick Lamar. No Enemies is one group reclaiming the power of protest songs for the twenty-first century. Founded in 2014 by Jamie Laurie and Stephen Brackett of hip-hop group the Flobots, No Enemies collaborates with a variety of movements and organizations to bring song to protests, rallies, and direct actions. No Enemies leaders develop "musical action plans" for each event, selecting songs appropriate to the cause and training participants to sing them. The results are transformative, turning ordinary protests into transcendent and powerful events.

Singing may be one of the most egalitarian arts of protest—after all, anyone with a voice can sing—but it's hardly the only medium to be used for social change. Public theater, for example, has had an equally vivid history as an art of resistance. While its roots go back to ancient Greeks (and likely farther), the contemporary seed of today's activist theater is a set of dramatic exercises developed by Brazilian director Augusto Boal in the late twentieth century. Collectively referred to as the Theatre of the Oppressed, they range from dramatic readings of news articles to enacting "invisible theater" in public spaces. Together, Boal's theatrical tools have allowed activists around the globe to creatively confront, expose, and process injustice.

Visual art, meanwhile, has a long tradition posing critiques of the status quo and proposing visions of an alternative future. By treating private property as a public canvas, for instance, graffiti is an inherently subversive art form—and its impact is only heightened when it tackles social issues. Sculpture and installation art can be effective media of resistance as well, as when conceptual artist Olafur Eliasson and scientist Minik Rosing arranged several car-sized chunks of ice from Greenland's melting ice caps in a public square in Paris during the pivotal 2015 climate change conference.

Even comedy can play a role in social transformation; in his 2015 handbook *Blueprint for Revolution,* protest movement veteran Srdja Popovic astutely notes that "fear is best fought with laughter" and explains that most cops, trained to deal with violent demonstrators, get flustered and thrown off balance faced with comic actions.[37]

In the twenty-first century, perhaps the most powerful art of resistance is the one most associated with antimarkets: propaganda. In a culture where Nike's swoosh and McDonald's golden arches are better known than the flags of foreign countries, visual branding can become a potent tool for solidifying group identity in an activist movement. Groups like *Adbusters* magazine and Popovic's Serbian rebel movement Otpor began co-opting the tools of branding from oligarchs in the 1990s. Today, from the Guy Fawkes mask of the Occupy movement to the alt-right's adoption of Pepe the Frog, the importance of a visual identity for furthering a social movement is a given.

As our world continues to shift, new ARTS OF RESISTANCE are emerging to critique and protest injustice. As we become increasingly reliant on computer code, hacker collectives like Anonymous are bringing ARTS OF RESISTANCE to the computer screen. And the guerilla interventions of tactical urbanism are making conceptual art out of the public right-of-way. The ARTS OF RESISTANCE of our grandchildren remain to be seen. But one thing's certain—whether through song, theater, code, or any number of other art forms, SACRED ACTIVISTS will continue to catalyze their causes through artistic expression.

FURTHER LEARNING

Simon, Ronald T., and Marc Estrin. *Rehearsing with Gods: Photographs and Essays on the Bread and Puppet Theater.* White River Junction, VT: Chelsea Green, 2004.

APPLYING THE PATTERN

Think about the work that you do and the causes you work for. What forms of art might fit in with that work? What artists in your community could you collaborate with? Are you an artist? If so, how could your art help engage others in your cause? In the causes of others in your community?

30. DISROBING THE EMPEROR

A key step in the life cycle of a social movement is exposing the illegitimacy of dominant narratives. Erode the moral authority of those in charge through creative public actions.

In Hans Christian Andersen's beloved nineteenth-century folk tale "The Emperor's New Clothes," a pompous ruler ends up the butt of a practical joke, as a group of opportunistic tailors persuade the emperor that they've woven him a robe invisible to anyone unwise or unfit for his or her position. Eager to defend his own standing, the emperor pretends to be impressed and spends a fortune to acquire thin air. As he parades down the street naked, convinced that he's wearing the finest regalia, the commoners are too afraid of being labeled as unfit to say anything. Only when an innocent child speaks up, asking why the emperor has no clothes, are the people free to acknowledge publicly what they already understood privately—their ruler is faking it, and they've all been duped.

The tale might be intended for children, but its message is tragically relevant. From long before Andersen's time on up to the present day, those in power have cloaked themselves in invisible robes of unearned authority. By insisting on their own virtue and wisdom, today's corporate CEOs and political leaders get away with blatant manipulation of the social contract. Fashion models are photoshopped to an unreal level of perfection. Dismal employment statistics are massaged to sound as optimistic as possible. Antimarket businesses tweak their business models to be slightly less destructive and proudly brand themselves as leaders in sustainability and social responsibility.

These crimes of doublespeak and hypocrisy have become so blatant, so commonplace, that we hardly even bother calling them out. Yet any successful campaign of DETHRONING THE ANTIMARKETS must do just that. Like the child in Andersen's story, we must say out loud what we're all thinking. In our case, however, we know exactly what we're doing. The most successful acts of disrobing are deliberate and strategic, planned with as much calculation as the lies they're aiming to discredit. One of the best strategies is to create "dilemma situations"—circumstances in which the powerful are forced to publicly choose between perpetuating an obvious lie or making an embarrassing admission of fault. Depending on the situation, there are several tactics that can effectively pull the robes from our emperors.

One of the most obvious approaches is through education. Infographics, articles, documentaries, and books can all reveal important truths and convey powerful voices. On the political left, television shows like *Democracy Now!* and *The Daily Show* are part of a cottage industry of outrage at the powers that be. But in a media landscape that's ever more democratic, polarized, and over-saturated, it can be hard to separate daring investigative reporting from paranoid conspiracy theorizing. What's more, the way we often find this media— through algorithm-driven newsfeeds—means that the only citizens that see it are the ones already predisposed to be swayed by it. These tools run the risk of preaching to the choir, of only reaching those that are already educated about the issue.

Whistleblowing is an effective tactic for delegitimizing the narratives of the powerful. Articles or films can be dismissed as biased or uninformed, but elites have a much harder time refuting information revealed in their own leaked emails and bank accounts. In the last several years alone, Edward Snowden's revelations of government surveillance, Julian Assange's trove of diplomatic cables, and the offshore banking revelations of the Panama Papers have each caused embarrassment and consternation among pilots of the antimarket, further eroding trust in the institutions that guide us.

Both journalism and whistleblowing take an intellectualized approach to state and corporate malfeasance, and their tactics of accumulating of facts, statistics, and bald-faced lies are useful for building court cases. Yet in the court of public opinion, these tactics alone are unlikely to succeed in TELLING THE STORY compellingly enough for everyone to be convinced. Fortunately, there is a third approach to DISROBING THE EMPEROR that acknowledges MULTITUDES OF KNOWING and moves beyond the head to tug at our emotions. Rather than words and images on screens, this approach uses the power of narrative and theater as its tools, and public space as its canvas, to create what NYU media studies professor Stephen Duncombe terms an *ethical spectacle*.[38] Drawing upon ARTS OF RESISTANCE like the Theatre of the Oppressed, such actions hack the public discourse to demonstrate the absurdity of official rules and narratives. At the beginning of Syria's brutal civil war, for instance, creative insurrectionists protested Bashar Al-Assad's oppressive regime by dying public fountains red with food coloring and burying loudspeakers playing anti-Assad songs in dumpsters, forcing the police to climb into the filth to shut down the dissent. Others focus on turning the tables, visiting injustice upon the powerful. Jacques Servin and Igor Vamos, better known as the Yes Men, have mastered a form of political prank they call *identity correction:* posing as official representatives of a company and publicly saying what the company would say if it was forced to be perfectly honest. Since 2003, they've shamed everyone from Dow Chemical to the World Trade Organization through spoof websites, publications, and public appearances.

Not all of us have the skills or ability to perform identity correction (and not all of us can afford to risk arrest to do so), but plenty of other forms of ethical spectacle are available to us, allowing us to show strength in numbers without putting anyone's safety at risk. Whether through informational media, whistleblowing, or various forms of COORDINATED NONCOMPLIANCE, we have a whole array of tools at our disposal for exposing the falsehoods of the powerful.

FURTHER LEARNING

Boyd, Andrew, ed. *Beautiful Trouble: A Toolbox for Revolution.* New York: OR Books, 2012.

APPLYING THE PATTERN

What "emperors" rule over your community? What images do they clothe themselves in? Who might be helping them stay robed? What is the alternative story to what they're telling? What could you or your community do to help disrobe them? Brainstorm ways to use journalism, whistleblowing, and ethical spectacles in your community—which ones seem most effective?

31. COORDINATED NONCOMPLIANCE

Boycotts, strikes, and sanctions may not always inflict economic pain directly. Nevertheless, they can be a successful tool for drawing attention to a cause and increasing public pressure for change.

In Ireland in 1880, after a dismal harvest season, a large landowner offered his sharecropper tenants a 10 percent reduction in their rent to account for their loss. The tenants, balking at the false show of generosity, demanded a larger reduction—and when that was turned down, they waged an isolation campaign against the landowner's local land agent. Farmhands stopped working in his fields. Merchants refused to sell to him. Even the post officer took part, withholding his mail. That land agent's name was Captain Charles Boycott, and within a matter of months, his last name had become synonymous with the protestors' tactic of targeted ostracism.

The word may have been new, but the gambit wasn't. Boycotts have been recorded at least as far back as ancient Rome, and the Qur'an tells of one among rival trading groups during the time of Muhammad. Yet most of these historical boycotts failed to achieve their aims—and modern-day boycotts, centered largely on consumer goods, hardly fare better. In a study of 133 corporate boycotts between 1990 and 2005, Northwestern University professor Brayden King found a mere 25 percent were successful at reaching their stated objectives.[39] In a similar study, French researcher Philippe Delacote pointed out that the politically and ethically motivated individuals most likely to participate in a boycott were unlikely to be large consumers in the first place and rarely had the ability to make a major impact in the product's bottom line.[4] Nevertheless, a select number of boycotts actually have resulted in meaningful change. What did they have in common? King's and Delacote's studies point to four success factors:

- *Get press.* Even if the boycotts themselves don't succeed, they can still have a measurable impact on a company's reputation. King's study found that corporate boycotts attracting significant media attention sent the corporation's stock price down 0.7 percent for every day the boycott continued, regardless of whether the boycott met its desired objective.

- *Keep a narrow and clear target.* Among his list of failed boycotts, Delacote cites a number of attempts that required consumers to memorize a long list of companies to avoid, or decode a complicated certification label. Inevitably, these attempts only ended up confusing well-meaning participants. The lesson? While it may be the case that any number of antimarket actors are worth targeting for a boycott, it's best to focus on one at a time.

- *Ensure an easy alternative.* One of the most successful boycotts of the last century was a consumer campaign to avoid buying table grapes in order to secure better rights for the California farmworkers who worked in the vineyards. The boycott was coordinated by Cesar Chavez—the leader of the United Farm Workers Organizing Committee—and while a large part of its success was due to Chavez' charisma and strategic savvy, it was also helped by the nature of the product being avoided. Grapes are just one of many summer fruits, and it was easy for millions of consumers to temporarily forego them in SOLIDARITY. But in the monopolies and oligopolies crafted by antimarket economics, many products have no appealing alternative, making a successful boycott much more challenging.

- *Get organized.* Despite the popular conceptions that most boycotts are grassroots initiatives, King's study concluded that the most effective were led by professional organizations with the experience, time, and media connections to ensure their message spreads far and wide.

Under these conditions, boycotts can indeed be a powerful lever for COORDINATED NONCOMPLIANCE. But what about situations in which there isn't a viable alternative to the offending company—or where the target isn't a consumer product at all? One strategy is a divestment campaign, in which governments, foundations, mutual funds, and other large institutions are pressured to sell their stock in a company or group of companies. The first widespread divestment movement, targeted against South Africa in the 1980s, is believed by many to have helped bring about the end of Apartheid in South Africa. More recently, a growing movement to divest from fossil fuel corporations has been one of several tactics of NONVIOLENT STRUGGLE in the fight against climate change. As with boycotts, the relative success of divestment has little to do with the direct losses sustained by removing investments—any shares of stock sold, after all, are likely to be purchased by another institution. Instead, divestment's goal is to tarnish the brand image and corporate reputation of the targets, reducing their share price and global standing.

Both divestments and boycotts are tactics of coordinated nonconsumption. But the principles apply equally well, if not more so, to the realm of production. Rather than consumers refusing to buy, in labor strikes, employees refuse to work. In this case, the stakes are much higher—besides losing their jobs, strikers frequently run the risks of arrest, injury, or even death on the picket line. But the rewards for a successful strike are equally powerful, resulting in real and meaningful increases in working and living conditions for thousands of families. Like boycotts, strikes have a long and checkered past. Their heyday was the progressive era of the early twentieth century, as increasingly organized workers used strikes to negotiate labor standards like the eight-hour workday, standards that have long since been taken for granted. Between 1910 and 1950, workers in the textile, coal, steel, and railroad industries organized strikes involving hundreds of thousands of people, winning public sympathy and successfully bargaining for higher wages and safer working conditions. But as the power of unions waned in the postwar era, so too did the frequency and success of strikes. When they do occur today, strikes are much smaller and largely defensive, launched in reaction to proposed cuts in salaries or benefits instead of a demand for better ones.

Like boycotts, strikes are more likely to succeed when they have clear, specific demands and when they're able to attract media attention. Another key factor is successful mobilization of the workers. Stephen Lerner, an organizer behind several successful janitors' strikes in the early 2000s, tells of how striking janitors in Los Angeles were put to work as full-time organizers, exponentially multiplying the power of their movement.[41] Equally important is generating community sympathy by TELLING THE STORY of the strike in a way that resonates with the general public.[42] Micah Uetricht offers a telling case study in his book *Strike for America: Chicago Teachers against Austerity*. Before striking for better wages, Uetricht explains, the Chicago Teachers' Union "spent years at a community level establishing themselves as fighters for a broad educational justice movement."[43] By the time the teachers finally did get on the picket line, polls showed two-thirds of minority parents supported them, despite the disruptions the strike caused in their families.

Like a moment of silence in a monologue or the negative space in a painting, COORDINATED NONCOMPLIANCE leverages the power of absence to push THE EDGE OF CHANGE along. From targeted boycotts of millions of consumers to the brave walkouts of hundreds or thousands of employees, there are many options for flouting the parasitic cycles of the antimarket. Even in the most dire situations, when nearly all of one's freedoms have been stripped, hunger strikes prove that our will to choose remains an inalienable right.

APPLYING THE PATTERN

What products or organizations are causing harm in your community that might be ripe targets for a boycott? Do you have a clear message, a way to get press, and a viable alternative for consumers? What unions are active in your community? How can you play a role of SOLIDARITY in supporting their struggles for better wages and working conditions?

32. TRUTH AND RECONCILIATION

For many people, the injustices of the past remain all too real in the present. Only through a process of public reckoning can grievances be heard and a journey of healing begun.

There is a paradox at America's core. Our country was founded upon visionary principles of egalitarianism, principles that have led to unprecedented prosperity for millions. Yet a great deal of that prosperity was only made possible through unspeakable acts of violence. The vast majority of U.S. citizens, for instance, live on land that was stolen unceremoniously from its previous stewards. As those stewards were killed off from European diseases and warfare, America's nascent economy was propped up by the slave trade, a slow-motion genocide that decimated families, towns, and entire cultures. Throughout the late nineteenth and early twentieth centuries, wave after wave of immigrants from Ireland, Italy, Russia, and elsewhere fled famine and persecution in their homelands, only to be reviled upon reaching the "land of opportunity." And in more recent times, our love-hate relationship with cheap immigrant labor has kept millions of undocumented migrants in a shadow society, one misstep away from being deported.

For the lucky ones whose ancestors weren't impacted by these horrors, all this history may seem like water under the bridge—if it's even considered at all. Most Americans grow up with a narrative of our history that glosses over the everyday plight of the marginalized, instead focusing on battles, presidents, and laws. No matter what the textbooks say, however, the wounds of generations past remain vivid and painful in the present. Whenever a black person is arbitrarily pulled over by a police officer, the specter of slavery and segregation is present. When Jews encounter anti-Semitism, echoes of the Holocaust reverberate. And when Native Americans are promised just about anything by the federal government, their faith is tainted by centuries of massacres and disregarded treaties.

One might argue that much has changed in the ensuing generations. Decades of NONVIOLENT STRUGGLE and proactive legislation have created more opportunities for society's downtrodden than ever before. "Sure," some argue, "we may have made some mistakes in the past, but isn't it time to move on?" And yet it appears that the echoes of past trauma may be more than just emotional. Advances in the emerging field of epigenetics show that the effects of severe stress can be transferred to our children's DNA, lingering for generations after the original harm. In one recent study at New York's Mount Sinai Hospital, researcher Rachel Yehuda examined the genetics of thirty-two Jewish Holocaust survivors, as well as their children, and found the same genetic markers of pronounced stress in both generations. Yehuda was able to determine conclusively that the children's genetic changes were a direct result of the Holocaust experiences of their parents—experiences that they themselves had never been through. In Yehuda's words, "trauma itself gets inherited."[44]

If the injustices of our ancestors are altering our very genetics and that of our children, whose responsibility is it to make things right? For many, the answer starts with an honest and compassionate dialogue about the sins of our shared past—a process often referred to as *truth and reconciliation*. As the name implies, TRUTH AND RECONCILIATION processes aim to give an objective accounting of past injustices and propose a series of steps toward collective healing. In the words of media theorist Douglas Shuler, processes of TRUTH AND RECONCILIATION create "a forum in which adversaries can approach each other without insisting on punishment or revenge."[45] They are RESTORATIVE JUSTICE played out in the public discourse.

The modern history of TRUTH AND RECONCILIATION began with governmental commissions launched in the 1980s to investigate human rights abuses under dictators in Latin America. Rather than assign blame or guilt, the purpose was to illuminate all sides of the story, engaging citizens in collective conversation about what happened. Since then, TRUTH AND RECONCILIATION commissions have been convened to investigate abuses in Canada's Indian School System, political assassinations under Pinochet's Chile, slavery in Mauritius, racial hate crimes in Greensboro, North Carolina, and many more.

The best-known TRUTH AND RECONCILIATION commission was held in South Africa to investigate the abductions, killings, and torture carried out under apartheid from 1960 to 1994. Over the course of two years, the commission took the testimony of approximately twenty-one thousand victims, culminating in a report detailing recommendations for a program of financial and symbolic reparations. Here in the United States, a renewed national dialogue around racism has inspired an effort, backed by national foundations and an array of grassroots leaders, to develop a national TRUTH AND RECONCILIATION commission to address the unresolved legacy of slavery and its aftermath.[46]

With the right support and timing, formal efforts like these play a critical role in accelerating healing across entire nations. But TRUTH AND RECONCILIATION need not happen at the scale of an entire society or nation. Nearly every local community has skeletons in its closet that may be invisible to some and painfully real to others—a decades-old gay rights riot that most have forgotten, a local street named after a racist leader, the site of a massacre that has gone unmarked. Merely by publicly remembering these incidents, we are initiating a process of TRUTH AND RECONCILIATION, acknowledging mistakes and opening space for a dialogue to occur. As a result of this dialogue, institutions may offer public apologies, pardons, or reparations. And while none of these are in any way sufficient to heal the wounds of generations past, they create the necessary conditions for allowing us all to move forward with dignity.

FURTHER LEARNING

Hayner, Priscilla B. *Unspeakable Truths: Transitional Justice and the Challenge of Truth Commissions.* 2nd edition. New York: Routledge, 2011.

APPLYING THE PATTERN

What traumas persist in your community? In your city? Your nation? Your history? Have they been acknowledged or suppressed? How are systemic injustices felt on the local and individual scale? How can you work to uncover the truths of these legacies and begin a process of reconciliation? How can you work within your community to identify the traumas and injustices in your history and start the process of healing them?

33. BREAKING BREAD

Sharing a meal together is a sure way to build trust.

If you really want to make a friend, go to someone's house and eat with him.... The people who give you their food give you their heart.

—Cesar Chavez

The kitchen is the focal point of many households, often serving as a gathering area on par with the living room. Across the ages, restaurants have been central to a city's culture, much more than mere places to absorb nutrition. From the New Testament's Last Supper to the northwest Native American potlatch feasts, it's clear that shared meals have played a historically outsized role in building social and cultural capital.

Today, food continues to show up in many of our relationship-building interactions. We solidify business relationships over lunch and woo prospective dates over dinner. In schools across the country, the cafeteria is a playing field where cliques are forged and broken. And our weddings, birthday parties, family reunions, and holiday celebrations would be woefully incomplete without some kind of shared meal.

What is it about eating together that allows us to let our guard down? In her book *Eating Together: Food, Friendship, and Inequality,* sociologist Alice Julier examines the many ways that meals implicate themselves into our social fabric. While some eating practices reinforce exclusion, eating much more often has a role of breaking down barriers. Those who ate together, Julier found, viewed their fellow diners of different classes, genders, and races as more equal than they would otherwise.[47]

But for all its stickiness as a social glue, the shared meal is no longer the unifying force it once was. As with many of the other building blocks of social capital, communal eating is on the decline. A 2015 report from the Food Marketing Institute found that nearly half of all meals and snacks are now consumed solo.[48] And of the meals we still share, many are compromised by digital media—a group of eaters alone together, staring at screens.

The good news is that shared meals remain a surefire way to bring people together. They are catalysts of the NEMAWASHI process and can pave the way for processes of TRUTH AND RECONCILIATION in matters large and small. But meals can come together in many ways. What processes for communal meals are most effective at achieving the group cohesion we're after? If a restaurant or productive dinner party host represents meal-via-hierarchy—reliable and efficient—potlucks are the network, unpredictable but equitable. As such, they're a particularly common strategy for building group intimacy, functioning like a kind of gift economy. Each person feels invested in the outcome and is given an opportunity to share stories, recipes, and cultural capital.

But like networked groups themselves, potlucks are not a panacea. Many people don't have time or knowledge to prepare a dish in advance, or they may feel intimidated about cooking for others. And given that more people than ever adhere to some form of dietary restriction, making a dish that pleases everyone can feel like navigating a field of culinary landmines. For regular gatherings with a relatively small and stable group of participants, the role of cook can be shared among the group on a rotating basis. Depending on the financial situation, organizations can hire a caterer, or they can host the gathering in a restaurant and let participants pick up their own tabs.

Regardless of the form, one thing is clear. The way food is shared says a lot about the values of the people and groups involved. How is the menu determined? Are the dishes made with processed or whole ingredients? If there is a caterer, is it a local or a corporate one? If the meal is at a restaurant, does it share the values of the community? Are the dishes culturally relevant? Is there enough food for everyone? What happens to the leftovers? Even if your organization is not focused on food as a part of its mission, it's important to think through the messages that the food is sending at any communal meal you have.

APPLYING THE PATTERN

What individuals or groups would benefit from sharing a meal? Which format of shared meal is most appropriate? How can you highlight different cultures via food? How often do you eat alone? Could you use those times when you usually eat alone to break bread with members of your community? How often do you share meals with your coworkers or with people you don't know? Think about those whom you could build community with over a shared meal—what individuals or groups could benefit? Which formats of shared meals would be appropriate? Which might not be?

34. LETTING LOOSE

Times of celebration are valuable in building trust and giving groups a stress-release valve.

Virtually every activist has struggled with the question of how to get beyond "preaching to the choir." A first step is to make "the choir" the sort of place lots of people will want to join.

—Tracey Mitchell

From running a SMALL BUSINESS to planning a campaign of NONVIOLENT STRUGGLE, the work of building a better world requires persistence and focus. We brave snowstorms to attend important meetings. We perform physically demanding labor till our muscles hurt. We surrender our leisure time to ensure the success of our campaigns. In times of particularly high stakes—a product launch, an election, a critical demonstration—we might even put our own well-being on the backburner to ensure that the group's work is successful.

Too much diligence, however, can be just as detrimental as not enough. After all, nobody wants to work for a cause that's no fun, even if they're getting paid for it—and especially if they're not. Successful groups make fun a *part* of the culture. They understand that regular and irregular moments of celebration— as small as a group cheer at the end of the meeting or as large as a multiday festival—are key to sustaining momentum and morale.

Celebrations and other social activities can serve several functions in the mechanics of group cohesion. Celebrations often serve as a temporary ZONES OF AUTONOMY, suspending the usual norms of a group. We're often able to share parts of our personality we otherwise suppress, adding new depth to our day-to-day relationships. Long after the party's over, the laughter we shared allows us to see each other as human beings, not just as collaborators on a project. In tense situations, LETTING LOOSE can be a reset button, allowing people to address or let go of conflicts. If LETTING LOOSE is done in celebration of an accomplishment—meeting a key deadline or winning a campaign—it creates the opportunity for people to informally reflect and express gratitude to one another for a job well done. Finally, celebrations can be great opportunities to welcome new people to a project or movement. For instance, by partnering with touring musical acts, the Permaculture Action Network has leveraged the energy of celebration to engage young people in permaculture projects happening in their own communities. At each show on the tour, the artists give a heartfelt pitch for permaculture and announce a project that will be worked on the following day. Swayed by the collective excitement of the show, dozens or hundreds of volunteers show up, learning about permaculture for the first time while lending their hands to acts of GADUGI.

With all these advantages, it's not surprising that researchers are beginning to confirm the measurable benefits of LETTING LOOSE—both for organizations and the people within them. Take, for instance, the informal socializing often labeled "water-cooler talk." At a day-to-day level, it might seem unproductive to spend ten minutes chatting with your officemate about weekend plans and pet memes. Yet a 2008 MIT Study led by Alex Pentland and Benjamin Waber found just the opposite. After gathering workplace data on information-technology specialists for a month, they concluded that informal interactions in a group actually appear to *increase* the amount of work that gets done.[49]

And it's not just productivity that improves when people let loose. Socializing with coworkers also appears to be directly connected to workers' health. A 2011 study by researchers at Tel Aviv University tracked 820 workers for a decade and found that a culture of workplace socializing was positively correlated with lower mortality rates.[5] People who hang out with their coworkers, in other words, are likely to live longer.

Hopefully, it doesn't take the lure of an extra few years of life to convince us to let loose. Ultimately, studies like these only confirm what we already know—communities are made stronger by regular moments of collective celebration. Far from being a distraction or guilty pleasure, LETTING LOOSE is a critical part of any successful social movement. And the worse the outside circumstances are, the more vital the ability to celebrate becomes.

APPLYING THE PATTERN

Is there a balance between work and celebration in your life? When was the last time you celebrated something special in your organization? What currently goes ignored in your community or personal life that deserves to be recognized and celebrated? What are some ways you can encourage informal socializing among the members of your community? How can you be inclusive of those who might be reluctant to socialize for personal reasons?

35. RiTES OF PASSAGE

Hold space for members of your community who are going through transformative experiences.

Among the Ndembu tribe in Zambia, both boys and girls are raised by the tribe's women, while the men live in a separate compound in the village. In their book *Risk Taking and Rites of Passage*, Scott Lawson and Lloyd Martin explain that, once Ndembu the boys come of age, the men "kidnap" them in the middle of the night and take them into the bush for six months. During the day, they're given hunting weapons and expected to fend for themselves, while in the evenings they sit with the men, who relate stories and wisdom from their past.[51]

Most of us in the overdeveloped world don't have quite so dramatic a transition into adulthood, but even so, we face a number of potentially terrifying transitions over the course of our lives: puberty, adulthood, marriage, becoming a parent, losing loved ones, the frailty of old age, and the inevitability of our own eventual death. Many of these transitions are marked by a specific kind of RITUAL AND CEREMONY we refer to as a *rite of passage*—a phrase coined by early twentieth-century anthropologist Arnold van Gennep. Graduation ceremonies, weddings, baby showers, and funerals are widely shared ritual expressions of life transitions. And while each one of these RITES OF PASSAGE unfolds differently, what they all share is a focus on involving the subject's greater community. In fact, the impact of the rite of passage on the community at large is often just as important as the impact on the subject. As youth and community development experts David Blumenkrantz and Marc Goldstein explain in a 2014 paper for *New Directions for Higher Education,* "A child's coming of age presents an opportunity for the whole community to examine, adapt and re-commit themselves to their social and cultural heritage."[52]

Today many of us lack a social or cultural heritage we feel comfortable calling our own. Perhaps it's not surprising, then, that the communal importance of the rite of passage has started to wane. Many of the rituals mentioned above have lapsed into perfunctory exercises, their original resonance reduced to a pale echo. Meanwhile, other RITES OF PASSAGE have been abandoned entirely, often leaving people scared and confused as they experience a dramatic life transition. Youth who don't participate in a confirmation, *quinceañera,* or bar or bat mitzvah may end up muddling through the transition to puberty without any acknowledgment from their greater community. Later in life, we're similarly expected to handle the loss of our parents or spouses on our own once the funeral ends. Lawson and Martin note that contemporary rituals marking the transition from adolescence to adulthood often take place away from home, through things like "gap years," mission trips, and other travel experience. While they may be successful in advancing personal growth, they leave both the youth and their community lacking a critical integration. "What these contrived rituals usually lack is a connection between a young person's liminal experience and the communities left behind. The young people miss out on having their connection to a stable community strengthened, and the community itself misses out on being renewed by new stories and adventures. An experience in isolation may result in temporary connections between participants, but the young people themselves have not been developed into citizens of their own family, church, school, or community."[53]

In short, we aren't meant to experience times of transition alone. They are community acts, times when we need our family and friends more than ever. By reframing RITES OF PASSAGE as collective experiences, the social capital of INTERDEPENDENT COMMUNITIES is strengthened in many ways. Those who haven't yet experienced those life transitions themselves can learn what may be on the horizon. Those who have, meanwhile, are given the opportunity to reminisce, relate, and offer advice, creating greater intergenerational ties. And by sharing experiences of joy, empathy, and grief as one, the community as a whole is brought closer together.

FURTHER LEARNING

Lawson, Scott, and Lloyd Martin. "Risk Taking and Rites of Passage." *Reclaiming Children and Youth* 20, no. 4 (2012): 37–40.

APPLYING THE PATTERN

What are the recent life transitions you've experienced? Did you feel seen by your community? Did you feel like you received adequate support from your community? What are the transitions you've witnessed? How might you support the people going through them? What rituals do you have for life transitions? What life transitions do you wish were supported by RITES OF PASSAGE in your community? If you could create RITES OF PASSAGE for them, what would they look like?

36. GADUGI

Communities are bound closer together when members provide communal labor for one another.

M ost of the patterns in this book focus on the interpersonal work necessary for building a better society. But the crafting of a better world is also bound to require plenty of physical labor: building homes, planting trees, restoring damaged landscapes, and so forth. This kind of work is repetitive and physically exhausting. It does not abide by our preferences for comfortable weather. It does not care about our emotions. For most of human history, manual labor has been necessary—it's only in the last century that a substantial portion of society *hasn't* been engaged in physical labor on a regular basis.

Imperial societies have tended to meet their labor needs through some combination of service and slavery, conscripting of vast numbers of citizens to leave their homes and assist with public works. By contrast, when Americans of European descent first ventured into the American West, labor often was the lonely work of grizzled pioneers. But in many other places and times, the physical labor necessary for survival has actually been a cause for celebration—because it wasn't performed alone. Around the globe, cultures evolved remarkably similar rituals that brought together their able-bodied members for temporary swarms of mutual aid and socializing.

Finnish villagers help each other build log houses through the thirteen-thouosand-year-old tradition of *talkoot*.

COMMUNAL LABOR IN OTHER LANGUAGES

Bayanihan (Filipino)

Gadugi (Cherokee)

Gotong-royong (Javanese)

Meitheal (Irish)

Mink'a (Quechua)

Naffir (Arabic)

Talkoot (Finnish)

The Sudanese host a group work party called a *naffir* to get the weeding and harvesting done in their fields. And among the Cherokee, labor-intensive annual tasks like shelling corn are accomplished with the ethic of *gadugi*, which simply means "working together." Despite the tremendous variation in cultural norms, climates, and the work that needs to be done, each of these traditions of communal labor features the same four elements:

Communal labor is local. Participating members generally live in close proximity to one another.

Communal labor is equitable. It rotates from household to household as the need arises, relying on no single home over the others.

Communal labor is the norm. Participation is voluntary, but there is strong cultural pressure to participate—especially if you've recently been on the receiving end.

Communal labor is celebratory. It doubles as an opportunity for participants to socialize and gossip. Invariably, the hosts express their gratitude and contribute to the atmosphere of conviviality by supplying food and drink.

Regardless of the culture, traditions of communal labor require solid reserves of social capital to incentivize enough people to participate and follow through on their reciprocal obligations. Perhaps it's no surprise, then, that most of these local traditions faded with the arrival of antimarket economies. One by one, families realized that they could avoid the cultural obligation of performing work for their neighbors by paying a stranger to do their own work. By turning labor into a quantifiable commodity, cash transactions made the INTERDEPENDENT COMMUNITY feel redundant.

Today, of course, physical labor has become thoroughly integrated into the monetary economy. But with the shift from communal labor to wage labor, the distribution of that work shifted. Instead of large groups coming together to build a house or harvest a field in a short timespan, this work is now performed by a small section of the population that moves from place to place, performing it day in and day out as needed. And because few people would willingly perform this kind of work unless they had no other choice, these tasks end up being performed by those with the fewest options: migrants, incarcerated laborers, and others at the bottom of society's ladder.

FIVE TIPS FOR A KILLER WORK PARTY

Communal labor can be a useful and inspiring act for everyone involved—but it takes a significant amount of prep work to do well. Happily, there are guidelines:

- *Be a discerning matchmaker.* Look for a genuine fit between participants and the activities involved. Make sure that the proposed tasks match the skill levels of the group.

- *Make participants feel invested.* Draw explicit connections between the labor involved and the interests and values of the participants. Explain the tangible improvement that their work will yield.

- *Make it easy.* Break down the day into a series of tasks, and determine the number of people appropriate for each one. If possible, delegate an experienced team lead in advance to answer questions. Provide clear written instructions to volunteers. Round up all the necessary tools and materials in advance.

- *Make it fun.* Provide healthy food, plenty of water, frequent breaks, and upbeat music, so everyone will feel inspired and nourished throughout the labor. Save time to celebrate your accomplishment at the end.

- *Expect a mess.* Despite your best intentions, something is bound to go wrong. Maybe the group gets everything done in half the allotted time— or maybe they take forever and have to leave before the first task is done. Have backup plans ready.

Yet even in our intensely money-dominated world, instances of communal labor live on. Old-fashioned barnraisings persist among Amish and Mennonite communities. The international nonprofit Habitat for Humanity recruits thousands of volunteers annually to help construct affordable housing along with the homeowners-to-be. And in the global permaculture community, *permablitzes* have become a common way for property owners to accomplish major installations while educating curious community members about new gardening or natural building techniques.

Communal labor isn't ideal for all physical work; it generally works best in situations that don't require extensive experience or skill. Any skilled services performed as part of the effort deserve fair compensation, whether in antimarket money or an HEIRLOOM CURRENCY. And despite the truism that "many hands make light work," *gadugi* is no cakewalk for the host: work parties require extensive planning and coordination to succeed.

Still, group labor remains ideally suited to many situations at THE EDGE OF CHANGE. Not only can it catalyze rapid results in the physical world, but it's also an indispensible tool for building social capital and INTERDEPENDENT COMMUNITY. There is something deeply fulfilling about communal labor that no amount of market logic can erase. Even among today's ephemeral, contingent communities, even in the midst of the antimarket's ruthless efficiency, we yearn to sweat alongside our peers and neighbors. We relive a ritual that our minds may have forgotten but that lives on deep within our bones.

FURTHER LEARNING

Berman, Sally. *Service Learning: A Guide to Planning, Implementing, and Assessing Student Projects.* 2nd edition. Thousand Oaks, CA: Corwin Press, 2006.
Permablitz Melbourne. *Permablitz Designers' Guide.* www.permablitz.net /wp-content/uploads/2011/10/PermablitzDesignersGuide1.pdf.

APPLYING THE PATTERN

Have you participated in any communal labor activities? What did—or didn't—make those activities meaningful or positive? Are there opportunities for your organization to host communal labor events? What other events are happening in your community that you can contribute to?

37. INTIMACY THROUGH ADVERSITY

Hard times bring people together. Whether it's a natural disaster, an interpersonal struggle, or a stressful assignment, difficult situations can be blessings in disguise for cementing meaningful relationships.

Whether global challenges or local tragedies, natural disasters or economic disruptions, breakdowns in the normal order often have a silver lining. With the playing field suddenly leveled, strangers from disparate parts of society become joined together in a common struggle. New connections are made, and ideas that would otherwise seem outlandish are given a chance.

Award-winning journalist Rebecca Solnit explored this dynamic in her 2010 book *A Paradise Built in Hell: The Extraordinary Communities that Arise in Disaster*. Surveying grassroots responses to Hurricane Katrina, the 1906 San Francisco earthquake, 9/11, and more—as well as decades of sociological research—Solnit concludes that "the image of the selfish, panicky, or regressively savage human being in times of disaster has little truth to it."[54] In fact, disasters consistently lead to innovation as people come together and forge solutions out of necessity.

Scholars of ecology are quite familiar with this Shiva-like dynamic of CREATIVE DESTRUCTION. They call it *disturbance*, and view it as a necessary component of healthy ecosystems. After a forest fire, new plants can take advantage of the sunlight formerly monopolized by the oldest trees. Some of those plants will grow to maturity, resulting in a remixed ecosystem that never could have existed before.

Just as in ecosystems, disturbance in our communities brings both crisis and opportunity, becoming CREATIVE DESTRUCTION. "In the suspension of the usual order and the failure of most systems," Solnit writes, "we are free to live and act another way."[55] The aftermath of a disaster, in other words, can become an unintentional ZONE OF AUTONOMY. And in under the right circumstances, the innovations gained from those periods of experimentation can last long after a return to normalcy. The remarkably successful WIR, an HEIRLOOM CURRENCY for businesses in Switzerland, had its origins in the cash-starved throes of the Great Depression. More recently, the networks of SOLIDARITY that emerged after Hurricane Sandy evolved into grassroots COMMONING projects like tool libraries, community gardens, and cooperatives that continue to make an impact.

This isn't to minimize the suffering caused by social disturbances or to imply that we should welcome them. But it is important to understand their potential as key leverage point for change, especially given the likelihood of more to come. While the late twentieth century offered a window of relative calm—at least for the world's affluent—the grim realities of climate change and resource depletion virtually guarantee disasters in the decades ahead.

On the bright side, we don't have to wait for tragic events like hurricanes or depressions to make use of INTIMACY THROUGH ADVERSITY. In fact, many group leaders make use of artificial adversities to accelerate processes of innovation and trust in their groups. Camp counselors and wilderness educators have long made use of exercises that force their campers to trust each other. And in the workplace or classroom, the looming deadline of a big project can compel members of a HUMAN POLYCULTURE to set aside their differences and come together.

FURTHER LEARNING

Solnit, Rebecca. *A Paradise Built in Hell: The Extraordinary Communities That Arise in Disaster.* New York: Penguin, 2010.

APPLYING THE PATTERN

What are some examples of adversity or social disturbance that you've witnessed or been party to? How did it alter the dynamics of the people involved? What new growth came from it? How can you employ artificial challenges to accelerate the NEMAWASHI process in your communities or organizations?

38. PRACTICING GRIEF

From personal tragedies to historical injustice to climate change and ecocide, we've all got a lot to mourn for. Acknowledging and validating each other's grief allows us to become more whole and work through our pain in a productive way.

Grief dares us to love once more.

Terry Tempest Williams

Grief is not a feeling. Grief is a skill. And the twin of grief as a skill of life is the skill of being able to praise or love life. Which means wherever you find one authentically done, the other is very close at hand.

Stephen Jenkinson

Death is a critical part of every life cycle. Without the death and decay of living matter, the ingredients of life would remain locked up, and natural systems would fall apart. In the garden, we harness that liminal area between life and death through the process of compost. By carefully adjusting the balance of carbon and nitrogen, moisture and heat, we create the right conditions for bacteria and fungi to work their remarkable alchemy, turning the broccoli stalks and potato skins of yesterday into the rich humus of tomorrow.

Grief is social composting. Just like bacteria in the compost bin, the process of grieving slowly disassembles that which has passed so that we can nourish that which is ready for new growth. Needless to say, there's no shortage of raw material out there to process. In his book *The Wild Edge of Sorrow*, therapist Francis Weller outlines no less than five distinct kinds, or "gates," of grief. The first gate entails the pain of loss, whether it's the death of a loved one or a painful romantic split. Then there's the internal pain of our own shame, guilt, and self-consciousness—what Weller terms "the places that have not known love." In the third gate, we grieve the sorrows of the world at large, from foreign wars to deforestation, while at the fourth we mourn for "what we expected and did not receive": the yearning for true community that none of us are allowed in our broken culture. Finally, there are the unresolved wounds of our ancestors: traumas such as rape, slavery, and genocide that we carry in our psyches and genes.

Owning up to all this pain is no easy task—and it's made worse by the fact that we're discouraged from sharing our pain in public. Our culture's aversion to death has taught us that grief is best processed alone or even suppressed

altogether. But if we deny our sorrows, the raw material of suffering never breaks down into the soil of healing, instead becoming toxic to ourselves and those around us. Rather, we must actively engage with grief in order to come out the other side healed. Grief, in other words, isn't something that happens *to* us. Much like composting, it's a practice—an active process.

That process is necessarily personal and can take any number of forms. But several insights from scientists, therapists, and other cultures give us some tips for healthy composting of grief. In a study published in 2014 in the *Journal of Experimental Psychology,* Harvard researchers Michael I. Norton and Francesca Gino explored the role that ritual plays in the face of loss. After interviewing 247 people about breakups or deaths of loved ones, they found a distinct correlation. People who performed their own rituals—burning photos of an ex or lighting a candle on the anniversary of a loved one's death—were less prone to grief than those without any ritual.[56] In their paper, Norton and Gino posit that the act of performing a ritual gives the griever a sense of control amid the chaos of loss.

While most of the rituals observed by Norton and Gino were performed individually, grief can also be effectively healed in group contexts. Funeral rituals around the globe tend take place in the presence of community, from the Irish wake to the Jewish *shiva* to the jazz funerals of New Orleans. And social support can be an essential aspect of the other four gates as well. Nicole Vosper, a British organizer, agroecologist, and designer, writes about her own process of engaging in collective action as a way of working through personal and societal losses. "We may start to compost this grief by actually investing time in projects that not only analyze and critically reflect, but create containers for us to share our feelings," explains Vosper. "We could do this by producing zines, writing articles, making art, doing talks and workshops. Even just gathering as friends."[57]

Whether it's tackled solo or collectively, through religious tradition or confrontational art, grief is as important to whole communities as compost is to the garden. Like BREAKING BREAD, RITES OF PASSAGE, and GADUGI, the process of grieving binds communities together, allowing us to develop compassion and HUMANIZE THE OTHER. After all, at some point or another, we all experience loss. By holding space for the loss of others, we are all made more whole.

FURTHER LEARNING

Weller, Francis. *The Wild Edge of Sorrow*. Berkeley, CA: North Atlantic
    Books, 2015.

APPLYING THE PATTERN

How do you process sorrow? What are your most vivid memories of feeling grief and sorrow? Using the framework of the five gates of grief, consider things you are grieving in your life? How does RITUAL AND CEREMONY inform or guide your process? How might you and your family or tribe begin to holding space for each other's grief? Where are you feeling tender and in need of expressing your sorrow? What lessons do you think your grief offers for making positive change?

39. DESIGN TOOL: POWER ANALYSIS

Who's on your side? Who calls the shots? What do they care about? Successful coalition building starts with a systematic mapping of influence.

Pick battles large enough to matter and small enough to win.

—Jonathan Kozol

In 2013, Denver's growing urban agriculture movement was running out of land: as the city emerged from the great recession into a real-estate boom, more and more urban farms on leased land were being kicked out to make way for high-end development. As a member of Denver's Sustainable Food Policy Council, I was part of a team trying to solve the problem by shifting urban farming from private to public land. Among the city's landholdings were thousands of acres of empty spaces in schoolyards, parks, rights of way, and vacant lots that never got used. By letting urban farmers use some of that space, the city could save hundreds of thousands in maintenance costs and address food insecurity at the same time.

To our minds, the scheme seemed like an easy sell. But as my fellow policy council members and I began asking around, we encountered one roadblock after another. Most city officials wouldn't agree to meet with us, and the ones that did offered bureaucratic explanations for why our idea could never work. Never mind that we'd seen plenty of examples in other cities proving the contrary. What had seemed like an easy win was quickly turning into a labyrinth of indifference and opposition.

What my gang of nascent policy wonks and I didn't understand was how to negotiate a key concept of NONVIOLENT STRUGGLE: pillars of support. Any time a movement pushes THE EDGE OF CHANGE, it's bound to encounter many forces pushing back. The status quo is held in place by institutional inertia—not just from government agencies, but also from businesses, media, religious institutions, and the education system. Each one of these institutions can be thought of as a pillar holding up a time-honored practice. But if you can convince enough of those pillars to shift their support, the practice crumbles, opening more space for innovation and justice.

Of course, shifting those pillars of support is no easy task, and it takes thoughtful strategy as well as brute force. That's the promise of POWER ANALYSIS, a design tool that can help you make better-informed choices about which pillars to shift and how. POWER ANALYSES have been conducted informally for decades, but the practice was systematized in 2003 by the Los Angeles community-organizing nonprofit Strategic Concepts in Organizing and Policy Education (SCOPE). Under SCOPE's model, the social designer starts by sketching vertical and horizontal axes, with the vertical axis representing relative power and the horizontal one relative opposition or support for your cause. Next, all the different stakeholders that might have a say in the issue are identified: government agencies, community groups, local media organizations, religious institutions, businesses, elected officials and others. Depending on the complexity of the issue, there may be a just handful of stakeholders or several dozen.

Once all the stakeholders are known, they can be plotted on the chart. If they wield a great deal of influence over the outcome of the issue, they are placed toward the top, while stakeholders with less power are at the bottom. Those that are vehemently opposed to your position are on the far left, and those that are the most in favor of it are on the right. Different categories of stakeholders are often indicated with different colors or symbols: institutions as boxes, individual people as circles, and the like.

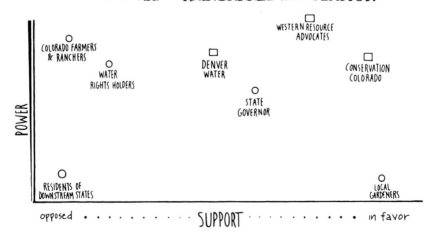

COLORADO RAINBARREL LEGISLATION

After performing a POWER ANALYSIS, you should be able to more clearly answer the following questions:

- *Who benefits from the status quo?* The truth is that even broken systems are usually working quite well for *someone*—more often than not, anti-market entities that profit from funneling capital out of a community. Depending on how an issue is framed, there may be many other stakeholders who also think they benefit. Understanding who has a stake in the status quo is critical in understanding what you're up against.

- *Who calls the shots?* What are the most powerful pillars of support for your issue? An influential special interest group that has the connections to shape policy? A bureaucratic regulatory apparatus? Faith institutions? Other than money, what else endows these pillars with legitimacy in the eyes of public opinion?

- *What narratives are being used to justify the current state of affairs?* We live in a world built, layer by layer, upon shared stories. Change comes when a story becomes obsolete and is replaced by a more satisfying one. The fight for a better future can be seen as a fight of narratives. How is the status quo being framed? What phrases, values, and narratives are being used to sell it? Where are the vulnerabilities in that narrative, and how can you develop a counter-narrative aimed at DISROBING THE EMPEROR?

- *Who needs to be swayed first?* In general, your goal is to move more and more of the stakeholders to the right side of the graph, toward support for your cause. As movement organizer Srdja Popovic puts it, "when you've managed to place yourself and your friends and just about the rest of the world on one side of the line and a handful of evil bastards on the other, you've won."[58] But most situations aren't so black-and-white. Many groups won't change their position until they see others do so, and some never will. Which stakeholders in your POWER ANALYSIS are likely to be early adopters, willing to go out on a limb in support of your idea? What are their specific desires that must be satisfied in order to feel comfortable supporting you? What narratives and messages will resonate with them?

- *How can the supportive stakeholders gain more power?* One way to tip the scales in favor of your cause is to convince the powerful to support it. But in some cases, an equally useful strategy is to empower those who already support it. That might mean gaining greater public visibility for the supporting stakeholders as a means of swaying public opinion. It might mean raising funds to increase their presence, or training them to become more involved in the legislative process. Use CAPITAL ANALYSIS to determine which forms of wealth the supporting stakeholders already have, and how they can leverage that wealth to grow in influence.

Working through each of those questions gives the social designer a much better understanding of the stakeholder landscape and their place within it. From there, it's should be relatively straightforward to identify THE EDGE OF CHANGE, the overlap between your vision and what's currently possible.

For my colleagues and me on the Sustainable Food Policy Council, a deeper understanding of the pillars of support helped our cause tremendously. After interviews with numerous city officials and members of the city council, we began to understand the story behind each group's hesitancies. The parks department had recently suffered bad PR from an unpopular renovation plan and was wary of proposing anything controversial. Denver Public Schools was concerned about allowing for-profit farms on public land, while members of city council wanted to make sure that there was a fallback plan if a farmer went out of business. As we gained knowledge about each of these concerns, we refined our approach, developing a more nuanced proposal, and one by one, each of the stakeholders began to relax its opposition. After a year and a half of conversation and elaboration, we sent our policy to the mayor, who gave our approach the green light.

Fortunately, our campaign ended with success and few ruffled feathers; not every instance of social change will be so painless. But whether you're advocating for more affordable housing in your neighborhood or a democratic revolution in your nation, the pillars of support matter—and meaningful change can only occur after analyzing and understanding those pillars.

PART 3

Organizations That Live

We can't make social change alone. Even at the community scale, creating a lasting, positive difference requires dozens of people acting in collaboration. It requires compassionate, driven leaders and team members with a diversity of skills. It requires dealing with uncomfortable issues like conflict resolution, apathy, burnout, and member turnover. In other words, it requires organization.

A church group, a business, and a protest movement each have vastly different objectives, norms, and cultures, but they all share some common challenges. Many institutions, for instance, are catalyzed by a single charismatic leader, yet most of them struggle to survive after that leader steps down. Though a great number of organizations are arranged in some form of hierarchy, many would like to make their participants feel empowered as co-creators. And nearly every group engaged in defending acts of COMMONING against the greed of the antimarket must reckon with the tension between earning revenue and fulfilling their mission.

Clearly, then, it's important for the social designer to have a good understanding of the patterns that allow groups to function at their highest potential and coalesce into "organizations that live." Two of the most fundamental patterns of group dynamics can be seen in the hierarchy and the network, the yin and yang of organizations. Hierarchy tends to be rigidly structured, with a multilayered chain of command that often gives rise to bloated bureaucracies. Networks, meanwhile, tend to be much more informal, with looser roles, smaller groups, and more democratic decision-making.

Incidentally, it doesn't take much searching to find both of these structures represented in natural systems across the scales of place and time. Hierarchies take the physical form of branching structures such as our lungs, watersheds, tree roots, or even the branches of the tree of life. Each of these structures demonstrates remarkable efficiency at *collecting* or *distributing:* our lungs collect oxygen and a river system collects water. A tree's roots collect nutrients from the soil and distribute sugars to its fungal partners, while the leaves on its branches collect sunlight.

Networks, meanwhile, are somewhat less visible, but no less impactful. The cells in our brains form an intricate network of neural pathways, and underground, microscopic strands of fungi form networks that can transport nutrients hundreds of feet. Spiderwebs are iconic networks, and the complex web of relationships among species within an ecosystem is one as well. If branching patterns are efficient, networks are *resilient.* Each one, in its own way, is able to withstand disturbance and create new solutions to complex problems. Yet this ability to innovate comes at a cost: maintaining all those interconnections takes a lot of energy. The human brain, for example, requires 10 percent of the oxygen in our blood despite being only 2 percent of the body's weight.

Back in the social world, these patterns play out with remarkable similarity. Most of our present-day institutions are organized as hierarchies, designed for scale and efficiency at collection and distribution. Businesses collect profits. Public school systems distribute social norms to impressionable youth. Government agencies distribute public services to citizens. Like the branches and canyons found in nature, these hierarchies tend to be resistant to change once they form and can be prone to weakness or collapse if one of the branches is cut off from the rest of the unit.

Anthropogenic networks, meanwhile, share the same traits for innovation and energy demand as their ecological cousins. Just like our brains, the internet—society's cranium—requires about a tenth of our energy supply to sustain itself, yet the innovations it yields are impossible to quantify. It takes much more time for a group to arrive at consensus than it does for a manager to make a unilateral decision, but the trust and enthusiasm gained by a group decision might very well make it worth it. Whereas hierarchies tend to circumvent forces of friction that might slow their flow, networks exist in situations where unpredictability is unavoidable. In fact, it's this continuous presence of challenge and conflict that often allows networks to come up with novel solutions.

	HIERARCHIES	NETWORKS
Natural Examples	• Watersheds • Lungs • Tree roots and branches • Circulatory and nervous systems • Wolf packs, primates	• Neurons • Mycelia
Cultural Examples	• Governments • Armies • Corporations • School systems	• The internet • Networks of friends • Grassroots social movements
Characteristics	• Energy efficient • Energy and information flows in just one direction • Vulnerable to disturbance • Found across scales • Resistant to change	• Uses lots of energy • Energy and information flows in all directions • Resilient • Limited in size • Adapts quickly

Whether in nature or culture, neither of these patterns exist in an isolated, "pure" form. Tree roots form cellular connections with mycelial networks to maximize their nutrient absorption. Within the levels of bureaucracy in a big business, there are usually formal or informal teams that function as networks. Networks are often more common in the early life of an organization, when many different ways of doing things are helpful. As it matures, the organization settles on a main set of activities and processes and, seeking to make them efficient, solidifies into a hierarchy.

Rather than an either/or situation, then, it's more of a both/and opportunity. The first two patterns in the section of the book explore networks and hierarchies in greater detail, with particular attention paid to the conditions that make each one more or less effective. NURTURED NETWORKS analyzes the importance of clear rules and norms for so-called horizontal groups, in which power is widely distributed; CONSENSUAL HIERARCHIES, meanwhile, investigates the factors that keep top-down organizations more equitable.

From there, the next several patterns articulate the common cycles and rhythms that emerge in both hierarchies and networks. HUMAN POLYCUL-TURES takes a deep dive into the optimal size of collaborative groups and the archetypal roles that make them effective. NEMAWASHI surveys the long-term stages of group cohesion, while STREAMS OF ENGAGEMENT explores several modes of interaction that groups slip in and out of throughout the course of a single gathering. The pros and cons of various voting systems are weighed in THE RIGHT WAY TO DECIDE, and the pulsing rhythm of large- and small-group activity is represented by the pattern CONVERGE AND DISPERSE.

The third cluster of patterns centers around group leadership. REGEN-ERATIVE MANAGEMENT makes the case that a healthy organization must be designed from day one to transcend the talents and personalities of its founders. NAMING NORMS suggests guidelines for how groups can establish clear com-munication. SKILLED FACILITATION highlights the unique position of the facili-tator and the many roles he or she is asked to play throughout a group process. Finally, CIRCLE DIALOGUE zooms in on a particularly ancient and common form of group interaction and its subcategories.

Every group beyond a certain size is bound to contain factions, subgroups, and competing interests, and the next three patterns of Organizations That Live share how these dynamics can strengthen rather than weaken group cohesion. THE CAUCUS is a meditation on the fractal balance between unity and divi-sion and on the importance of creating space for both. CALLING OUT, CALLING IN offers a pathway for maintaining compassion while holding one another accountable, and RESTORATIVE JUSTICE introduces a model of conflict resolu-tion that's constructive rather than retributive.

The final two patterns, DOCUMENT THE PROCESS and MEASURING SUCCESS, concern strategies for tracking and institutionalizing group wisdom, and finally, the design tool of TEAM ANALYSIS that closes the section offers an approach for analyzing the skills within a group.

40. NURTURED NETWORKS

Horizontally structured groups can be more innovative and resilient than hierarchies—but only if they are thoughtfully designed and cared for.

Movements are airplanes. Without a pilot at the helm, they will crash.

—Srdja Popovic

The Occupy movement of 2011 will be remembered for many things, including the resurgence of the radical left and the injection of income inequality into the national conversation. But for all these achievements, many Occupy chapters were fraught with a frustrating lack of momentum. Saddled with long-winded public meetings and constant bickering, the movement eventually splintered under the weight of its own vague ambitions.

As is often the case, these flaws came from the noblest of intentions. Starting from the astute observation that our society's top-down institutions systematically disempower those at the bottom, Occupy's organizers established as their decision-making process consensus-based general assemblies—a form of radical decentralization in which every voice has the opportunity to be heard. While righteous in theory, this move to abolish power structures ended up backfiring, as meeting after meeting was derailed by newbies with naive ideas and disgruntled citizens using their time in the spotlight to rant about their own private cause. With no clear leader to guide the process, power struggles became a continual source of rancor and frustration.

Occupy was hardly alone. Time after time, activists fed up with the rigid, slow-moving hierarchies of corporations and government have turned to horizontal networks to embody romantic ideals of a fully participatory society. These kinds of leaderless groups can be powerful and innovative in the right contexts, but all too often, we think "no authority" means "no leadership" and allow these groups to be tanked by large personalities, unproductive bickering, and passive-aggressive behavior.

In her classic 1972 essay "The Tyranny of Structurelessness," feminist Jo Freeman argued persuasively against the perils of leaderless groups. "A 'laissez faire' group is about as realistic as a 'laissez faire' society," Freeman quipped. "The idea becomes a smokescreen for the strong or the lucky to establish unquestioned hegemony over others. This hegemony can be so easily established because the idea of 'structurelessness' does not prevent the formation of informal structures, only formal ones."[59]

Getting rid of hierarchy, in other words, doesn't actually erase unequal power dynamics. It just makes those dynamics less obvious. Without any rules for engagement, power rather quickly accrues to the loudest voices in the room, regardless of whether those voices actually have the best ideas.

In the last several years, social psychologists have begun to confirm Freeman's anecdotal warnings with data. In a series of studies at Ohio State University professor Amy Brunell tried to quantify the impact of narcissism on group dynamics. Simulating situations as diverse as class elections and desert-island survival strategies, Brunell and her colleagues found that people who scored highly in narcissistic traits such as self-esteem and a desire for power were much more likely to end up in leadership positions—despite the fact that they were *no more likely* to make wiser decisions than others.[6]

Some of us have stronger opinions. Some of us are more likely to speak up. And some can be very long-winded. Whether due to genetics, personality, or just how much sleep we had the night before, power imbalances are likely to exist in even the most tightly knit groups. That's just community. But rather than let these imbalances wreck the group, smart leaders are able to cultivate "NURTURED NETWORKS": horizontal groups that have just the right amount of structure to thrive. These groups engage in NAMING NORMS at the beginning and throughout the process. They employ SKILLED FACILITATION to ensure everyone's voice is heard. They follow THE CREATIVE PROCESS, setting clear goals and engaging in defined phases of various STREAMS OF ENGAGEMENT. They create mechanisms for people to be held accountable to their actions and for the group to CONVERGE AND DISPERSE.

With these structures in place, the horizontal groups we cherish actually do have a fighting chance against the top-heavy bureaucracies of antimarket forces—and a truly democratic society might just come with it.

FURTHER LEARNING

Freeman, Jo. "The Tyranny of Structurelessness," www.jofreeman.com/joreen
/tyranny.htm, originally published in *The Second Wave* 2, no. 1 (1972).

APPLYING THE PATTERN

Are you part of any leaderless groups? What are they like? Do you notice any
subtle or informal hierarchies are present in the group? How do those informal
structures aid or impair the group's efforts? Does your group have the too little
or too much structure to succeed? What practices could your group adopt to
become more of a NURTURED NETWORK?

41. CONSENSUAL HiERARCHiES

In order to stay equitable, hierarchical structures need to be limited in scale and operate with a basis of trust and consent.

Bureaucracy is a ubiquitous presence in our culture. Many of the institutions we interact with on a daily basis—the public school system, the bank, the grocery store, the federal government—have some form of many-leveled hierarchy. All share the same pyramidal organizational arrangement and, not coincidentally, the same resistance to change, exploitative character, and lack of accountability.

With this preponderance of unresponsive institutions, it's easy to jump to the conclusion, as many have, that hierarchies are necessarily a destructive force and have no place in an equitable society. And yet there are countless examples of hierarchical organizations that have been effective, accountable—and yes, even empowering. SMALL BUSINESSES, food cooperatives, sports teams, and local trade unions are just a few examples of hierarchically structured organizations that frequently work in a satisfactory way for everyone involved.

Natural systems would also seem to support the theory of the healthy hierarchy. While we have much to learn from systems that operate via *emergence*—the phenomenon of the "hive mind" or the "wisdom of the crowd," in which decisions spring naturally from a group—they're hardly the animal kingdom's only model for group decision making. Plenty of species exhibit hierarchical behavior, with a small group making decisions on behalf of a much larger pack. In a 2014 paper, Princeton researchers Iain Couzin and Albert Kao developed a statistical model to examine the effectiveness of group decisions in chaotic, "real-world" contexts. After exploring several different variables, Couzin found a distinct evolutionary advantage to hierarchies in cases where there were many kinds of information to process. "Smaller groups actually tend to make more accurate decisions," he explains, "while larger assemblies may become excessively focused on only certain pieces of information."[61] But "smaller groups" doesn't mean that the size of the whole pack or herd is small—just the decision-making group: "Organisms can exhibit highly coordinated movements despite vast numbers of individuals.... Even when groups are large, the number of individuals contributing to a group's decision may be relatively small."

The question isn't "Are hierarchies evil?" but rather "*When* are hierarchies evil—and when are they helpful?" Fortunately, organizational psychologists have been asking variations on that question for decades. Although their findings haven't always been adopted by the institutions that surround us, they offer key insights to the social designer. According to these findings, a few key elements are necessary in order for hierarchies to remain healthy:

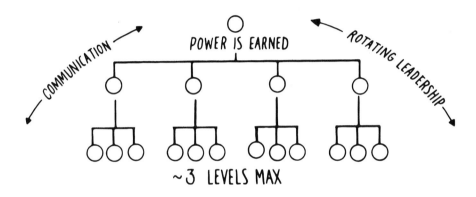

- *Power must be earned.* Members of a group must trust the people making decisions on their behalf. That means, presumably, that the decision makers are well known among the group and that they have a track record of making good decisions. It also means that the group has the ability to remove a decision maker who isn't meeting its long-term needs, whether through a regularly scheduled election or a vote of no confidence.

- *Power must be shared.* No matter how much trust and support any given decision maker earns, no single person can be expected to completely understand the needs of a community. History tells us, moreover, that power held too long decays into a tool for corruption and personal gain. Contemporary hierarchies use tools like term limits, boards of directors, and co-leadership to encourage diverse leadership and protect against abuse of power. Tomorrow's hierarchies might employ any of these tools and more to ensure that authority doesn't stagnate in any one person or group.

- *Communication must be open throughout all levels of the hierarchy.* Hierarchies, by nature, tend to excel at one-to-many pronouncements. But in order for hierarchies to be *consensual,* communication needs to be able to flow in the other direction as well, from the bottom to the top. Every member of a hierarchy, no matter how lowly their status, should feel empowered to access the decision makers. This creates very real constraints on the total size of the hierarchy, limiting it to the zone of reciprocity (150 people or so—see RELATIONSHIP ZONES). Time and time again, organizational psychologists and management consultants have found that larger hierarchies, blanketed with too many layers of bureaucracy, are breeding grounds for disengagement and corruption.[62]

APPLYING THE PATTERN

Analyze the hierarchies you are a part of or interact with—in what ways are the efficient? Inefficient? Enabling? Repressive? What would you do to make them more consensual? Contrast the effective hierarchies with NURTURED NETWORKS— what are the advantages and disadvantages of each? The balance between them?

42. HUMAN POLYCULTURES

Group work happens most effectively in teams of four to seven, with a healthy balance of skills and perspectives represented in the group.

From ecological restoration to RESTORATIVE JUSTICE, the work of healing our society tends to be social. But as we learn from RELATIONSHIP ZONES, different kinds of work are best done by groups of specific sizes. And while large crowds may be vital for acts of NONVIOLENT STRUGGLE and GADUGI, the majority of our collaborative efforts happen in groups that are well within the zone of intimacy. Even sophisticated projects that require hundreds of minds—say, building a social movement or a feat of civil engineering—inevitably break up into smaller and smaller project teams, with each team settling in the zone of intimacy.

What accounts for this relatively small size of collaboration? As it happens, it's less about the size of the group itself than about the number of connections between members. Take a group of four people. Among those four, there are six possible one-on-one connections, or dyads. This makes for relatively easy decision making—with only six relationships, chances are low that any one pair has destructive tensions or irreconcilable differences, and only a couple of conversations can be happening at once.

With the addition of another group member, there are still only ten dyad connections to manage. But as the group adds more members, the connections begin to multiply rapidly. By the time there are eight people, the number of dyads rises to almost thirty, creating all kinds of opportunities for hecklers, cliques, and distracting side dialogues. In permaculture terms larger groups simply have too much *edge* to be effective. In many cases, these bloated groups end up having only a handful of active members, with the rest lurking unproductively in the background and going along with whatever the active members think—a phenomenon commonly referred to as *groupthink*.

So what size is best? Perhaps unsurprisingly, the institutions that have studied this the most are the largest ones, with the most resources at stake: large businesses.

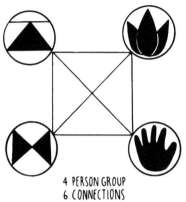

4 PERSON GROUP
6 CONNECTIONS

5 PERSON GROUP
10 CONNECTIONS

7 PERSON GROUP
21 CONNECTIONS

8 PERSON GROUP
28 CONNECTIONS

6 PERSON GROUP
15 CONNECTIONS

Management experts Marcia Blenko, Paul Rogers, and Michael Mankins recommend seven as the optimal group size, claiming that each additional member beyond that reduces the effectiveness of the group's decision making by 10 percent.[63] Jeff Bezos, the founder of Amazon, has taken a more whimsical approach with an internal policy called the "two pizza rule": no working groups larger than you could feed with a couple pizzas.[64]

It's one thing to understand the ideal size for an action group, but that's just the beginning. At least as important is the group's *composition*. What skills and personality types are represented in the group? Are they the right ones for the job? A helpful ecological model for thinking through this challenge is the polyculture, an association of species that mutually support one other. A classic polyculture, grown for thousands of years in North and Central America, is the "three sisters" of corn, beans, and squash. In this polyculture, the corn provides support for the climbing beans, while the beans add nitrogen to the soil to help fertilize the corn. Meanwhile, the squash acts as a groundcover, protecting the soil from the hot sun and preventing weeds from sprouting. And the three plants, when eaten together, provide a nearly complete source of nutrition for humans.

In many cases, people are the same way, especially when we're working toward a common goal. Each person brings a different set of skills and perspectives to a situation. In the best cases, those skills and perspectives balance each other out perfectly, and the group becomes greater than the sum of its parts. While people's skills aren't as static as those of plants, we often find ourselves playing similar roles in groups. With tools like TEAM ANALYSIS, we can systematically track those roles and assemble groups designed for maximum effectiveness. While the archetypes we come across are many and subtle, it's still worth calling out some of the most common characters. The following list is adapted from one articulated by Starhawk in *The Empowerment Manual,* along with several other roles I've come across in my own work.

ELDERS

George Santayana's oft-repeated aphorism reminds us that those who cannot remember the past are condemned to repeat it. Elders are those who help us remember the relevant parts of the past (whether the grand sweep of history or last year's meeting). They keep us from reinventing the wheel or wasting our energy on distractions and tangents. The definition of an elder can vary—it certainly need not be tied to a person's age. Rather, it's about having more experience than others in the group, as well as the ability to distill that experience in ways that give insight to the present circumstances.

Elders lead by example. Regardless of whether they identify themselves as elders—most won't—elders are respected by those around them for their commitment, leadership, and balance. But like everyone else, elders are fallible. And at the end of the day, they're people too, with their own blind spots, agendas, and ideologies. Groups with strong elders must be mindful of succumbing to mythologizing or hero worship, while elders themselves must stay vigilant of letting their wisdom creep into entitlement.

Elders

Grandparents

Tribal elder councils

Professors emeriti

Jimmy Carter

Mavis Staples

Maya Angelou

RADICALS

We are creatures of habit—and for good reason. Changing our lifestyles, habits, and institutions isn't just scary; it's also a lot of hard work. When we're consumed with the daily struggles of raising kids, meeting deadlines at work, and paying the bills, the idea of erasing the present system and starting over sounds overwhelming and impractical. And so we stick with what we know, even if it is against our own best interests.

Radicals are those in our midst who have the vision and courage to propose another way of doing things. *Radical* comes from the Latin word *radix,* "root," and contemporary radicals tend to be motivated by a desire to address the root cause of an issue. In the same way that eldership is archetypically associated with old age, radicalism is seen as a trait of youth. But experience and radicalism are not mutually exclusive, and it's certainly possible for one person to embody both elder and radical roles at the same time.

The ideas of the radical may not be practical or even possible—but that's not always the point. By providing an alternative vision, they can show the rest of us possibilities that lie outside the existing order, giving us the inspiration and motivation to push THE EDGE OF CHANGE.

Radicals tend to have a fiery energy—and like an actual fire, their efforts can cause collateral damage or get out of hand without care and intention. In the wrong circumstances, their urgent and uncompromising approach can actually set back a cause, alienating potential allies or obscuring valuable opportunities for compromise. And radicals with selfish intentions can become demagogues, exploiting our fears and weaknesses and inciting violence in the name of change.

Contemporary Radicals

Bernie Sanders

Ted Cruz

Russell Brand

Julian Assange

Angela Davis

Corky Gonzalez

MENTORS AND APPRENTICES

Like an elder, a mentor has a wealth of experiential capital. But whereas elders deploy their experience in service to the group as a whole, a mentor has chosen to nurture a specific person or CAUCUS of people within the group. And the apprentice, in turn, has set the intention of learning from the mentor.

Mentor-apprentice arrangements can take all sorts of forms. Apprentices can be mentored in a specific skill, a role in a group, or a stage of their life cycle. Some mentorships, like residencies in medical school, have become institutionalized and are considered a requirement for acceptance into a field. Some consist of little more than a handshake agreement. Some last a few weeks, while others, like the guru-student relationship in India, may entail a lifelong commitment as serious as a marriage.

The economic arrangement can also vary—sometimes an apprentice pays a mentor for their help; sometimes vice versa. Either way, it's important that both parties recognize the value of the relationship and commit to their roles. Good

Common Mentor-Apprentice Arrangements

WWOOFing

Internships

Big buddy programs

Med school residencies

Trade union apprenticeships

Student teaching

mentors act with patience and compassion, allowing their apprentices to fail and learn from their mistakes. Good apprentices, meanwhile, trust in the abilities of their mentor and recognize their own limitations.

Mentor-apprentice relationships have an inherent power dynamic, and as such, the relationship requires wisdom and maturity to succeed. Mentors are often tempted to abuse their authority, either trivially, in the case of a supervisor making his or her intern do meaningless tasks, or gravely, in the case of a sports coach sexually abusing his or her students. To prevent these situations, it's important for mentors to have circles of accountability and for apprentices to have unbiased parties of recourse they can turn to without fear of reprisal.

GRACES

Many HUMAN POLYCULTURE roles are outward facing, focused on maximizing the group's external impact. But in the midst of getting the work done, group members can easily neglect to care for each other and themselves, lapsing into burnout or interpersonal conflict. Graces keep an eye on a group's *internal* dynamics to make sure that doesn't happen. They're the ones who ensure there's coffee and snacks available at the meeting, the ones who pull aside a withdrawn-looking participant to check in about his or her day, and the ones who remember to send a thank-you card to the special guest.

In short, graces ensure that everyone feels nurtured, both physically and emotionally. But don't assume that a grace is female; while nurturing may be seen as a "feminine" quality, there are plenty of ways that men can act with grace. Perhaps because of its feminine associations or its less public nature, the vital role of the grace is all too often overlooked, and all-star graces can be underappreciated. No matter their gender, graces should be cautious of becoming *overly* accommodating, putting their own needs on the back burner to make sure others feel welcome.

Famous Graces

Marge Simpson
(*The Simpsons*)

Deanna Troi (*Star Trek*)

Jackie Onassis Kennedy

Father Mulcahy (*M.A.S.H.*)

Mary Magdalene

NETWORK WEAVERS

Sometimes meaningful change is as simple as facilitating an introduction. Network weavers are those who seem to know everybody and are always eager to make connections. By using their reserves of social capital for the greater good, they help spin the fabric of interdependence that leads to true communities.

Network weavers tend to be gregarious, helpful, and socially active within their circle. Some can put you in touch with people in high places, while others will find the right people for your community advisory board. Because they are so social, network weavers can easily become overcommitted and can be hard to pin down. But understanding the network weaver's own needs and motivations—even if it's just telling them some folks *they* need to know—will go a long way.

Network Weavers

Benjamin Franklin

Harriet Tubman

Mark Zuckerberg

Susan B. Anthony

Andy Warhol

Rick Rubin

GRIOTS

Most of the time, groups are too caught up in the day-to-day tactics of getting things done to consider their efforts in the context of THE LONG GAME. We might not be aware of the historical circumstances that brought us to the current point.

Throughout history, many cultures relied on storytellers that shared a community's legends and oral history through song and storytelling. In West African cultures, the name *griot* is given to these traveling bards.

Today's griots are similarly able provide insight about a community's collective identity through the power of narrative. Combining the patterns of SANKOFA and TELLING THE STORY, they show us how we ended up where we are now by digging up historical details and referencing age-old themes.

The contemporary griot's medium may be song, like the griots of West Africa—or it might be documentary film, blogging, tweeting, or PowerPoint. Regardless, griots have the ability to distill the chaos of data in everyday life into a powerful narrative that connects present situations to age-old traditions, themes, and struggles.

Famous Griots

Bob Dylan

Joni Mitchell

Michael Pollan

Ken Burns

Simone de Beauvoir

W. E. B. Du Bois

Kendrick Lamar

TRANSLATORS

While legally enforced segregation may be a thing of the past, cultural segregation is more pronounced than ever.

Whether you live in a rural exurb or a gentrifying inner-city neighborhood, the chances are that you have many neighbors who aren't like you—and whom you struggle to connect with. We pump fuel side by side at the gas station before driving off to completely different kinds of jobs. We experience the same snowstorms and heat waves just feet away from each other, but from homes that look, sound, and smell like two different countries. We interpret the same current events through glaringly divergent narratives of reality.

These are cultural edges of twenty-first-century society. In the right circumstances, they can provide wonderful opportunities for mutual learning. All too often, however, our differences have become so large that common ground can be hard to find. Translators are the individuals that bridge those gaps. With direct experience in multiple realms of society, they help the rest of us navigate between them, explaining each reality to the other along the way. While literal translation between languages might be part of their skill, just as important is the

Famous Translators

Jorge Ramos (the Latino community and American media)

Commander Worf (the Federation and the Klingon Empire)

Ta-Nehisi Coates (black America and white America)

Malala Yousafzai (Middle-Eastern women and Western society)

The Lorax (the trees and the factory owner)

ability to code switch, jumping fluidly between the jargon, cultural references, and tone of one culture and those of another. Like network weavers, translators can relate to a wide variety of people as a result of their own experience straddling cultural boundaries. And like griots, they often possess great communication and storytelling skills.

In ideal circumstances, translators use their skills to foster greater collaboration between willing parties. But the most challenging test of the translator comes in cases of the STREAM OF ENGAGEMENT called *conflict transformation*, when they may be called to serve as a mediator or negotiator as well. In these cases, translators must walk the line between appeasement and truth, without merely saying what each side wants to hear.

HELPING HANDS

When I was in college in New York City, I would occasionally drop in for a weekly event called Grub—a free community meal cooked with ingredients rescued from the trash. The event was hosted in a collective house in Brooklyn, and I still remember the aphorism scrawled above its sink: "first the dishes, then the revolution."

Those six words sum up nicely the importance of helping hands to any effective human polyculture. No matter how glamorous the ultimate goal, any attempt at social change entails any number of menial tasks to succeed. For every hour of the exciting stuff, there countless hours that someone has to spend behind the scenes performing data entry, shoveling dirt, knocking on doors—or doing the dishes.

Requiring little creativity but lots of time, these tasks of STEWARDSHIP rarely receive much recognition from the group itself, let alone the general public that benefits from the work. It's no surprise that they're often left to those in the group at the bottom of the (formal or informal) ladder: the newest member, the unpaid intern, or the one with the least privilege.

Sometimes the other group members are truly too busy to be a helping hand— in which case they ought to make sure

Common Helping Hands Roles

Cooks

Janitors

Administrative assistants

Mechanics

Research assistants

Spouses or partners

that the people doing the dirty work are recognized and honored. But all too often, we avoid being a helping hand out of selfish convenience, simply because we have the status within the group or society at large to do so. By sending signals that certain kinds of work are beneath certain people in the group, we reinforce patterns of privilege and exploitation, lowering morale and the sense of group unity.

But when each person shows a willingness to be a helping hand, regardless of his or her own status, the other members of the group feel empowered and are more willing to pitch in. Ideally, our human polycultures will function with the expectation that everyone from the leader on down will be a helping hand some of the time. First the dishes, then the revolution.

MAVENS

Servant leaders hold the vision for a group, and helping hands may do much of the day-to-day work. But somewhere between the two are likely to be tasks that require a specific, specialized skill: graphic design, perhaps, or Spanish translation. In fact, the inability to perform such tasks can often create significant bottlenecks, holding a group back from success.

This is where mavens come to the rescue. Specialists par excellence, mavens elevate a specific skill into an art form, allowing groups to overcome their technical hurdles to thrive. Whether it's coding or carpentry, mavens apply an ethos of persistence, care, and craftspersonship to whatever it is they do, honing their skill over years of hard work.

Depending on personality, luck, and the nature of their discipline, some mavens may be widely acknowledged and celebrated in their community. All too often, however, mavens are unsung heroes, toiling away without much credit while undervaluing their own talent and time. What's more, the obsessive nature of the maven can shift from asset to liability; mavens can get so lost in their own craft that they become aloof and reclusive, struggling to connect with others.

Famous Mavens

Buckminster Fuller

Georgia O'Keeffe

Han Solo

Madonna

Prince

J. Robert Oppenheimer

SERVANT LEADERS

One of the natural world's most dazzling illustrations of synergy is the principle of additive color. No matter how clearly we understand the physics behind it, the act of combining all the colors of the visible spectrum into a clear white beam continues to delight the eye.

Imagine, now, that each role in a human polyculture is a distinct color on the spectrum, with its own personality and best uses. When combined into one beam, they behave just like light, creating a bright, pure beam that can cut through the darkness of ignorance and violence. In this metaphor, the servant leader acts as the prism, deftly combining the right human polyculture roles together at the right time in service to a larger goal.

Even in the most democratic organizations, *someone* needs to make the decisions. As described in NURTURED NETWORKS, groups without leaders can easily fall prey to tyranny of structurelessness. Driven, hardworking, and charismatic, servant leaders can adopt each of the other human polyculture roles to catalyze community action, without allowing their ego to get in the way.

Servant leaders know when it's important to weave networks together, and they know just which story to tell to motivate and inspire a group. As helping hands, they set an example by working longer and harder when necessary. As facilitators, they may serve the role of a grace, creating the conditions for everyone in a community to speak his or her mind.

Of course, no one person embodies every role as an expert. Servant leaders have done the necessary reflection to understand which roles they lack within themselves and are capable at empowering others around them to fill the gaps. They also take seriously the "servant" part of their title, always ensuring that they're pointing the group's beam of light toward justice and ecological harmony.

Just as an individual shouldn't feel typecast into the role of maven or grace, no one person should monopolize the role of servant leadership in a group. Whether it's organized as a CONSENSUAL HIERARCHY or a NURTURED NETWORK, a well-functioning group employs a culture

Famous Servant Leaders

Mother Teresa

Nelson Mandela

The Dalai Lama

Albert Schweitzer

Jesus

of REGENERATIVE MANAGEMENT to nurture qualities of the servant leader in each person.

FURTHER LEARNING

Rath, Tom. *StrengthsFinder 2.0.* New York: Gallup, 2007.

Starhawk, *The Empowerment Manual: A Guide for Collaborate Groups.* Gabriola Island, BC: New Society, 2011.

APPLYING THE PATTERN

In your experience, what are the differences between working in a group of seven or smaller, versus a group of eight or much larger? What personal characteristics of your own come out when working in groups of different sizes? What are some prominent or personal examples you can think of for each of the roles described above? Which roles do you identify with or find yourself in most often? Have any of these roles been missing in groups you work with?

43. NEMAWASHI

Every group goes through a distinct process of "forming," "norming," and "storming" before the members can work together cohesively. Honor this process and allow it to take its time.

Just like people themselves, groups of people have a life cycle. Generally, that cycle starts with a lot of excitement and energy, but before too long, the going gets tough. Financial challenges, personality conflicts, differences of opinion—any number of things can send the group spinning out of control, its original idealism devolved into squabbling over petty differences. In many cases, this infighting deflates the energy so much that the group falls apart. What's the trick to avoiding group implosion? It's not about avoiding conflict; instead, we need to learn to honor conflict as a healthy and necessary part of the group life cycle.

In his book *In the Bubble,* futurist John Thackara describes the use of the Japanese word *nemawashi* to encapsulate a whole process of community building—a process which many of us Westerners seem to have forgotten. The word literally means "turning the roots," referring to the transplant shock a plant experiences when put in new soil. In colloquial Japanese culture, however, NEMAWASHI refers to the process of the members of a group getting to know each other. Implied in the term is the recognition that every group goes through a distinct series of phases, and honoring the steps is vital to healthy group success.

Generally, NEMAWASHI takes place within HUMAN POLYCULTURES—groups of three to ten that are brought together via circumstance rather than blood ties. Ideally, the end result is an INTERDEPENDENT COMMUNITY, a group of people who need each other, who can accomplish things as a team that they can't alone. Each member trusts his or her peers and feels secure about his or her role in the group.

Here in the United States, a more familiar framework for the NEMAWASHI process is Bruce Tuckman's four-stage model of group development, originally proposed in 1965. While Tuckman's model is ordered as forming, storming, norming, performing, my own observation of group dynamics has led me to switch the middle two phases:

- *Forming*. The forming phase is when people come together around a common goal, often led by a charismatic champion. This is usually a time of enthusiasm and high energy, where anything seems possible. It is a time for visioning sessions, manifestos, and BREAKING BREAD.

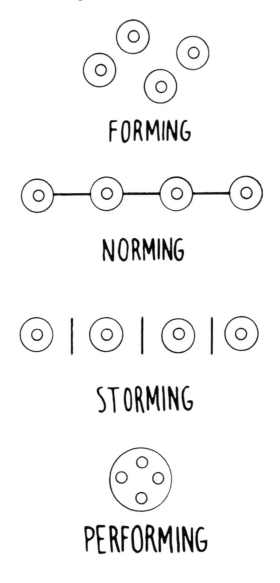

FORMING

NORMING

STORMING

PERFORMING

- *Norming.* Next comes the norming phase, where the group determines the types of behavior and members of the group that are acceptable. This can happen deliberately—as in a process of NAMING NORMS—or unconsciously, when one person's specific patterns of behavior or language are replicated by the rest of the group. It's generally the phase in which rituals are established, when meeting times and processes start to become formalized, and when people begin to differentiate their respective roles in the HUMAN POLYCULTURE.

- *Storming.* After norming comes storming—the phase of conflict. This conflict can take many forms—the tension between elders and radicals, financial struggles, a disconnect between the vision of champions and the day-to-day needs of mavens, members getting burnt out, or any number of external pressures. Regardless of its proximate causes, conflict frequently leads to a shakeup of group membership or identity, resulting in what some have labeled as the subphase *mourning*.

  But just as a storm can bring much-needed moisture to a parched landscape, this phase of NEMAWASHI can bring the group to a new level of cohesiveness. With healthy conflict resolution strategies and SKILLED FACILITATION, the storming phase actually brings the group closer together, creating INTIMACY THROUGH ADVERSITY and establishing a new level of trust between group members.

- *Performing.* With this trust in place, the group can finally enter the last phase of the cycle: performing. The group is then able to become even closer through LETTING LOOSE.

Understanding the process of NEMAWASHI allows us to consciously design the groups we're a part of. In fact, the connections between NEMAWASHI and THE CREATIVE PROCESS are striking—*forming* is equivalent to setting goals, while the *norming* phase mirrors analysis and assessment. *Storming* represents the messy process of design itself, in which potential conflicts among sectors are resolved into a harmonious whole. Finally, the *performance* phase represents the implementation of the design, in which the original goals of the group are made real.

Of course, no group will proceed through these steps as clearly as they are outlined here. Just as THE CREATIVE PROCESS is realistically more of a looping spiral than a straight line, the various stages of NEMAWASHI are continually intermingling throughout the lifecycle of a group. The important thing is to be aware of which phases are at play and to navigate them with clarity.

APPLYING THE PATTERN

Has the NEMAWASHI process been apparent in groups you have been a part of? Can you identify examples of each stage of NEMAWASHI with your group experiences? Have your groups ever gotten hung up in a stage? How might you be more intentional about fostering this process in the future?

44. STREAMS OF ENGAGEMENT

Collaborative teams cycle through multiple modes of interaction over the course of their work. Groups that understand when and how to employ each of these modes will find themselves on sure footing.

Should we brainstorm solutions before or after getting community feedback? How many people should we invite to the planning meeting? How do we deal with the tension between the two founders?

Running collaborative groups entails a continuous stream of questions such as the ones above. Considered one by one, these choices may not have a dramatic impact, but each one becomes another brick in the edifice of a group's culture. As a whole, the way we make these many small decisions can mean the difference between an inspired, confident, and cohesive group and one that feels disjointed and unfocused. One of the most important ways to keep groups moving in the right direction is to ensure that effective leaders and SKILLED FACILITATORS structure interactions to fit the specific reasons each group comes together.

Sometimes people want to learn about a topic and explore it as a group. Often group meetings are places for participants to brainstorm ideas or narrow down a list of ideas that have already been generated. Sometimes, they are forums for resolving disagreement, dispute, and conflict. And, quite frequently, the main goal is to work through tactics and logistics.

Each one of these catalysts necessitates a different set of conditions. Conflicts aren't likely to be resolved, for instance, unless the territory is perceived as neutral, and each side has a chance to share its perspective. Successful brainstorming requires a mindset of creativity and suspended judgment, while collaborative action demands a more focused and pragmatic approach.

Since 2002, the National Coalition for Dialogue and Deliberation (NCDD) has worked with groups of all sizes to enhance their effectiveness. Through their work, they have discovered that nearly all group interactions can be categorized into one of several "streams of engagement." Like the four steps of nemawashi, the streams of engagement unfold in sequence, and their steps closely mirror THE CREATIVE PROCESS. But whereas nemawashi is a long-term process that involves building trust over time, the streams of engagement are much more fluid, with a group switching between them numerous times in a single meeting. The following list is based on NCDD's framework, with some additions based on Starhawk's work.

EXPLORATION

Exploration is the process of gathering the information necessary to make well-informed decisions. This first stream of engagement can be seen as a conceptual "inhalation" of facts, ideas, people, and tools. In fact, exploration has as many forms as there are MULTITUDES OF KNOWING. Sometimes an outside facilitator or expert guides the learning of group members. Sometimes the exploration is more peer-to-peer in nature, with members of the group sharing knowledge with each other. And sometimes a group is engaged in a process of shared exploration, each gaining and sharing knowledge as they go.

Regardless of how the exploration process is conducted, it can easily feel

Examples of Exploration

- Hands-on workshops
- Community listening sessions
- Hearing different members' opinions on an issue
- Researching best practices
- Focus groups and surveys
- Site survey for a permaculture design

overwhelming in its scope. A number of questions tend to arise: Is it better to go broad or deep? At what point has enough information been gathered to move forward? Which data points are relevant, and which are meaningless noise?

These questions can be answered more easily by setting boundaries and goals for the exploration process in advance. What is the timeframe of the exploration process? What sources of information are most valuable? Are they qualitative or quantitative? How will information be collected, processed, and analyzed?

Another common pitfall is the temptation to jump to solutions while still exploring. Most of us are conditioned to be problem solvers, and as a result, we start thinking of answers before we fully understand the problem. It might help, therefore, to use signs, buddy systems, or other strategies to help group members to keep an open mind during the exploration process.

ASSESSMENT

Assessment is the process of analyzing information to determine its relevance to the group. If exploration surveys what's out there, assessment attempts to deduce what it means, TELLING THE STORY of the data gathered.

Assessment demands pattern identification skills and a gift for narrative, qualities of the griot. Like exploration, it is often a small group activity, although SKILLED FACILITATION can bring assessment processes to larger groups. Good assessment requires having the right analytical tools at hand, as well as a space that's conducive to creative thinking.

Examples of Assessment

- Finding common themes in a series of interviews

- Developing a POWER ANALYSIS for an issue

- Performing SECTOR AND ZONE ANALYSIS for an issue

195

VISIONING

Visioning is the process of generating ideas that will lead a group toward a common aim. In the best cases, the process also helps generate social capital and the momentum for positive change.

The best visions start with a grasp of the whole concept and then proceed to articulate how each of the different parts express that whole. This is actually the reverse of how our task-oriented brains tend to work, and it can take some retraining to avoid becoming stuck in the details of some particular part of the vision.

For visions to be practical and actionable, participants need to have a deep knowledge of context—new businesses need to understand their target market; ecological designs need to know the ecosystem; activist campaigns must understand the needs and motivations of the key stakeholders; and social change initiatives need to know the community. If this knowledge isn't already present, the group might have explore and analyze that information first. In many cases, no single person has the full picture, so close collaboration is critical.

As the most creative stream of engagement, visioning is often quite inspiring

Examples of Visioning

- Developing a business model
- Listing potential agenda topics for a meeting
- Brainstorming ideas
- Creating a concept design for a permaculture site
- Thinking of potential mission statements
- Creating a shared vision for the future of your community
- Rezoning your neighborhood

and fun—so fun, in fact, that teams often get stuck there, continuing to dream up new solutions instead of picking one to implement. But visions are only as good as the change they help create in the real world, so groups with "vision addictions" would be well advised to find ways to keep moving through the creative process.

EDITING

Editing is the process of selecting the best choice or choices from a pool of potential options. The group that did the visioning process usually participates in editing. In fact, the two often occur near-simultaneously, with groups generating and eliminating ideas in rapid succession.

However, there's a real value in separating the two. Restricting the visioning to coming up with ideas helps relieve the filter and expands creativity, while setting aside a specific time for editing allows for more focused deliberation.

Indeed, the key to productive editing is having clear agreements about the decision-making process. What, for instance, is the limiting factor—the one variable that will determine how many total ideas can be considered? For some groups, it might be time, while others

Examples of Editing

- Determining the agenda topics and their order

- Running financial models to choose the most realistic business

- Selecting grants to award among a pool of applications

- Choosing plant varieties to grow on a farm

- Picking specific policies to advocate for

might be limited by space or budget. There should be a clear set of criteria to determine the relative value of different ideas. And, most importantly, groups need to know who has the final say. Will it be a consensus decision determined by everyone, a majority vote, or a unilateral choice by a leader?

CONFLICT TRANSFORMATION

Conflict transformation is the process of identifying and resolving differences among members of a group—whether those differences stem from logistical disagreements or centuries-old patterns of exploitation.

When groups have cases of hurt feelings and interpersonal strife, conflict transformation draws on processes such as TRUTH AND RECONCILIATION, RESTORATIVE JUSTICE, and nonviolent communication to allow each side to understand the other and find a path forward. In many cases, however, conflict transformation takes a much more prosaic form—building consensus among stakeholders or group members with competing interests.

Regardless of the nature of the conflict at hand, successful transformation rests on a few key factors. You want as few people involved as possible, as long as all sides of the issue are represented. The participants

Examples of Conflict Transformation

- Creating a policy platform among a mix of diverse stakeholders

- Distributing chores between roommates

- Navigating tensions between new residents and existing ones in a gentrifying neighborhood

- Resolving competing visions of an organization's future

need to feel comfortable with the space and ground rules, and they must trust the facilitator's neutrality. Finally, the process itself needs to result in an acknowledgment of each other's situations and a plan for shared commitments.

COLLABORATIVE ACTION

Collaborative action is the process of planning and executing a shared vision. Through countless small decisions, groups move from idea to reality, making adjustments along the way. Collaborative action is often more tactical than strategic, and it comes with corresponding shift in HUMAN POLYCULTURE roles. Whereas visioning is often facilitated by servant leaders and conflict transformation is mediated by elders or graces, collaborative action is the work of mavens and helping hands. Often, collaborative action is best undertaken through action plans, which provide participants with incremental goals and clear lines of accountability. It also helps to MEASURE SUCCESS, using qualitative or quantitative indicators to provide the team with feedback as they go.

Like exploration, collaborative action flows most smoothly in groups of three to six—ideally, ones in which everyone knows each other's strengths and feels comfortable being their true selves. Collaborative action can often feel tedious, but RITUAL AND CEREMONY can be used skillfully to connect it to the big vision.

FURTHER LEARNING

National Coalition for Dialogue and Deliberation, "Engagement Streams Framework," 2014, http://ncdd.org/rc/item/2142.

APPLYING THE PATTERN

Think about projects you've worked on within a group. Can you identify examples of the STREAMS OF ENGAGEMENT in those group interactions? What streams were strongest? What streams do you think were lacking, and how could you encourage them?

45. THE RIGHT WAY TO DECIDE

Group decisions can be made via majority, plurality, consensus, or any number of other forms. Understand each of these decision-making processes, and apply the right one in the right context.

When I was in high school, I dreaded hanging out in large groups. It wasn't about social anxiety around crowds; instead, I was simply frustrated by how long it would take coordinate anything. Should we meet at the mall? A park? One of our homes? Should we go to a movie, play laser tag, or go swing dancing? We spent more time driving around deciding what to do than actually doing it.

If only this was just a teenage thing. Unfortunately, adults in loosely organized groups get caught in decision-making traps all the time. We're too polite to rule out another person's silly idea or too confrontational to make everyone feel invested in compromising toward consensus. We lack the necessary information to make an informed decision or get too lost in the weeds to understand the fundamental choice that needs to be made.

Decision making in hierarchies, meanwhile, frequently presents a mirror image of these traps. Those in power make critical choices based on gut feelings or their own limited knowledge, without a full understanding of how those choices will affect staff workload, prior progress, or buy-in from the group. At its worst, it results in poor choices that disempower group members.

Fortunately, effective groups can remedy both of these pitfalls by thoughtfully choosing a decision-making process and sticking to it. Every group has the opportunity to negotiate its own balance between the efficiency of a unilateral decision and the participation of a larger group. In fact, there is an entire subdiscipline of political science devoted to voting theory, tasked with finding the best decision-making technique for a given set of circumstances.

The first step to figuring out the right way to decide is determining which decisions ought to be made by which parts of the group. Does the whole team need to have a say in what food will be served at the next meeting? Does everybody trust a subgroup to decide the name of the next event or the wording of the mission statement? Part of the answer will likely depend on how established the group is. As members get further along in the NEMAWASHI process and establish more trust, they tend to feel more and more comfortable delegating decisions to individuals or CAUCUSES.

Once you determine *who* is voting, then you can move on to *how*. There are two fundamental decision-making strategies: majority and consensus. But in the same way that hierarchies and networks work best in combination, each of these strategies can be seen as opposite ends of a spectrum, with many permutations possible in between.

The most popular decision-making process in use today is the *majority process*, developed by army engineer Henry Martyn Robert in 1876, after a disastrously facilitated church meeting. Loosely based on parliamentary procedure of the era, the book that's come to be known as *Robert's Rules of Order* has served as the protocol for corporate boards, fraternities, and parent-teacher associations ever since. Making a decision according to *Robert's Rules* generally looks something like this:

1. Someone puts forth a proposal.

2. The proposal is discussed.

3. As discussion winds down or as time runs out, someone makes a motion to vote based on the proposal and any modifications.

4. Someone else seconds the motion.

5. A yes-or-no vote is taken, and the motion passes if a majority are in favor.

Whether we knew we were following *Robert's Rules* or not, most of us have probably participated in a decision-making process that used those steps. In contexts with high levels of trust and little disagreement, it proceeds quite smoothly and efficiently.

But this kind of majority process—the default for most groups—can be lacking in a number of ways. In a vote between two options, for instance, it can disempower 49 percent of the group. In *Robert's Rules* and most majority voting protocols based on it, there's no requirement to incorporate opposing viewpoints and therefore no reason to engage in dialogue. This is especially problematic in groups that embrace diverse perspectives, which are generally the kinds of groups we would like to nurture.

In response to these challenges and others with majority voting, some groups have adopted a process called *consensus*. Originally developed by the Iroquois Confederacy and formally refined by the Quaker Society of Friends, consensus process has its contemporary roots in the Movement for a New Society, a Philadelphia-based alliance of activist groups operative in the 1970s and 1980s. The basic steps of consensus are as follows:

1. Someone puts forth a proposal.

2. The proposal is discussed, sometimes with a nonbinding "straw poll" to gauge the level of support.

3. Someone makes a revised proposal based on the original and any modifications.

4. A vote is taken, but instead of just yes or no, there are three possible positions—yes, stand aside, or block—and the proposal passes if nobody blocks.

Consensus process is rooted in the subtle distinction between *unity* and *unanimity*. While the popular meaning of the word *consensus* implies a unanimous agreement, decision-making by consensus isn't predicated on full support for an idea: the "stand-aside" vote, for instance, allows people to express reservations without blocking. By allowing all concerns to be voiced—and by empowering every person with the ability to block a decision—a consensus vote measures the *willingness to move forward* despite minor concerns.

Like the networked structure that it represents, the consensus process can be vastly more equitable and innovative, but it also requires more energy. As a result, consensus works far better in smaller groups at the zone of cooperation and smaller. Beyond thirty people or so, there are simply too many people to satisfy, and chances increase that someone will block.

Many consensus processes are hamstrung by trying to appease one or two dissatisfied members, increasing the time and conflict involved in making a decision. These situations can be curtailed by adopting *decision thresholds,* in which consent doesn't have to be unanimous. This can be particularly useful for larger groups or for a situation in which there are several appealing options to choose from. The group should decide well in advance whether to adopt decision thresholds during the process, and it should be consented to by everyone—including by the stalwarts.

Many other processes provide a middle ground between simple majority and pure consensus. In the year 2000, mathematician Warren Smith conducted simulations of many voting methods to see which produced the most satisfactory outcome for the largest amount of people. The winner was a process called *range voting*, in which participants rank each choice by their preference, and the choice with the highest average rank is declared the winner.[65] Since Smith's study, range voting has become a ubiquitous part of our lives in the form of crowdsourced online ratings for restaurants, apps, and just about everything else. Range voting can be an efficient protocol when there are a set number of discrete choices, such as candidates for office or venues for an event.

In the context of facilitated groups, a common variation on range voting is called *dotmocracy*. Participants have a limited number of dots to spread among a discrete set of options and can choose to concentrate all their dots on one option or spread them out over several. Popular since the 1980s, dotmocracy is useful as a quick way to gauge relative levels of support for a range of ideas. But the rapid process of dotmocracy can also be a weak point, as it can encourage participants to vote without careful deliberation of the issues. As a result, dotmocracy works best in combination with dialogue before and after the voting process.

CONDITIONS FOR MAKING GOOD DECISIONS

Regardless of the decision-making method chosen, facilitators have a number of important factors to consider:

- Does the group have all the necessary information to make a well-informed decision?

- Are the right people involved? Are those most affected by the decision part of the process? If not, how will you communicate with them to ensure that they are bought in and actually implement or support the decision?

- Do the options under consideration truly represent all possible alternatives—or are they all minor variations on a theme?

- Is the decision-making process being guided by principles of SKILLED FACILITATION? What are the mechanisms for preventing the loudest voices from dominating the conversation? How can you prioritize the voices of the unheard?

- Are you spending the right amount of time on the right topics? It can be easy to go around in circles debating a minor topic and leave only a few minutes for much more important ones.

DECISION-MAKING MODEL	IDEAL GROUP SIZE	PROS	CONS	NOTES
Majority Voting	Zone of trust and larger (10 or more)	Uses democratic participation in the process. Fast. Effective for decisions with low stakes.	Can leave members feeling like they have lost, leading to lack of identification with group. Tyranny of the majority often overwhelms minority views, encouraging factions to form within the group.	At a minimum, it's important to have thoughtful and inclusive discussion prior to any major "majority rules" decisions.
Consensus	Zone of cooperation and smaller (2 to 30)	Has a high level of team involvement and can lead to strong, well-supported decisions. Often leads to completely new solutions, which the team arrives at in the course of its discussion.	Can become time-consuming, especially as groups get larger. May be difficult to reach a consensus.	Develop good practices to ensure that each person participates in the decision-making process. Define the decision topic clearly, and remain sensitive to the team's process.
Unilateral—Decision by Authority	One person or small team deciding on behalf of others.	Very fast. Appropriate when there is complete trust in the person or group making the decision. Good for time-sensitive decisions, and ones where the team doesn't need to give input to support and implement the decision.	Does not maximize the strengths of the individuals in the group. Less buy-in.	
Dotmocracy and Range Voting	Zone of trust to zone of familiarity (10 to 150)	Good for quickly choosing between many options.	Can result in decisions that nobody fully supports. System can be gamed to influence a favored outcome.	

This combination of range voting and deliberation is formalized in the *crowdwise process*, developed in the United Kingdom by Perry Walker of the New Economics Foundation. Crowdwise begins with a range vote, in which a range of options is presented, which stakeholders rank according to their preference. But instead of that vote determining the winner, participants then enter into a discussion about each option and seek opportunities to combine or eliminate them. A second range vote is conducted on these revised options, and the process is continued until one option remains.

Clearly, the majority voting most of us are used to is just one out of a constellation of strategies available to groups and facilitators, with each one offering different opportunities and challenges. But with so many options, deciding how to decide can easily drag down the momentum of group. As a rule of thumb, it's better to spend two minutes finding a good process than twenty minutes finding the *best* process. If only I'd followed that advice in high school.

FURTHER LEARNING

Kaner, Sam. *Facilitator's Guide to Participatory Decision-Making.* 3rd edition. San Francisco: Jossey-Bass, 2014.

APPLYING THE PATTERN

How do the groups or organizations you work with make decisions? Have you seen it work effectively or ineffectively? What techniques from this section might be better alternatives? Try one of them and consider how it worked. How did the group do with it? What would you do differently next time?

46. CONVERGE AND DISPERSE

In seeking a dynamic balance between collaboration and autonomy, well-functioning groups embrace a rhythm of coming together and breaking apart.

A healthier world is one in which everybody participates. Engaging all perspectives leads to a richer understanding of the issue at hand, as well as more realistic solutions. And as a matter of equity, patterns such as SUBSIDIARITY, CITIZEN GOVERNANCE, and LEADERSHIP FROM WITHIN remind us that key decisions about policy, land use, business, and more should be made by those most affected by the outcome.

But while it may be ideal to involve as many people as possible in solving a problem, there are practical limitations to doing so. Trying to make even the most basic decisions in large groups can lead to intractable differences of opinion. Conversely, the tendency of people in large gatherings to go with the flow can lead to groupthink, a lack of due diligence, and the drowning out of the voices of the unheard. Even without these dramas, mundane logistics like coordinating meeting times with many people can drain a group's energy.

In short, making decisions as a large group can be tedious or even impossible, with the challenge increasing exponentially as the size of the group grows. So how do groups balance the benefits of democratic participation with the pitfalls of big gatherings? Through continuously managing the size of the group to fit the task at hand, in an ongoing cycle of coming together and breaking apart.

First, it's important to recognize that teams move through many STREAMS OF ENGAGEMENT while performing transformative work. During a single meeting, a group might start with an introduction circle (RITUAL AND CEREMONY), engage in a brainstorming session, debate the merits of a particular policy, and wrap up by discussing action items and deadlines. THE RIGHT SIZE for each one of these types of engagement can vary wildly. Explaining instructions, for instance, is most efficiently done with the entire group in one place, but problem solving is usually a disaster with more than ten people at a time.

If you've ever worked for a company or gone to school, this should look familiar. Most contemporary classroom environments employ a mix of lectures, individual assignments, breakout groups, and team projects in order to keep things interesting and meet diverse learning styles. And whether you're on a construction crew or working at a tech start-up, your typical workweek is likely to consist of various combinations of solo work and small group work, punctuated by the occasional gathering of the full team.

FOUR EFFECTIVE PATTERNS OF CONVERGENCE AND DISPERSAL

Spokescouncils. As successful groups grow in size, it becomes harder to make decisions with everybody participating in each discussion. Split the team up into working groups or committees, and designate one person from each to act as the "spoke" or representative to the organization as a whole.

Pair share. Most of us—especially introverts—are far more likely to be honest, articulate, and vulnerable when sharing our thoughts one-on-one than in front of a big group. Having participants discuss a topic in pairs before recapping their discussion in front of the whole group be a powerful technique for everything from introductions to conflict transformation.

Tributary brainstorming. For something intended to be inspiring and productive, group brainstorming sessions can be maddeningly tedious and circular. Most brainstorming "turns on the hose" of group conversation all at once, drowning out ideas that might take time to form and encouraging off-the-cuff ideas that might not be the most inspired. Instead, model the flow of tributaries in a watershed—start with individuals writing down their ideas alone, then have them compare notes in small groups, and finally have each group report their results to the whole team.

Festival. Longtime rituals like parades and big sports games derive much of their power from the convergence of many disparate individuals. If you're feeling a lack of cohesion among your community, consider planning a big event designed explicitly to bring people together under the banner of celebration.

The *idea* of CONVERGE AND DISPERSE is already second nature to most of us. But the way we currently do it *in practice* doesn't always lead to the best results. That's where THE CREATIVE PROCESS comes in. By employing a design approach to these group dynamics, we can analyze each step of a process and determine when it makes sense to bring the whole group together and when to split into individual or small-team work. The chart below shows the rough sizes that are appropriate for each STREAM OF ENGAGEMENT.

	Zone of Intimacy (3–10)	Zone of Trust (10–25)	Zone of Cooperation (25–50)
Exploration	x	x	
Assessment	x		
Visioning	x	x	x
Editing	x	x	
Conflict Transformation	x		
Collaborative Action	x		

APPLYING THE PATTERN

When have you worked in large groups when smaller ones would have been more effective, or vice versa? Have you worked with a group that effectively converged and dispersed? Can you think of times when converging and dispersing would have been helpful in groups you've worked in? How can the pattern of CREATIVE DESTRUCTION inform this pattern?

47. LEADERSHIP FROM WITHIN

Although outsiders can play key roles of support and influence, authentic change must come from within the ranks of the affected community.

It is a contradiction in terms to use the two words "disorganization" and "community" together: the word community itself means an organized, communal life; people living in an organized fashion.

—Saul Alinsky

The principle of SUBSIDIARITY makes the common-sense assertion that important decisions should be made by the people with the most at stake. After all, those with the most to gain or lose are likely to know the most about the context, and they're the ones who are likely to care the most about the eventual outcome. But while these concepts may seem obvious, they're rarely adhered to in practice. All too often, policy is steered by special interests seeking profit while disregarding the basic needs of everyday citizens. Large NGOs working on behalf of the disenfranchised are run by college-educated whites. Even public-input processes often seem perfunctory and opaque, making a mockery of CITIZEN GOVERNANCE.

The side effects of unaccountable decisions made by special-interest groups are manifold, reading like a checklist of the twenty-first century's most pressing social problems: environmental toxins, economic stagnation, failing school systems, and institutional discrimination, to name but a few. Some of us can fret over these challenges from the sidelines, but those living with the consequences of decisions they didn't make suffer daily under their weight. This cumulative wear releases a steady stream of stress hormones, which have been shown to lead to everything from heart disease to cancer. In 2010, a study by the National Institutes of Health actually put a number on the effect of this stress, estimating that black women are biologically 7.5 years older than their white counterparts.[66]

These consequences are psychological as well as physical. Across every continent, entire generations of society are growing up without real hope for change or the tools to create it. Native Americans languish on reservations, cut off from society at large and their own ancestral territory. Minority youth growing up in impoverished cities and suburbs have little chance of higher education or meaningful employment. Throughout the Global South, hundreds of millions make do in informal settlements at outskirts of megacities, scraping by on pennies a day.

When our children are growing up with nothing to live for, it's no wonder they turn to alcohol, violence, and crime as adults. Mateo Nube, an organizer for California-based activist group Movement Generation, has seen the effects of these unaccountable decisions up close and makes a clear connection between these conditions and antimarket practices that extract capital from communities. "We live under an economic system that has predetermined there are places and people that are actually completely disposable."[67] In the same way that consumer culture sends mountains of used goods to the landfill, entire generations within a culture are being thrown away.

Yet Nube's metaphor also presents us with the seed of an alternative future: "We need to be thinking about the concept of 'zero waste' not only as it relates to stuff, but as it relates to people."[68] What would a zero-waste concept of people look like? Social movements of the recent past provide instructive examples. In the mid-twentieth century, independence movements throughout the Global South sought to escape the yoke of European colonialism and reclaim suppressed cultural heritage. Here in the United States, the free food and education programming provided by the Black Panthers echoed this struggle for self-determination. Beginning in the 1960s and 1970s, organizers like Saul Alinsky and Paulo Freire began to systematize this approach to bottom-up organizing, empowering community after community with the tools to speak out on their own behalf.

Using tools from these leaders and others, most of today's most successful social movements recognize the centrality of leadership from within. Across the northern forests of Canada, women of dozens of First Nations have declared themselves Idle No More, successfully blocking many oil and gas projects on their ancestral homeland. At the southern tip of Florida, the Coalition of Immokalee Farmworkers has run a decade-long campaign for better pay and labor protections for their backbreaking work. And throughout the United States, young undocumented immigrants have banded together as a movement of Dreamers, each one facing the threat of deportation to speak out for access to education and other rights.

In December 1996, a diverse group of forty organizers and activists met in Jemez, New Mexico, to strategize around issues of globalization and trade. Among other outcomes created during that gathering was a set of principles, titled the Jemez Principles for Democratic Organizing, which provides a handy blueprint for cultivating leadership from within:[69]

- *Be inclusive.* From planning meetings to staffing decisions to board membership, organizations seeking leadership from within must commit to involving those most affected—even when it requires more discussion, planning, time, and conflict.

- *Emphasize bottom-up organizing.* Leadership from within necessitates ongoing work to build a strong base, engaging people at all levels of leadership and cultural status.

- *Let people speak for themselves.* As much as possible, both internal and public conversations about injustice should involve the voices of people directly affected by it. When people are needed to speak on behalf of a group, structures of accountability should be in place to ensure that they speak as accurately as possible.

- *Work together in solidarity and mutuality.* The struggle for a better world involves an interconnected web of communities and causes. It's critical to recognize this interdependence by supporting individuals and groups with complementary goals and values and by striving to incorporate those goals and values into our own work. Advocacy groups of African Americans and advocacy groups of Latinos, for instance, should advocate for one another as well. Sustainability organizations should take cues from justice groups, and vice versa.

- *Build just relationships among ourselves.* The culture of an organization matters. An institution's norms, both written and unwritten, should reflect the values of mutual respect and justice that we're seeking to create in the world at large.

- *Commit to self-transformation.* The most profound change starts high in the watershed. As servant leaders, it's incumbent upon us to walk the walk, embodying the values and ideals of the organizations we're a part of and tending to our own self-care.

Fifty years after Freire and Alinsky began their careers, the *idea* of LEADER-SHIP FROM WITHIN is widely recognized—but examples remain rare in practice. As much as most of us agree with the theory, the fact remains that most social change organizations are still founded by outsiders. Those who have not been affected by most forms of injustice have, by definition, more access to intellectual, social, and financial capital needed to start an organization. The problem is that it's difficult to transition an organization to being led from within once it's already started. Without meaning to, our words, actions, and very presence can send disempowering signals from the very first steps of the NEMAWASHI process.

Does that mean that there's no place for allyship and SOLIDARITY in social change? Hardly. In fact, many communities welcome engagement and help from outsiders. It's just that doing so respectfully requires a shift in our narratives, from seeing disempowered communities as our clients to thinking of them as our bosses. Rather than selling a community on our solutions, the ally's job is to help create the conditions for a community to articulate its own problems and come up with its own solutions. As a rule of thumb, outsiders should refrain from getting involved unless they're invited in by community itself. Once in the game, meanwhile, it's important to engage on the terms of the most affected, checking in on a regular basis to make sure that our actions are being guided by—and held accountable to—those doing the leading.

Does this style of organization-building takes more time to launch? Absolutely. Does it entail more individual soul-searching and interpersonal conflict? Most likely. But once we remind ourselves that the process is just as important as the goal, dedicating ourselves to leadership from within is the obvious choice. And as we walk the path laid out by the Jemez principles, we're sure to find ourselves gaining more and more momentum as we go.

FURTHER LEARNING

Green, Mike. *When People Care Enough to Act: ABCD in Action.* With Henry Moore and John O'Brien. Toronto, Inclusion Press, 2007.

APPLYING THE PATTERN

Are the organizations you work for or with directed by members of the community? If not, how can you integrate the community's voices into your work? What members of the community might you invite to dialogue about this? What organizations in your community are directed from within? How might you collaborate with them?

48. REGENERATIVE MANAGEMENT

Successful leaders are always seeking opportunities to cultivate leadership within others.

Brilliant personalities can make amazing things happen—rally people to their cause, raise awareness, make a revolutionary technology, pass laws. But an organization centered around one person's personality is also dangerous. After all, even geniuses aren't infallible, and at some point, the wisdom of the founder will fail. More fundamentally, what happens when the founder moves on? No matter how committed someone might be to begin with, their interests, time, family commitments, and financial circumstances are bound to change as they move through their own life cycle And even if someone remains committed to a single organization till the end of his or her life—well, then what? There's still THE LONG GAME to consider.

Plenty of organizations fall apart or limp along once their charismatic founder leaves. A 1984 study of the newspaper industry, for instance, found that newspapers of all kinds were most likely to fail during times of leadership transition.[7] Two decades later, a review of corporate mergers estimated that 55 percent of leaders brought in to manage a merger from outside either firm failed at their job within eighteen months.[71]

In response to these dismal statistics, consultants and strategists have developed an array of succession-planning advice for leaders thinking of stepping down. But even these strategies are often too little, too late. The smoothest transitions are those that were planned from day one. From the earliest stages of an organization, founders should be thinking about how to "design themselves out of a job," slowly building a group culture that institutionalizes sound decision making and nurtures LEADERSHIP FROM WITHIN.

Susan Kenny Stevens is a nationally known consultant specializing in nonprofit life cycles. In her book *Nonprofit Lifecycles: Stage-Based Wisdom for Nonprofit Capacity*, Stevens outlines four stages of founder succession for nonprofits that apply equally well to REGENERATIVE ENTERPRISE, SMALL BUSINESS, and other organizations:[72]

1. *Sole organizational ownership.* The founding and early life of the organization. The founder is the one calling all the shots, getting everything done, and so on.

2. *Separation and delegation.* "The founder is moving from being 'the one' to 'one of.'" Staff or board members (or a mix of both) are brought on; the founder stops doing everything but is still in charge of everything.

3. *Shared ownership and interdependence.* Ownership is transferred from the founder to the board and to the management. "The founder's gift has gone public. It is now co-owned by the community represented by the board and staff."

4. *Founder legacy.* The founder steps back from operations, identifies the values and ideas he or she want to leave behind, and seeds them throughout the organization.

No matter what stage in the organizational lifecycle an organization finds itself in, it's worth thinking about regenerative management. And not just for founders—all the people in the group who have positions of responsibility ought to think about how to institutionalize their decision-making process and approach. There are some strategies for moving an organization through the stages of succession:

- *Know what you're looking for.* Organizations are continually growing, evolving, and facing new challenges. The leadership skills necessary at the founding of an organization (adaptability, vision), might be completely different than those needed by one poised for growth (evaluation, fiscal discipline). Be clear about what values you're looking for in a new leader, and don't assume you should be looking for someone as close in strengths to the old leader as possible.

- *Nurture servant leaders.* Build an internal culture of SUBSIDIARITY, in which each person is empowered to take on as much responsibility as he or she would like. Allow everyone to play to their strengths, while challenging their weaknesses.

- *Spread the power.* Heed the pattern of DOCUMENT THE PROCESS, and try to write down the personal knowledge in your head. Train others in your organization to do the things you know how to do—even if they're not as good at it as first.

- *Provide continual feedback.* Provide kind but critical feedback to encourage group members to learn from their mistakes.

- *Embrace change.* Organizations are continually encountering new challenges and opportunities, and sometimes the next level of growth demands a rethink of earlier assumptions and long-held institutional processes. Encourage solutions that change with the context, while creating systems and policies to ensure that the group's core values stay the same.

- *Be willing to let go.* Many founders find themselves wanting to take back control long after they've formally committed themselves to stepping back. This pattern is so well known that it has a name: *founder's syndrome*. A necessary part of regenerative management is placing enough faith in your team that you are willing to see them make decisions differently than you would—and know that that's okay.

FURTHER LEARNING

Stevens, Susan Kenny. *Nonprofit Lifecycles: Stage-Based Wisdom for Nonprofit Capacity.* N.p.: Stagewise Enterprises, 2002.

APPLYING THE PATTERN

Are you the founder or leader of an organization? Do you have a plan for the organization once you're gone? Think about the organizations you are a part of. Are they one-person shows, or do they encourage others to show leadership as well? Are they planning ahead on how to transition leadership? If not, how can their practices change so that they will be more long-lived?

49. NAMING NORMS

Every group has its own rules about what kinds of behavior are encouraged and discouraged. Effective groups make those rules transparent, name them early in the NEMAWASHI process, and continue to revise them as the group evolves.

As a college student, I loved the process of comparing ideas, writing about them, and debating them with my peers. In high school, I'd been on the speech and debate team for several years, and I'd lost my fear of speaking up in a group, so when it came time for class discussions in college, I was always among the first to raise my hand and share my opinion. It wasn't until years later that I thought about how my constant comments took the floor time away time from others who might have been more shy or introverted. In my enthusiasm to dive into the material, I'd neglected to consider how my presence was affecting other students' ability to contribute.

Fortunately, my undergraduate enthusiasm had few side effects besides an eye-roll or two. But the same dynamics that I stumbled into are writ much larger in other contexts. During the norming stage of NEMAWASHI, all kinds of spoken and unspoken rules of participation are established—rules that can either engage or exclude. Sometimes these signals of disempowerment are sent blatantly, as a result of the spoken rules of the group. But much more frequently, they're delivered via unspoken and unconscious mechanisms—the way people dress, their posture and body language, the jargon and slang they use, and the way they're facilitated. Without negotiating the norming process carefully, groups can inadvertently shame, shun, or otherwise disempower their members, with detrimental consequences on the group's performance and society as a whole.

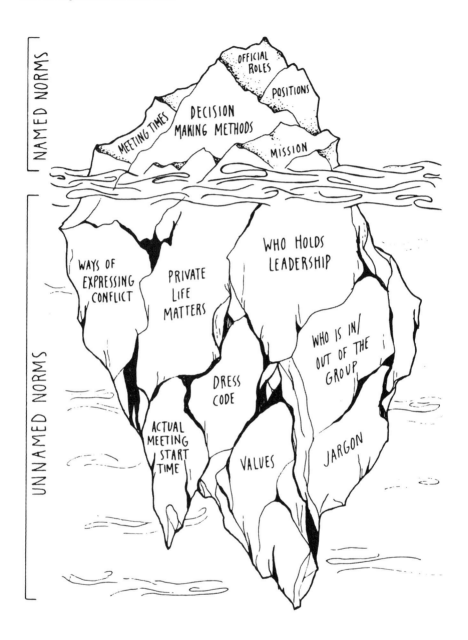

As organizers, facilitators, and changemakers, it's up to us to have our antennae out for these disempowerment signals and to work proactively to disrupt them. In many cases, this is as simple as making the invisible rules visible. Through facilitated discussion, group members can get the rules of engagement out on the table and commit to holding each other accountable to them. Here are just some of the norms that a group might want to consider as a team:

- *What are the goals of the group?* Is everyone on the same page about what the group is trying to accomplish, and by when? Is there a need for a written mission statement or list of key values?

- *How does the group make decisions?* Carefully weighing the opinions of each group member often results in more thoughtful choices but can take a while. Simple majority votes are more efficient but less equitable. Find THE RIGHT WAY TO DECIDE for your group that balances these two approaches. Are key choices determined by a majority vote? A consensus process? Through subcommittees?

- *What are the rules for membership?* Who gets to join, and what is the process for acceptance into the group? Under what circumstances might someone get asked to leave? Consider THE RIGHT SIZE for the group. What is the minimum number of people it needs to function? What is the size beyond which it would become cumbersome and ineffective? Are nonmembers welcome at group gatherings? If so, in what capacity?

- *How are discussions facilitated?* SKILLED FACILITATION is usually a critical factor for group effectiveness. Who is responsible for setting agendas, keeping discussions focused, and transforming conflict? Does one person act as facilitator for all meetings, or does the role rotate among members? Are there certain conversations that call for bringing in an outside facilitator?

- *Who has authority?* Whose words hold more weight within the group? Are there formal positions of authority? If so, do they correspond with the informal power dynamics?

- *How does the group communicate?* During group dialogue, conversation might flow through any combination of CIRCLE DIALOGUE techniques: freeform "popcorn" discussion, raising hands, or using a talking stick or fishbowl layout. Meanwhile, communication outside of face-to-face meetings has its own set of norms to consider. Do group members feel okay communicating via email? Text message? Voicemail? How formal are the expectations about the language used? What hours and times of day are considered acceptable to reach out?

- *What steps are the group willing to take to be inclusive?* Is translation provided for non-English speakers? Childcare for parents? Can the meeting times be shifted to accommodate members' work or school schedules?

There's no limit to the amount of unspoken norms that might affect group performance—but there *is* a limit to how many can be addressed openly. Having a conversation about each of the above questions could be exhausting and counterproductive. Therefore, groups should be intentional about which norms are most important to discuss for their particular context. Later, as the group goes about its business and its culture continues to evolve, facilitators, leaders, or others can maintain an awareness of how well the spoken norms are being adhered to, and if there are any unspoken norms that need to be addressed.

COMMON COMMUNITY COMMITMENTS

Co-creating group commitments can be a useful exercise to name norms at the beginning of a group process. By asking participants to name their own commitments and asking the rest of the group if they consent to following them, a culture of participation is established right at the outset. That being said, facilitators might want to come prepared with a list of community commitments that they can suggest if needed. Having run this exercise several dozen times, I've come up with a list of the most common commitments:

- *Step up and step back.* This commitment invites those who are normally quiet to step up and challenge themselves to participate, while asking frequent participators to step back to allow others room to speak. It can be casually self-enforced or implemented more intentionally through giving participants a limited number of "comment stones" that are turned in when the participants speak in the group.

- *Confidentiality and trust.* Participants commit to keeping the information shared within a group confidential—an important precondition for creating a space where participants are comfortable being honest and vulnerable. A formal explication of this commitment is called the Chatham House Rule, which states that "participants are free to use the information received, but neither the identity nor the affiliation of the speaker(s), nor that of any other participant, may be revealed."

- *Punctuality.* A commitment to respecting each other's time by starting and ending meetings at the agreed-upon time. Keep in mind that punctuality is valued differently across cultures, so this may not be a universally desired commitment.

- *Diligence.* Participants commit to bringing their full selves to the task at hand, agreeing to unplug from other distractions and engage with their brain, heart, and body.

- *Meet people where they are.* This commitment acknowledges that each person has different experiences, abilities, and skills, and it pledges that nobody will feel ashamed of where they are in their path.

- *Speak only for yourself.* It's all too easy to state opinions as facts, especially during heated or controversial conversations. By asking participants to preface their own opinions with statements like "I believe" or "I feel," this commitment acknowledges that feelings might differ.

APPLYING THE PATTERN

Think about the norms that you, your organization, or your community have. Which norms are explicit, and which norms seem implicit? Would someone coming into one of these groups for the first time be aware of the norms? How could you go about clarifying the healthy group norms without disempowering any of the group's members or allies?

50. SKILLED FACILITATION

Even the most experienced groups benefit from having someone to keep discussions effective and on track.

One person can have a vision. Two can have a productive dialogue. But the nitty-gritty of constructive social change can be worked out only in groups. From the tribal council to the boardroom to the covert gathering of revolutionaries, collaborative meetings are the foundation of democratic decision making. With more people comes more complexity to manage, though, and meetings of all kinds are susceptible to infighting, grandstanding, unclear processes, and other ills that dampen their effectiveness. With all these downsides, it's no wonder that meetings are reviled by white-collar professionals and radical organizers alike.

Even so, collective deliberation remains the only viable alternative to rule by decree. If we want our meetings to be as productive as possible, one of the most effective interventions is skilled facilitation. With the right person guiding a conversation, an unfocused brain dump can turn into an outpouring of creative energy, a spat of bickering can be transformed into an emotional and cathartic dialogue, and an overwhelming goal can be split into a series of discrete tasks with group members taking ownership of each one. In each these cases, facilitators live up to the Latin etymology of their title: *facilis,* "easy, nimble." Drawing out the wisdom within the group, they make difficult processes flow more easily.

Depending on a group's place in the unfolding of NEMAWASHI—as well as which STREAMS OF ENGAGEMENT are called for in the moment—a facilitator may be called to perform any number of roles. There are the prosaic functions of setting agendas, keeping discussions focused, and making sure to DOCUMENT THE PROCESS. There are the improvisatory efforts of mediating conflict and responding to unexpected turns in the conversation. And there are more abstract roles:

ensuring full participation from group members, sensing and responding to the mood of the room, and guiding groups through RITUAL AND CEREMONY to help them reach their highest potential.

Like the servant leader in a HUMAN POLYCULTURE, a good deal of the facilitator's skill lies in the ability to juggle these competencies and to understand the right role to play at any given time. Here are some of the most important archetypes of skilled facilitation:

- *The facilitator is a conductor.* Perhaps more important than anything else is managing the mood and energy levels of a gathering. Facilitators are able to structure the right activities in the right order and at the right pace to achieve the best results. They use icebreaker rituals to get people comfortable at the beginning of a meeting and debriefing rituals to help them feel a sense of closure at the end. In between, they relieve tension with games, humor, or personal anecdotes; call for breaks when the energy is flagging; and allow a group to struggle when it is working through a particularly challenging situation.

- *The facilitator is a polymath.* Experienced facilitators are fluent in multiple modes of group interaction and know how to incorporate them in any number of cultural and social contexts. They are conversant in the STREAMS OF ENGAGEMENT and are equally comfortable leading groups through brainstorming sessions, task-oriented planning efforts, or resolving conflicts. They understand the rhythms of CONVERGE AND DISPERSE, breaking groups apart and bringing them together.

- *The facilitator is an interior designer.* The meeting place matters. A gathering held in a windowless classroom is likely to lead to an entirely different set of interactions than, say, a gazebo filled with cushions and birdsong. No matter the setting, facilitators make the most out of the space available to them, adjusting everything from lighting to the decorations on the walls to encourage the desired outcome. Learning environments might be filled with inspirational posters and books. Brainstorming sessions ought to have plenty of open wall space or table space to document ideas. CIRCLE DIALOGUE and other democratic conversations require seats that are facing each other. In addition to the space itself, skilled facilitators make good use of physical tools of the meeting—ranging from talking sticks to digital projectors—to keep things moving in the right direction.

- *The facilitator is a gardener.* As discussed in NAMING NORMS, the right group culture can make a tremendous difference in how effectively a group is able to achieve its goals. In many cases, facilitators are tasked with nurturing that culture. This aspect of the facilitator's job is about creating a climate of participation, in which all participants feel welcome and able to engage. It means affirming tentative statements and paraphrasing muddled ones. It means actively discouraging side conversations, unproductive arguments, and individuals claiming the floor for their own soapbox speeches. And it means asking tough questions when the conversation is sliding into groupthink.

- *The facilitator is a neutral party.* Groups place an extraordinary amount of trust in their facilitator—and a key part of earning that trust is maintaining neutrality. As the Canadian Institute of Cultural Affairs puts it, every facilitator "has to have an unshakable belief that the group itself has the wisdom and creativity needed to deal with the situation."[73] Even when that wisdom and creativity is going against the facilitator's own opinion or beliefs, the facilitator must encourage constructive dialogue. Of course, there are many situations where someone's prior history might make such objectivity impossible—and in that case, a truly neutral third party should be called in to facilitate.

- *The facilitator is a psychologist.* Much about what humans communicate to one another is said without words. Are there silences in the conversation? If so, do they feel uncomfortable or thoughtful? Are people slouching in their seats or leaning into the conversation with arms crossed? Are two people in the corner exchanging worried looks? Are participants hurriedly making notes or checking Facebook on their phones? Much like the grace in a HUMAN POLYCULTURE, facilitators are sensitive and responsive to nonverbal cues, adjusting the length and nature of activities to keep people engaged and supported.

- *The facilitator is a jazz musician.* No matter how much planning goes into a group process, things will go off-script—sometimes in a major way. SKILLED FACILITATION often entails adapting to changing situations on the fly, improvising new solutions as they go. In the words of group coach Brian Stanfield, "the facilitator has to know how to balance the process on the one hand and the results of the process on the other, and to harmonize the needs of the participants at any one moment with the total demands of the task."[74]

- *The facilitator is a role model.* They use COMMITMENT PRUNING, grounding rituals, and other strategies of self-care to ensure that they're able to give their best in each situation. They put in the necessary time in advance to prepare, and they develop documentation after the fact with the help of note takers. Good facilitators are always looking to improve their craft, constantly learning new skills and information and seeking constructive feedback to help them grow.

These archetypes give a broad overview of the skills necessary to facilitate fairly and gracefully. Each situation calls for different roles to be emphasized, and each facilitator will embody some of these roles more masterfully than others. With these variations in mind, it's important to consider a couple more factors when choosing a facilitator. When a group member is willing and capable, it's often easier and more effective for conversations to be facilitated internally. Sometimes, however, it can be better to bring in an outside party—for instance, if a big decision must be made and every group member must act as a participant, or in situations when the facilitator must truly be unbiased.

You should also consider the frequency of facilitation. Even when acting as a true steward of the group's intelligence, facilitators have an undeniable power over the flow of a conversation, determining who gets to speak and deciding when to allow dissent and when to avoid it. Given this fact, some NURTURED NETWORKS choose to rotate facilitators on a regular basis to keep any one person from accruing too much influence. On the other hand, it can be confusing and counterproductive for a group to continually have to adjust to different styles and skill levels of facilitation. Ultimately, each group must decide for itself which qualities of SKILLED FACILITATION to emphasize and how to incorporate them into their culture.

FURTHER LEARNING

Butler, Ava S. *Mission Critical Meetings: Eighty-One Practical Facilitation Techniques.* Tucson, AZ: Wheatmark, 2014.

Kaner, Sam. *Facilitator's Guide to Participatory Decision-Making.* San Francisco: Jossey-Bass, 2014.

Killermann, Sam, and Meg Bolger. *Unlocking the Magic of Facilitation: Eleven Key Concepts You Didn't Know You Didn't Know.* Austin, TX: Impetus Books, 2016.

APPLYING THE PATTERN

Think of a time when you've participated in a poorly facilitated gathering. What made the facilitator ineffective? Which of the qualities above did they lack? How have gatherings within your organization been facilitated? Is there an upcoming gathering you will be a part of? If so, outline a facilitation plan using the techniques in this pattern.

51. CIRCLE DIALOGUE

Groups of people discussing and deliberating in a circle is the oldest, most democratic, and most elemental form of decision making. Although not without its limits, the circle is a good template for group discussion at the RELATIONSHIP ZONES of trust and collaboration.

Circles are ancient. For as long as humans have had campfires, we've gathered around them, telling tales, sharing our wisdom, and making group decisions. In a circle, everyone is able to see one another, with the implication that everyone has an equal say. But as we settled, urbanized and specialized our skills, many of our groups literally began to turn their backs on the circle. Battalions were arranged in single-file lines and grids. Places of production snaked into ever-longer lines as industrialization grew in its complexity. And classrooms and places of worship arranged participants in rows facing a speaker, who often mounted a raised platform to face the audience. Each of these institutions arranged people in ways that underlined the unequal power dynamics they had instituted.

Still, circles remain a part of our daily life in contexts as diverse as family meals, business meetings, and college seminars. Perhaps that's because their usefulness as a pattern of dialogue remains unparalleled. The very form of the circle demands that we pay close attention, encouraging participants to be genuine and vulnerable as they share information and opinion. Circles don't tend to countenance the presence of wallflowers, nor do they tolerate soapboxes.

By reincorporating circle dialogues into more of our group interactions, we may find ourselves listening more deeply, developing better ideas, and empowering each other more fully. The social designer has many variations of the circle dialogues to choose from, ranging from the nearly hierarchical to barely controlled chaos. Depending on the number of participants and the group norms around who has the right to speak and when, the CIRCLE DIALOGUE can be optimized for the right purpose.

COUNCIL DIALOGUE

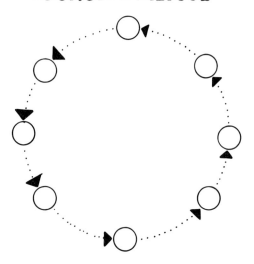

The council dialogue is an age-old practice guided by a simple set of rules, in which members engage in deep listening to each other's perspective. Jack Zimmerman and Virginia Coyle's book *The Way of Council* identifies council practices across a number of traditional cultures, from the Iroquois Confederacy and Hawaii to ancient Greece and the Muslim world.[75] Since 1979, the Ojai Foundation has been at the forefront of reviving council dialogues for use in contemporary contexts. Council dialogues usually employ a few common elements—a facilitator to solidify the group's intention and keep an eye on the ground rules; RITUAL AND CEREMONY to open and close the space; a talking piece that passes from hand to hand, marking who has the right to speak; and an agreement that no person can speak twice until all have spoken.[76] Councils can have a prescribed order, often proceeding clockwise or counterclockwise around the circle, or they can work with a "popcorn" order, allowing participants to speak whenever they feel called to do so. In terms of size, council dialogues work best within the zone of trust, with fifteen or so people, because waiting for too many people to speak can become a drag on the group's momentum.

FACILITATED CIRCLE DIALOGUE

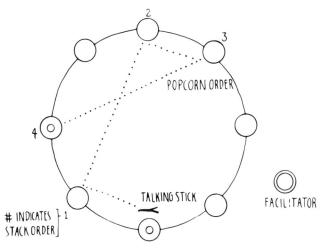

Less formal than a council, facilitated circle dialogues are ideal for freeform discussion in medium-sized groups of five to thirty or so. As the name implies, these circles are led by SKILLED FACILITATION, so the discussion is managed in a much more active manner than a council would be. The facilitator might, for example, keep time, document the group's ideas on a board, or keep a running "stack" of speakers following the order of raised hands. As a natural arrangement for many STREAMS OF ENGAGEMENT, most of us have likely participated in facilitated circle dialogues without even realizing it.

STORY CIRCLE

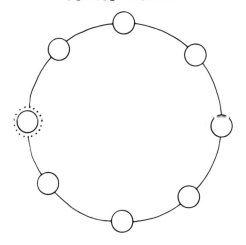

Like most contemporary classes and performances, story circles have a clear leader who does most of the talking. But while most classrooms and stages feature rows of seats aligned toward a speaker, story circles embody a setup in which everyone faces each other, and the leader sits in the circle along with everyone else. With the shift from stage to circle, the signal is sent that the "audience" is, in fact, an integral part of the performance. As such, story circles are ideal arrangements for CONSENSUAL HIERARCHIES of anywhere from a handful of people to several hundred.

FISH BOWL DIALOGUE

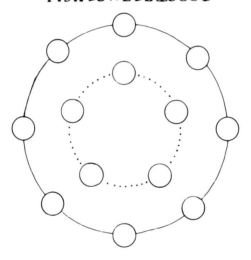

Sometimes there are too many people for a full group to be involved in a CIRCLE DIALOGUE. In other instances, the situation may benefit from only certain people being given the right to speak, with others encouraged to observe and bear witness. Fishbowl dialogues offer a solution to both of these challenges by creating a circle within a circle, in which the center circle can speak while the outer one observes. Fishbowls can therefore balance the efficient, freewheeling nature of small group discussion with the inclusion and transparency of more public meetings. While not typically conducted in the round, panel discussions can be considered a variation on the fishbowl, as can courtroom proceedings. Fishbowls are often employed in the context of conflict mediation, including in the RESTORATIVE JUSTICE practice of dialogue circles. It's important to note that the tiered nature of the fishbowl creates a rather overt hierarchy of power, one that must be acknowledged and carefully managed. Without careful facilitation, members in the center can feel intimidated, while those on the edges may feel disempowered. Depending on the context, it may be appropriate to rotate members from the inner circle and outer one, and vice versa, or allow proscribed periods of comment and dialogue from the outer circle.

FURTHER LEARNING

Zimmerman, Jack, and Virginia Coyle. *The Way of Council.* Wilton Manors, FL: Bramble Books, 1996.

APPLYING THE PATTERN

What experiences have you had with circle dialogues? Are they used in your groups or organizations? In what situations might they be effective in your organizations? What barriers to effective circle dialogue do you anticipate, and how could you plan to minimize them?

52. THE CAUCUS

Members of a group who share a common interest need the space to develop their own subgroups—especially if they come from marginalized backgrounds.

Most of the time, building unity is a fundamental goal for our groups. We want to establish coalitions, to highlight our shared values, to achieve consensus. In an increasingly fractured and polarized age, it's imperative that we continue to build bridges between causes, races, classes, and ideologies. And yet the language of unity threatens to obscure an equally important dynamic of healthy communities—that of distinction. One of America's strengths, after all, is that it is a melting pot of immigrants from across the globe. But over the generations, the dynamics of forced assimilation have continually threatened to melt away all our distinctive flavors into a bland mush. This homogenizing impulse goes against the grain of ecological systems, which thrive by staying both interconnected *and* diverse. In ecosystems, it's the differences between individuals, species, and microclimates that allow unique solutions for novel challenges, driving resilience, innovation, and change.

A 2015 study published in the *American Journal of Sociology* confirms that this balance is equally critical for social systems as well. In the study, Damon Centola and his colleagues looked at how social innovation spreads in different kinds of networks. "Networks that are very diffuse make it hard for ideas to catch on, while networks with very strong group boundaries make it almost impossible for ideas to spread. A network that was moderately 'grouped,' however, was most conducive to spreading complex ideas."[77] So as much as we need to build bridges, we also need to claim and reclaim our separateness and to gather in spaces that reinforce our distinct identities. This is the role of the caucus—a family within a tribe, a village within a city. The concept of the caucus is a distinctly American one, with the term believed to come from *kaw-kaw-was,* the Algonquian word for *counselor.*[78] European colonists appropriated the idea in their early efforts at representative democracy, and it eventually became a key concept informing early framers of the Constitution.[79] Since that time, caucuses have emerged within state and national legislatures to advocate for causes and identities of all stripes. Today, the U.S. Congress has hundreds of such groups, ranging from the Asthma and Allergy Caucus to Wildlife Refuge Caucus. While many of these alliances are relatively inconsequential, a select few, such as the Out of Iraq Caucus or the House Freedom Caucus, have managed to wield outsized impact on the political discourse.

Beyond its usual association with informal political coalitions, THE CAUCUS is a useful concept for many other contexts. Identity-centered social struggles like the women's liberation and gay rights movements have demonstrated the power of THE CAUCUS to effect social change. And at a community scale, immigrant enclaves, internet chatrooms, addiction support groups, and afterschool clubs each offer specialized bubbles of mutual interest and dependence in the midst of larger communities. In these informal situations, a caucus provides a space of mutual SOLIDARITY and understanding, allowing members of a specialized group to express themselves more fully than they can in society at large.

But the biggest strength of THE CAUCUS—its ability to isolate—can also be its Achilles' heel. If caucus members spend too much time within their bubble, they run the risk of losing touch with the rest of society, leaving their own culture out of step with THE EDGE OF CHANGE. Ultimately, the success of a caucus lies in its in-between-ness, its ability to both divide and connect. Without the temporary bubble of a caucus to retreat into, individuals are isolated and disempowered; without a larger group for THE CAUCUS to connect with, members can lose themselves in their own world and fail to capitalize on their collective power. Just as smaller groups gain their best productivity through a pulsing pattern of CONVERGE AND DISPERSE, larger groups benefit from cycles of caucus and collaboration.

APPLYING THE PATTERN

Who are the subgroups in your organizations? In your community? Are you a member of any of them? What groups might benefit from a caucus? What are their focuses? Do they have the space to both work on their own and enter into the community? How might you help facilitate them?

53. CALLING OUT, CALLING IN

An important part of acknowledging privilege is pointing out instances when our peers abuse it, while doing so in a compassionate and respectful way.

Whether or not a group has gone through an intentional process of NAMING NORMS, there are likely to be times when those norms are violated. Perhaps someone is speaking out of turn or hogging too much of the spotlight. Perhaps some members are abusing their privilege or making assumptions based on race, class, or gender that are unintentionally hurtful or offensive.

In such cases, it's all too easy to roll one's eyes and maybe complain about it later in private. But what happens if left unchecked? Those behaviors become normalized within the group—regardless of what the stated norms may be—and perpetuate oppressive dynamics that the group is trying to dismantle. Permaculture designer and organizer Uma Lo explains, "Every microaggression that goes unaddressed reinforces a system that shames women, people of color, trans and gender-non-conforming folk for wanting to be whole, to be seen, understood, and respected; and the invisibility of the harm done (a broken feedback loop) perpetuates the inequality."[8]

It's an important part of disciplined groups to hold each other accountable to the ideals of the group—a practice often termed *calling out*. Over the last decade, a new wave of social justice activists have used the rhetoric of calling out to highlight the ways in which privileged groups are unintentionally silencing others. From mansplaining to #oscarssowhite, many of today's contemporary justice memes are bold, unapologetic critiques of what most people have long perceived as normal.

The shock-tactic approach of calling out can be a powerful tool for highlighting unacknowledged privilege in a public forum. But what happens when the target isn't a fictional bro in an online video, but a member of your zone of trust—someone whom you see and interact with on a regular basis? In that case, approaching the situation with righteous anger—however well deserved that anger may be—could backfire, causing hurt feelings, defensiveness, and a retrenchment of positions. What if the situation could be addressed from a place of empathy and shared values? That's the premise behind a practice that activist and author Ngọc Loan Trần terms *calling in:* "I start 'call in' conversations by identifying the behavior and defining why I am choosing to engage with them. I prioritize my values and invite them to think about theirs and where we share them. And then we talk about it. We talk about it together, like people who genuinely care about each other. We offer patience and compassion to each other and also keep it real, ending the conversation when we need to and know that it wasn't a loss to give it a try."[81]

While it may be most associated with dynamics of privilege, calling in isn't just a tool for DECOLONIZATION. Ultimately, it's a helpful approach for addressing any form of norms violation, from showing up late to a meeting to rushing a decision-making process. Regardless of the situation, calling out and calling in take courage. It's never easy to confront someone about their behavior, and it's especially tough when that person is in a position of relative power due to his or her official title, age, gender, or skin color. It's important, therefore, for groups to do what they can to establish a culture of safety and support that makes the process easier.

While the greater challenge almost always rests with the person doing the calling, it's important to acknowledge that the other side of the exchange can be painful as well. I've been fortunate to be around people who were brave and insightful enough to point out times when I've stepped outside the values of inclusiveness and DECOLONIZATION. Every time, my default reaction was denial and defensiveness. I've learned not to take that default reaction at face value and instead to take time to let my emotions settle. In most cases, the person calling me in was right.

All in all, dialogues of calling out and calling in can be some of the most challenging conversations a group has. Few people are excited to enter conflict transformation mode and bring up issues of personal missteps and social prejudice. Yet because of their challenging nature, these conversations can also be some of the most important for the evolution of the group, as well as for the individuals within it. When approached with mutual respect and compassion, calling in increases our understanding, inspires us to grow, and expands THE EDGE OF CHANGE.

HOW TO CALL SOMEONE IN

In her book *Witnessing Whiteness: The Need to Talk about Race and How to Do It*, education professor Shelly Tochluk offers the following strategies for calling in people within your zones of intimacy, trust, and cooperation.[82] While her list was written specifically about race, it can apply just as effectively to other situations of disempowerment.

1. *Begin slowly.* There is no need to speak out on every new piece of knowledge all at one time if our friends or family are not asking for more. These are our closest relationships. We have plenty of time to initiate people into this way of seeing the world. Besides, jumping in too quickly might very likely only push them away.

2. *Speak from the heart.* Refer to recently acquired information and how it has been personally affecting. Ask only for them to listen and to try and understand why you feel as you do.

3. *Demonstrate excitement.* If we offer some of our new realizations with excitement and interest, we stand a better chance of getting people on board. A sudden shift into anger alienates and makes our journey less appealing.

4. *Challenge sensitivity.* Using the previously described strategy of expressing our personal emotional reaction to statements can be extremely helpful when we need to challenge something said within a dialogue.

5. *Be humble.* Becoming angry with our families, friends, and colleagues for not seeing issues of race as we do is a sure way to get shut down and turn them off.

6. *Pick battles carefully.* Some people just are not ready to hear what we have to say. Reserve energy for moments when our efforts can make a difference. Retreat and come back a different day, or a different year, depending upon the individual.

7. *Plant seeds.* Know that we plant seeds every time we witness actively. We might not see immediate results, but some new epiphany might be growing in someone that will someday emerge, even if we never see the tangible results.

8. *Extend the invitation.* Invite family, friends, and colleagues to join this journey with you. Ask someone to watch a movie that features a racially provocative theme with you. Invite someone to attend a culturally or racially diverse art show, musical performance, or other event with you. Ask questions and prompt conversation to see what people are thinking.

FURTHER LEARNING

Tochluk, Shelly. *Witnessing Whiteness; The Need to Talk about Race and How to Do It.* 2nd edition. Lanham, MD: Rowman and Littlefield, 2010.
Trần, Ngọc Loan. "Calling IN: A Less Disposable Way of Holding Each Other Accountable." *Black Girl Dangerous*, December 18, 2013, www .blackgirldangerous.org/2013/12/calling-less-disposable-way-holding-accountable.

APPLYING THE PATTERN

When have you seen behavior in your groups that needed calling out? How was it handled? Have you ever called someone else out or been called out yourself? How did it feel? What would you have done differently? How can you do it more compassionately in the future? How can you be more open to being called out yourself?

54. RESTORATIVE JUSTICE

A justice system rooted in revenge and retribution will only perpetuate more of the same. But bringing victim and perpetrator together in a process of conflict transformation can propel both parties to grow and heal.

One of the most sickening manifestations of antimarket logic is the commodification of punishment. The war on drugs and other "tough on crime" policies over the last several decades have created an invisible world of suffering behind bars. Today, the number of Americans in jail is equal to the entire population of the city of Houston, Texas—a 700 percent increase since 1970. Our government spends over $80 billion every year to house and feed its inmates, the majority of whom are in prison for nonviolent crimes. What's more, this carceral state compounds inequalities in race and class, creating a feedback loop of structural oppression that author Michelle Alexander has famously dubbed the "New Jim Crow."[83]

Our criminal justice system may be particularly egregious in scope, but it's just one instance of a cultural paradigm of retribution that extends far beyond lawbreakers. From common parenting techniques to discipline in the school system, we have erected a social model of "correcting" unacceptable behavior that uses punishment, isolation, and force, while neglecting attempts at mutual understanding or rehabilitation. It's no accident that our top-heavy society has this coercive, retributive mindset. For nearly fifty years, critics like Michel Foucault argued that our approach to justice evolved as just another way of maintaining institutional, top-down power, in the same way that antimarkets enforce top-down forms of currency and business.

But just as our growth-obsessed economics is only one approach to exchange, the discipline-and-punish model of conflict resolution is but one among many. In fact, it's a relative newcomer to the scene. Despite the tremendous diversity of cultures and customs in traditional societies, internal conflicts throughout the world appear to have been settled in a remarkably consistent way: through face-to-face dialogue mediated by an impartial council of elders and often formalized through public RITUAL AND CEREMONY.

In the thousand-year-old *sulha* process of the Middle East, for instance, disputes are arbitrated by a group of community leaders called a *jaha*. After both parties agree to the *jaha*'s terms, they participate in a public ceremony that involves each side tying knots in a white flag, short speeches from the *jaha,* and sharing meals in each other's homes.[84] Among the Acholi of Uganda, families of the victim and perpetrator share a bitter drink made from the *oput* tree, symbolizing the bitterness of conflict.[85] Nearly identical processes can be found among traditional societies in Thailand,[86] the Navajo people of the American Southwest,[87] and scores of other indigenous groups. The key element that makes these systems work is social capital—strong bonds between community members that hold them accountable to one another. But now that nearly all of us live in communities much, much larger than 1,500 individuals—the point at which Dunbar's zone of suspicion begins (see RELATIONSHIP ZONES)—that intrinsic accountability has vanished.

Is it possible, then, to have a bottom-up approach to justice in today's cosmopolitan, itinerant world? If the past four decades of restorative justice is any indication, then the answer is a resounding yes. The restorative justice movement originated in the 1970s in Kitchener, Ontario, when a probation officer managed to convince a local judge that bringing victims and offenders together for a process of reconciliation would benefit both parties. The probation officer was right; the model became institutionalized in Kitchener and began to spread beyond it.

As restorative justice began to be applied to more and more communities and institutional contexts, its implementation evolved accordingly. Practitioners developed a whole ecosystem of tools and techniques, such as victim support circles, mediation processes, and compensation protocols. Programs began to involve not just victims and perpetrators in the process but also relatives, teachers, and social workers. Today, restorative justice is used in thousands of schools and criminal justice systems throughout the world, and there are several organizations dedicated to its practice. Research has confirmed its efficacy. Convicted youth participating in restorative justice programs are less likely to recidivate,[88] and schools that employ it report both fewer disciplinary actions and better grades.[89]

Critical to the success of restorative justice programs are the principles of *fair process,* involving as much agency and transparency as possible. In a landmark

1978 study, John W. Thibaut and Laurens Walker discovered that successful examples of justice without coercion all set clear expectations, involved individuals in the decisions that affected them, and sought to explain why decisions were made.[9] Ted Wachtel, founder of the International Institute for Restorative Practices, explains it this way (emphasis added): "human beings are happier, more cooperative and productive, and more likely to make positive changes in their behavior when those in positions of authority do things *with* them, rather than *to* them or *for* them."[91]

If our current justice system is an outgrowth of antimarket thinking, restorative justice is the approach of SUBSIDIARITY and COMMONING, in which local communities are empowered to solve problems at the most local level possible. With this power comes the understanding that all community members—not just the police force or judicial system—are responsible for maintaining peace. Even if we no longer reside in small, tightly knit communities, the development and maintenance of social capital remains just as important now as it was with the Arab, Ugandan, and Navajo processes of the past.

FURTHER LEARNING

Van Ness, Daniel W., and Karen Heetderks Strong. *Restoring Justice: An Introduction to Restorative Justice.* 5th edition. London: Routledge, 2015.
Zehr, Howard. *The Little Book of Restorative Justice.* Intercourse, PA: Good Books, 2002.

APPLYING THE PATTERN

In what ways have you been a victim of injustice? A perpetrator? What were the consequences of those situations—were they restorative or punitive? If it was punitive, what restoration work could have been effective? If you are in a position of authority, how might you integrate RESTORATIVE JUSTICE into your work?

55. DOCUMENT THE PROCESS

"Learning organizations" adapt and grow by constantly trying out new ideas and institutionalizing the ones that work.

A few years ago, I was asked to join an ad hoc organizing committee for a multiday educational festival. Along with a talented group of organizers spread across the country, I helped develop marketing materials, reach out to local communities, solicit workshop leaders, assemble panel discussions, locate projection equipment and tents, and organize registration logistics. All of us had been involved in planning events before, but there was no template for *this* event, and we shared the distinct feeling of trying to build a bike while simultaneously trying to ride it.

Thankfully, everything came together in the end, and the festival was a great success. But in our haste to make the whole thing work, we failed to document many of our decisions and steps. As we packed up, headed home, and went back to our hectic lives, all the knowledge we'd gained about what to do (and what not to do) slowly dissipated. When it came time to plan the festival again a couple years later, the new organizing team was compelled to start from scratch.

Time and time again, we get so swept up in pushing THE EDGE OF CHANGE that we neglect to keep track of what we are doing. Even if we understand the value of documenting our work, investing extra time in something that will only be useful a year from now can easily be given little priority—especially when our checklist of items to do ASAP feels impossibly long. By the time the dust settles on a project, the process of how we got there can be a blur of rushed meetings, half-completed spreadsheets, and sleep-deprived snap decisions. But when documentation gets lost in the shuffle, so does any opportunity for objective feedback or MEASURING SUCCESS.

These situations are classic cases of what psychologists term *hyperbolic discounting:* the tendency to value short-term needs over equally important long-term ones. But with the right systems and group culture, we can turn this spiral of erosion into a SPIRAL OF ABUNDANCE, systematizing our success.

Documentation is about more than just our future selves; it's also an important part of REGENERATIVE MANAGEMENT. If you want an institution to exist independently from the skills and talents of any one individual, it's critical that each person documents his or her own knowledge and shares it with colleagues or successors. Documentation might also be valuable for all kinds of external groups. Community members might wish to see your steps as part of a process of transparency and accountability. Potential funders may want to examine documentation to ensure that their resources will be spent efficiently. And another organization that would like to launch a similar project in another city might benefit from seeing how you went about achieving your success.

There are all kinds of ways to document your work as you go. The most straightforward and obvious include keeping the minutes of meetings, taking photos of notes and brainstorming sessions, and keeping journals and blogs. But there's no need to limit your creativity there. You could film a short video diary after every meeting. You could capture important flows in diagrams and bubble charts. You could even develop a story or ritual that encodes important steps of a process.

In our goal-obsessed culture, it's easy to forget that the process can be just as important as the end result. How we get there is just as important as where "there" is. And by keeping track of where we stride, we allow ourselves to retrace our journey—and we allow others to follow in our footsteps.

APPLYING THE PATTERN

In what ways are you and your organization innovating? Who might be able to learn from your failures and successes? How can you document your work to help your own organization, as well as others who can learn from you? How can you balance innovation with STEWARDSHIP?

56. MEASURING SUCCESS

Lasting impact cannot be gauged solely on the basis of inspiring anecdotes or external attention. Develop procedures to accurately quantify your influence, and use the data you measure to inform your decisions.

Along with a dedicated team of facilitators and organizers, I started teaching permaculture design courses in Denver in 2012. Right away, we could see that the trainings were changing peoples' lives—students would routinely get in touch to tell us about how they had switched their careers, transformed their backyards, and powered up their activism as a result of the course. But after a few years of teaching the class, a colleague approached me with a question I'd never before considered: "How can you prove that the course is worth people's investment?" We were hearing only from the satisfied customers, she pointed out, and a lot the information we were teaching could be found for free online. What made the experience of our course worth a thousand bucks? Other than a handful of anecdotes and some phrases straight from the flyer, I couldn't come up with convincing argument.

The experience taught me the value of balancing our success stories with unbiased measurements. Even if we acknowledge MULTITUDES OF KNOWING beyond the numeric, it's hard to deny that the right statistic can turn someone from a doubter to a believer. For many initiatives, MEASURING SUCCESS is becoming less and less of a choice; as grants become more competitive, funders demand to have proof that their money is being put to good use. But even if funding isn't an issue, finding ways to track our impact ought to be important a simple matter of personal improvement. After all, who wouldn't want to know if their blood, sweat, and tears are paying off in the form of real, measurable change?

MEASURING SUCCESS begins with picking the right indicators. Like the odometer, tachometer, and fuel gauge on a car's dashboard, well-chosen indicators give a quick snapshot of the social impact and financial health of our work. Internally, indicators create accountability, letting you know if you're actually making an impact and where you need to reassess. And to the outside world, they serve as proof that you that your work is meaningful and worth paying attention to.

Some indicators are easy as taking a count—how many people are served by a program, how many trees have been planted, how many jobs have been created, how many people attended an event. But many of these numbers give a limited picture of true impact. An event or program might be well attended but poorly executed. A city might plant a million trees but end up killing half of them within a few years due to neglect. A job might be created—and quickly lost.

To accurately MEASURE SUCCESS, it's sometimes necessary to identify indicators that don't immediately present themselves numerically, things like feelings, stories, and ideas. How has someone's life been improved by a program? How are the trees improving the ecosystem? How has the community become more interdependent? This kind of qualitative information can be difficult to track, and it's hard to measure with certainty.

Still, even the most intangible indicators can be estimated with the right skill and advance planning. Ecosystem impacts can be gauged through soil tests and biodiversity counts. Changes in a cohort's knowledge can be tracked via surveys at the beginning and end of the program. Scientifically valid evaluation is a sophisticated science, and it can often require a lot of time, talent, and technology—and money. But for situations where the budget is tight and the required margin of error somewhat loose, a basic understanding of experimental design and a little patience can go a long way.

Whether they're simple or sophisticated to track, the best indicators are ones that can cover four bases:

- *Relevance.* Is your indicator actually tracking the right thing? You might have hundreds of people showing up for your events—but if they're not leaving any different, the absolute number is irrelevant.

- *Validity.* Is the indicator being measured accurately? As pollsters can tell you, it's all too easy to get respondents to answer questions the way you want them to, whether consciously or unconsciously. Make use of those with the specialized skills to design surveys to eliminate bias.

- *Verifiable.* Can you document how you measured the indicator? If the process were repeated, would you be likely to get similar results?

- *Usefulness.* It's unwise to spend too many resources measuring situations that you can't change. Indicators are helpful only to the extent that they actually allow you to make better decisions.

Once the information is captured, you can put it to use in TELLING THE STORY of your organization, moving from "what" to "so what?" Depending on your audience, this could take the form of a graph, an online video testimonial, or even just a single compelling statistic. Either way, having data to back up your organization's mission will go a long way toward convincing funders, community members, partners, and other stakeholders that you're the real deal.

After that challenge from my friend, our permaculture teaching team began to evaluate what our students had learned more thoroughly. We designed more self-assessments into the curriculum, asked students to fill out feedback forms at the end of every class, and began following up with past participants a year after the training. We soon learned, to our surprise, that some things we hadn't been teaching very well at all. Fortunately, the overall numbers were solid, and the students' number one takeaway was the community they had formed—something that no amount of YouTube videos or library books could replace. Armed with this information, we changed the parts of the curriculum that weren't working and proudly began to tell the story through statistics.

SURVEYS

- able to reach a large number of people
- takes skill to develop unbiased survey questions
- challenging to capture compelling stories

FOCUS GROUPS

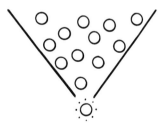

- touch more people in less time than interviews
- useful for people to bounce ideas off eachother
- risk of participants influencing each other
- familiar and accessible location
- facilitator should be skilled and unbiased

ONE·ON·ONE INTERVIEWS

- much more in depth
- relatively time consuming to schedule, interview, & analyze
- often requires incentive for participation
- take care to be culturally sensitive

SECONDARY SOURCES

- includes peer-reviewed literature, magazine articles, & public data sets
- helpful to distill patterns, but need to understand limitations of applicability to the situation

FURTHER LEARNING

Hunter, David E. K. *Working Hard and Working Well: A Practical Guide to Performance Management.* N.p.: Hunter Consulting, 2013.

APPLYING THE PATTERN

How does your organization collect information? What kinds of information are you collecting? Does it fit the criteria above? How do you plan to use what you collect? What will success mean to your organization, and how will the information you collect measure that success? Are there things you're collecting that are irrelevant? How might you streamline the process?

57. DESIGN TOOL: TEAM ANALYSIS

Successful human polycultures require a balanced team of members who trust one another. Using team analysis, we can investigate the strengths and challenges of our collaborative groups.

Depending on its size, purpose, structure, and the composition of its members, every group has its own microculture that evolves as it moves through the process of NEMAWASHI. Even so, there are plenty of common patterns to be found in the roles assumed by members of the group and how they interact. The HUMAN POLYCULTURES pattern dives into what some of those roles are. Team analysis applies our understanding of those roles to systematically make our groups function better.

To conduct a team analysis, gather as many members of your group as you can. If you'd like, perform an opening RITUAL AND CEREMONY to get the group present and engage in a process of NAMING NORMS to make sure you've established a safe space where everyone can be honest and vulnerable.

As THE CREATIVE PROCESS suggests, it's best to start a team analysis by thinking about the bigger picture. What are the goals of the group? How long do you intend it to be around? Keeping in mind the characteristics of each of the RELATIONSHIP ZONES, what is THE RIGHT SIZE range for the team? What is the minimum number of people necessary to enact its vision—and what is the largest it can grow to and still remain efficient and effective?

Next, draw a mind map of each of the people in a group. Look through the labels listed in HUMAN POLYCULTURES and try to identify who in the group plays what role. Keep in mind that each person is likely to play multiple roles and that those roles might be fluid over time. There also might be disagreement among the group members about who embodies each role. There's no need to attempt to arrive at consensus; instead, merely make note of the dispute and use that information as additional fuel for your analysis.

Once you've discussed the roles currently being played, you can run down the list of HUMAN POLYCULTURE archetypes and dive into each one in more detail:

- Does the team have a servant leader? Which other HUMAN POLYCUL-TURE roles does he or she possess, and which roles will have to be played by others?

- Who are the elders in the team? Who are the radicals? Do the relationships between group members contain healthy respect or unhealthy rivalry? To they complement each other or are the competing for the same niche?

- Is the work of helping hands spread evenly throughout the group, or is it concentrated in a few people at the bottom of the pecking order?

- What critical skills does the team need to succeed? Which members of the team are the mavens who currently possess these skills? Of the remaining skills, which can be learned by the team's current members? Does the team need to bring on new members or establish new partnerships to gain those skills?

- How well connected is the team to its potential allies? Which other groups is it lacking connection to? Who are the network weavers and translators that could help it become more connected?

With this analysis complete, your group should have a much clearer picture of how each member sees himself and each other in relationship to the team as a whole. What patterns did you notice in each person's assessment? What general themes emerged for improvement?

PART 4

Envisioning
the Ecommony

Gross National Product counts air pollution and cigarette advertising, and ambulances to clear our highways of carnage. It counts special locks for our doors and the jails for the people who break them. It counts the destruction of the redwood and the loss of our natural wonder in chaotic sprawl. It counts napalm and counts nuclear warheads and armored cars for the police to fight the riots in our cities. It counts Whitman's rifle and Speck's knife, and the television programs which glorify violence in order to sell toys to our children. Yet the gross national product does not allow for the health of our children, the quality of their education or the joy of their play. It does not include the beauty of our poetry or the strength of our marriages, the intelligence of our public debate or the integrity of our public officials. It measures neither our wit nor our courage, neither our wisdom nor our learning, neither our compassion nor our devotion to our country, it measures everything in short, except that which makes life worthwhile. And it can tell us everything about America except why we are proud that we are Americans.

—Robert F. Kennedy

Capital. *Currency. Dollars.* In daily use, these terms tend to overlap and blur into one another. When an analyst calls a business *undercapitalized,* for instance, he or she usually means that it's lacking enough dollars to perform in a certain way. When we refer to *currency exchange,* we're generally referring the relative values of things like dollars, yen, euros, and pesos—state-sanctioned currencies issued by central banks.

Viewed through an ecological lens, however, these terms begin to coalesce in very different ways. Take the word *capital,* for instance. Whereas most MBAs will use the term to refer to cash or hard assets like buildings and equipment, ecological economists see capital as *any form of stored value.* As discussed in COMMONING, capital can take the form of a clear blue lake, the decades-old knowledge of a place, or an intimate network of community members.

Similarly, the definition of *currency* becomes much broader when applied beyond conventional economics. From a systems standpoint, currency can be seen as *a medium that measures and regulates the flow of capital* throughout that system. In most ecosystems, for instance, water serves as a currency, dictating the flow of nutrients and energy. Blood serves a similar role in our bodies. Favorites, likes, shares, and star ratings have become the dollars and cents of our online identities, regulating the flow of social capital in the digital universe.

So where does this expansive view of *capital* and *currency* leave our third term? With so many forms of currency, it's clear that limiting our understanding of the word merely to dollars and its central-bank-issued relatives is like equating humans and mammals—oversimplifying a vast and ancient group into a single recent member of that group. Studying *Homo sapiens* can only teach us so much about bats, porcupines, or dolphins. In the same manner, dollars and their state-sponsored kin barely scratch the surface of the possibilities that other forms of currency possess to measure and regulate capital in the human systems of exchange we call *economies.* Like any form of currency, dollars are designed for certain outcomes and contain certain assumptions built into their structure. As a currency that is generated primarily via loans, for example, dollars are predicated on an ever-increasing supply of interest-bearing debt to function. While the stocks and flows represented by our terms *capital* and *currency* are fundamental to ecosystems and economies alike, the specific behavior of accumulation represented by *dollars* is peculiar to our day and age.

This section attempts to break apart the constraints set by current ideas about capital and currency, and sketch the outlines of an economy centered around local control, restoring capital, and long-term thinking—a commons economy, or *ecommony.* The section opens with a survey of some of the other currencies available to us, starting with THE GIFT—the currency of love—and continuing with a variety of HEIRLOOM CURRENCIES designed to occupy more specialized niches than the one-size-fits-all dollar. Of course, no matter how enthusiastically we embrace gift economies and timebanks, central bank–issued currencies are likely to remain in our lives for some time to come. Recognizing this reality, the FINANCIAL RAM PUMPS pattern shares strategies for redirecting their flow—away from the plunder and inequality they're designed for and toward developing place-based economies of the commons instead. DEBT FORGIVENESS, meanwhile, reminds us of another tool for liberating our communities from the grip of antimarket currencies, one that's been around for as long as debt itself.

From there, the patterns start to hone in on what economies of the commons look like at the granular level. If the shareholder-owned corporation and central bank are the twin pillars supporting the antimarket economy, HOUSEHOLD ECONOMIES and the SMALL BUSINESS form the indivisible units of the ecommony. Groups of such households and businesses, in turn, can become a robust, interlinked network through the process of IMPORT SUBSTITUTION, in which communities slowly relocalize by meeting more and more of their needs through suppliers close to home.

What will it look and feel like to conduct business in such a network? For one thing, many organizations are likely to be REGENERATIVE ENTERPRISES, financially self-sustaining organizations whose primary purpose is to heal natural and social systems. And many will choose to adopt the principles of XERIC ENTERPRISE, minimizing their overhead expenses to make it through difficult times. In a closed-loop economy, our current modes of capital investment hardy make sense; instead, companies will embrace the ethos of the COMMUNITY-SUPPORTED ENTERPRISE, blending the roles of investors and customers. Another set of roles to be reintegrated is management and labor, a marriage that can result in worker cooperatives, employee stock ownership plans (ESOPs), and other forms of EMPLOYEE OWNERSHIP. And in order to ensure their goods and services are broadly accessible, many institutions will step away from the century-old rule of "one product, one price" and embrace some form of DYNAMIC PRICING.

The two design tools at the end of the section offer systems for examining our present-day institutions through the viewpoint of the ecommony. CAPITAL ANALYSIS uses the "eight forms of capital" framework developed by Ethan Roland and Gregory Landua to reflect on the forms of wealth present in an organization or community. And within the realm of a specific enterprise, the BUSINESS MODEL CANVAS provides a template for designing institutions that replenish communities, ecosystems, and our pocketbooks all at once.

58. THE GIFT

The gift is the currency of love. It is the most ancient form of exchange and forms the glue of INTERDEPENDENT COMMUNITIES.

Ko Maru kai atu, ko maru kai maika ngohe ngohe. (Give as much as you take, all shall be very well.)

—Maori Proverb

It's often said that the more one gives, the richer one becomes. Anyone who has donated to charity, volunteered their time for good cause, or surprised a loved one with a thoughtful present knows that the act of giving brings satisfaction to both the giver and the receiver, weaving a relationship that goes beyond the simple value of the goods and services exchanged. In fact, this process of building social capital through gift has long been an integral part of INTERDEPENDENT COMMUNITIES throughout the globe. From northwest Native American potlatch ceremonies to the karmic philosophies of Hindu and Buddhist thought to the Jewish directives of *tzedakah* (charity) and *tikkun olam* (healing the world), virtue and social status have long been tied to a willingness to give freely.

But as Europeans navigated the transition from a theistic to a scientific worldview, and as community-centric morality gave way to a utilitarian ethos of personal gain, gifts became much less important. Today, nearly 250 years after Adam Smith enshrined this morality in *The Wealth of Nations,* his vision of a society driven completely by self-interest has become the foundation for nearly every institution that governs our lives. As a result, more and more of our human interactions have substituted the free offering of services, materials, or property with currency-mediated transactions. It's not hard to see why: when exchange is depersonalized into a set of hard calculations, prices can be precisely set to match demand, and capital can flow farther and more quickly than before. In an economy that's designed to reward efficiency and return on investment, the gift economy is a square peg in a round hole.

But while the switch from gift to transaction seems rather simple and straightforward on the surface, it masks a much more profound loss in our communities. Transactions, focused as they are on the exchange of objects, revolve around quantitative ideas of value. But in a gift exchange, the actual objects passing from one person to another aren't the point. As anthropologist Chris Gregory explains in his classic text *Gifts and Commodities:* "What a gift transactor desires is the personal relationships that the exchange of gifts creates, and not the things themselves."[92] Gifts are markers of reciprocity—they establish, acknowledge, and maintain relationships of interdependence.

Early twentieth-century sociologist Marcel Mauss was the first Westerner to assert that gifting was a fundamental aspect of culture, more widespread than any other form of economic exchange. To Mauss, seeing gifts as merely an economic system is missing the whole point. Gifts are spiritual transactions, in which the giver gives part of his or her very identity to the recipient and, by so doing, affirms their sacred kinship.

Marshall Sahlins, one of many distinguished anthropologists following in Mauss's footsteps, makes the distinction between two different kinds of gifts. Most rituals of gift-giving we practice today are what Sahlins terms *balanced reciprocity:* when we give a friend or extended family member a present to commemorate a birthday or anniversary or to celebrate a holiday, there's often an unspoken expectation that the favor will be returned when the next opportunity rolls around the calendar. These gifts of balanced reciprocity, then, are subtle forms of barter. By spreading the transaction out over time, the giver and receiver alternate roles, creating cycles of obligation that, at least in theory, keep the relationship maintained.

Generalized reciprocity, by contrast, is when giving and receiving are decoupled. The giver gives spontaneously, without expecting something in return. Without the prospect of getting something back to incentivize the giver, generalized reciprocity demands even more generosity. Perhaps unsurprisingly, Sahlins notes that this form of selfless giving is most prevalent within the RELATIONSHIP ZONES of intimacy and trust, while rituals of balanced reciprocity tended to dominate larger groups.

Regardless of which kind we use and when, the health of our communities is in no small way dependent on recovering the art of the gift. Many of the patterns that build community—BREAKING BREAD, PRACTICING GRIEF, RITES OF PASSAGE, GADUGI—revolve around people freely sharing their knowledge, food, labor, or other forms of capital as a way of cementing relationships. And on a individual level, giving enlarges our own hearts, connecting us more deeply with the rhythms of exchange at the heart of any complex system.

FURTHER LEARNING

Eisenstein, Charles. *Sacred Economics: Money, Gift, and Society in the Age of Transition.* Berkeley, CA: North Atlantic Books, 2011.

APPLYING THE PATTERN

How does receiving or giving a gift make you feel? What's the most meaningful gift you've received? Is there a feeling of joy and gratitude, obligation and power, or some combination in the acts of giving and receiving? What needs does your community have that you can meet by giving?

59. HEIRLOOM CURRENCIES

No single currency can adequately serve the many needs we have for exchange. Encourage a multiplicity of currencies, each one intentionally designed to meet a specific need.

We take it for granted that nearly all our transactions are filtered through a single means of exchange: currency issued by a central bank. To be sure, the currency's name and purchasing power varies from country to country, and it might appear as paper bills, handwritten checks, or bits on a screen. But whether we're handing our neighbor a $20 bill for mowing the lawn or negotiating a $20 billion corporate merger, we're all at the mercy of the same massive currency system. As media and social theorist Douglas Rushkoff puts it, "Central currency is the transactional tool that has overwhelmed business itself; money is the tail wagging the economy's dog."[93]

It wasn't always this way. While central currency has been around for millennia, it was largely used for public works, taxes, and trade, and rarely made its way into the lives of everyday people. For the vast majority of recorded history, the vast majority of humans in any given culture met their transactional needs through a patchwork of GIFTING, bartering, IOUs, and other informal means of exchange. Debt-based antimarket currencies didn't evolve until the Middle Ages, and even as recently as the mid-nineteenth century, U.S. citizens used any number of locally issued banknotes for most of their day-to-day transactions. But as interstate trade expanded, the inefficiency of converting between thousands of fluctuating exchange rates became too burdensome, and the U.S. banking system consolidated into today's form shortly after the Civil War.

What remained was a currency monoculture, a single form of exchange that dominates our lives like nothing else. Like an invasive weed, dollars are relentless in finding new economic landscapes to exploit. In the process, they've choked out not only local forms of cash but also the less tangible and informal exchange mechanisms that are so critical to INTERDEPENDENT COMMUNITY. Our cultural identity is now shared through Netflix instead of folk tales. A community's cohesion, once cemented through town halls and neighborly gossip, is now at the mercy of Starbucks and Facebook. The communal work parties of GADUGI have given way to the transaction of labor for hire. This currency monoculture has all the downsides of an agricultural one: systemic risk, loss of local diversity, and a focus on quantity over quality.

The good news is that we need not confine ourselves to one currency. Even in the midst of dollar's dominance, we can water the seeds of new and ancient currencies, allowing alternative means of exchange to flourish once again. Just as heirloom crops are bred to maximize flavor, shelf life, or nutritional content, we can breed other currencies to meet other needs—incentivizing IMPORT SUBSTITUTION, encouraging neighborly interaction, or properly valuing the HOUSEHOLD ECONOMY, to name a few.

Over the last several decades, as recognition of the dollar's flaws has grown, more and more communities have begun to experiment with developing heirloom currencies. Many haven't lasted long, largely due to fierce headwinds of the central-bank system. Many couldn't get enough traction from a community bewildered at the idea of complementary currency. Some of those that did receive critical mass have been perceived as a threat to central-bank currencies and were shut down. Paul Glover, founder of Ithaca Hour, has emphasized that every local currency needs at least one full-time networker to "promote, facilitate, and troubleshoot" currency circulation.

Nevertheless, each one has been an opportunity to learn, and a small but growing body of scholarship around currency design has emerged. Currencies come in a bewildering array of variations, but they can be roughly grouped into four categories: local cash, mutual credit, time banks, and cryptocurrencies.

LOCAL CASH

Local cash supplements the national system of bills and coins with a local one, usually pegged to the national one in value. It's generally used within a bounded geographical region—often a city or network of towns—and is accepted by participating businesses. Local cash is intended for day-to-day exchange between individuals and SMALL BUSINESSES, and it works similarly to dollars for those sorts of transactions. Because of this similarity, it's one of the easiest kinds of HEIRLOOM CURRENCIES for communities to get used to. But national currencies have a crucial feature that most local cash systems leave out: interest. As a result, there are no loans, no expectation of growing the total supply—in other words, no imperative for growth. Rather than being lent out in large chunks by a small group of banks, the flow of local cash is directed by the cumulative spending choices of community members, building social capital in the process.[94]

One of the most successful early instances of local cash was implemented in the Brazilian city of Curitiba. In exchange for collecting trash and recycling across town, slum dwellers were given bus tokens and plastic chips that could be redeemed for fresh produce. The system was wildly successful, resulting in cleaner streets, healthier residents, and increased transit use. Eventually over 70 percent of households in the city participated, receiving over a million bus rides and 1,200 tons of food in the process.[95]

In the past few decades, dozens of local cash systems have been launched; some of the most successful are the ones in Ithaca, New York; Brixton in England; and the Berkshire region of western Massachusetts. Still, many smartly designed initiatives fail within a few years, and even the brightest stars manage to capture only a few percent of a community's total economic activity. So what's the secret sauce for sticking around and scaling up? In 2015, the London-based New Economics Foundation released a report examining failure and success factors for local cash systems.[96] Among their findings were that successful local cash systems found ways to encourage business-to-business transactions, had stable systems of governance, and created buy-in from a critical mass of establishments—a process that often took years.

MUTUAL CREDIT

If local cash functions somewhat like a simplified dollar system, mutual credit systems are glorified IOUs. They start from the premise that, in a relatively closed economy, most credits and debits end up cancelling each other out. Say, for example, that Andre pays Bella $33 for a haircut. The next day, Bella buys $33 worth of groceries from Cam, who later spends that same $33 on bike parts from Andre. Since each person's transaction was of equal value, the money itself was redundant. Even if none of the three had a single cent to their names, they could have gotten the same goods and services without anybody feeling cheated.

Rarely, of course, do transactions align so simply in the real world. But by tracking everybody's relative credits and debits, mutual credit systems allow the same sort of moneyless transactions on a much more sophisticated scale.

As long as each individual gives as much as he or she receives in the long run, actual dollars become irrelevant. For this reason, mutual credit systems are ideal for communities that lack access to financial capital but have plenty of self-contained economic activity.

The Swiss Wirtschaftsring (WIR) is among the oldest and most successful mutual credit systems of the modern era. Established in the depths of the Great Depression, when Swiss francs were in scarce supply, the WIR allowed small and medium-sized businesses to exchange goods and services without using money. As the Depression eased, organizations continued to rely on the WIR. By 1993, one in six Swiss businesses were using it, conducting annual trades equivalent to 2.5 billion francs.[97] The LETSystem, developed by Michael Linton in British Columbia, was designed in the 1980s as a mutual credit platform that could be used by any community. Today, over 1,500 LETSystems are active across the world, while platforms like the Community Exchange System are harnessing the power of the internet to make mutual credit systems that are digitally operated and global in scope.

TIME BANKS

Time banks are a variation on mutual credit systems, but with a crucial difference. Instead of basing their unit of value on an existing antimarket currency, they measure hours. Underlying this approach is an explicit ideological orientation. In order for a time bank to work, its users must subscribe to the radical proposition that an hour of a doctor's time is equally valuable as an hour of a janitor's. The earliest known time bank was the Cincinnati Time store, established by American anarchist Josiah Warren in 1827. Warren was several generations ahead of his time, though, and his store fizzled after a few years. Time-based exchange didn't reappear on the alternative economic radar until 1980, when Dr. Edgar Cahn established TimeBanking.

Contemporary time banks tend to operate in hyper-local geographic areas, anywhere in size from a single neighborhood to a medium-sized city. Because it's tricky to incorporate the cost of goods into the time bank model, they're usually limited to exchanging services and skills. Members list their needs and skills in a central exchange, and matches are mediated digitally or by a human broker. Time banks tend to excel at capturing value that antimarkets miss—they can put to work people whom the broader economy won't employ, and they offer a market for services that central currencies don't always value.

CRYPTOCURRENCIES

The most recent genre of HEIRLOOM CURRENCY is cryptocurrencies: decentralized exchange media that use cryptography to secure transactions and control the creation of new units. The most well-known cryptocurrency is the Bitcoin, developed in 2010 by an enigmatic programmer with the pseudonym Satoshi Nakamoto. Designed to facilitate secure, anonymous transactions over the internet, Bitcoin and its cousins revolve around blockchains, giant digital ledgers of every single transaction made using that currency. A currency's blockchain isn't held centrally, but rather in a network of computers, which encode every transaction with a digital watermark. All that encoding takes massive amounts of processing power, so the people who lend their computers to the cause are rewarded with brand new units of currency. Because no single entity controls the blockchain, fraud and counterfeiting are practically impossible.

As with any new technology in its nascent stages, cryptocurrency has its share of downsides. Its anonymity has made it attractive to all kinds of cybercriminals, from hackers to arms dealers, and the price of cryptocurrencies relative to antimarket currencies fluctuates wildly. Finally, the exorbitant amounts of electricity used by blockchains—$100 million a year for Bitcoins alone[98]—makes them one of the most carbon-intensive currencies imaginable. Even so, many see great promise in the blockchain's potential for decentralized, secure global exchange. In 2016, the global consulting firm Deloitte even went so far as to predict that countries would be creating their own cryptocurrencies within five years.[99]

CATEGORY	WHAT KINDS OF COMMUNITIES AND ECONOMIES FIND IT USEFUL?	AT WHAT SCALE IS IT MOST APPROPRIATE?	PROS	CONS
Local Cash	Person-to-business cash transactions. Good for communities with high interest in relocalization.	Local or regional.	Keeps money circulating locally. Builds social capital. No built-in imperative for growth.	Tied to ups and downs of central bank currency. Can be difficult to achieve buy-in for a critical mass of merchants, especially if they have nowhere to spend the local cash.

CATEGORY	WHAT KINDS OF COMMUNITIES AND ECONOMIES FIND IT USEFUL?	AT WHAT SCALE IS IT MOST APPROPRIATE?	PROS	CONS
Mutual Credit	Business and individuals who lack access to traditional capital. Ideal for catalyzing IMPORT SUBSTITUTION.	Mostly used on a local scale.	Credits created by members themselves. No repayment schedule or interest. Statement of accounts is public for transparency.	Inability to attract significant participation by established businesses. No absolute requirement for settlement, so there must be a limit of the debit balance a member is allowed to carry.
Time Banks	Groups and individuals with skills and services— especially ones undervalued by the antimarket economy.	Neighborhood or city scale.	Incentivizes people to help other members of their community. Honors services of those traditionally undervalued.	Difficult to integrate with exchanging goods. Not everyone will agree that each person's time is of equal value.
Cryptocurrencies	Anyone seeking anonymous, secure transactions online.	Global scale.	Cheaper and more secure than spending antimarket currencies online. Has potential to scale large enough to replace current currency system.	Anonymity is a boon to nefarious actors. Blockchain processing uses lots of CPU power. Does little for local communities.

FURTHER LEARNING

People Powered Money: Designing, Developing, and Delivering Community Currencies. London: New Economics Foundation, 2015. http://community -currency.info/wp-content/uploads/2015/06/ccia-book-people-powered -money.pdf.

APPLYING THE PATTERN

Do any HEIRLOOM CURRENCIES exist in your community? Are there opportunities to create one? What would the pros and cons be for each model in your own community? Which of your needs or your organization's needs can be met outside the official currency system?

60. FINANCIAL RAM PUMPS

Central currencies like the dollar are designed to increase inequality, but skillful interventions can sometimes reverse part of that flow to achieve more beneficial aims.

O f the many dilemmas and paradoxes of life at the dawn of the Anthropocene, one of the most vexing is that our primary form of currency is fundamentally mismatched to the needs of healing our society. Central-bank-issued currencies like the dollar, euro, and yen are all based on a growing supply of debt and require economic growth to work. Given this design feature, it can hardly be seen as a fluke that our currencies flow toward activities that are efficient, homogenous, and expected to create a quick profit. The liquidation of natural, social, and cultural capital into an ever-expanding pool of financial capital is part of the fundamental structure of debt-based currency. As surely as water at the top of a mountain finds its way to the ocean, these currencies find their way to activities that erode other forms of capital.

In the long term, the only way to avoid this trap may be through a restructuring of our financial system—designing HEIRLOOM CURRENCIES, detangling central banks and central governments, and deploying any number of other innovations in the service of DETHRONING THE ANTIMARKETS and creating local economies of COMMONING. But for the everyday changemaker without access to such levers of power, that's not a very satisfying prescription for change.

Fortunately, there's much that each of us can do to build regenerative economies even within the context of a growth-addicted society—and an ingenious little device called the *ram pump* provides us with a perfect metaphor for how it can be done. Ram pumps use the principles of hydraulics to capture energy from flowing water and send a small portion of that water (usually 5 to 10 percent) back uphill. This water can be stored at the highest point of the site. In an intelligent site design, the water moved by the ram pump can serve a multitude of uses before it finally leaves the property.

The lesson of the ram pump is that, with some skillful engineering, we can temporarily send energy in a counterintuitive direction without any extra effort. If dollars are designed to flow downhill, increasing inequality and exploitation, then a financial ram pump is any strategy that redirects currency to flow uphill in the service of equity and regeneration.

For most of us, the most familiar mechanism to reverse the flow of dollars is philanthropy. In the United States alone, more than $350 billion was donated to charitable causes in 2014, a sum representing about 2 percent of the country's total GDP.[10] The recipients of these donations—nonprofits, foreign aid organizations, religious charities, and others—are often on the front lines of social change and provide an essential safety net to billions of people. Yet the scale of the charitable sector means that it can end up having the same excessively hierarchical tendencies as the antimarkets that fund it. Many of the largest nonprofits and NGOs are run very much like corporations, with the same lack of accountability, a revenue-driven mindset, and a disregard for principles of SUB-SIDIARITY and COMMONING.

While charitable giving has its place, then, it's hardly perfect—and it's far from the only mechanism for getting dollars to flow uphill. COMMUNITY-SUPPORTED ENTERPRISE lets customers become investors, providing up-front funding in exchange for future goods or services. Local lending circles can function as grassroots banks, creating an economic ZONE OF AUTONOMY that keeps central bank–issued money within a community. And DYNAMIC PRICING strategies—such as pay-what-you-can and sliding scales—can open up access to goods and services to populations that usually that can't afford them.

Together, these strategies can act as powerful tools of redirection, channeling currencies that were designed for centralization into supporting acts of small-scale, distributed COMMONING. Still, they are only a partial solution for the necessary work of rethinking our systems of exchange. For all the value that these strategies provide, they do nothing to rewrite the rules of the currency itself and therefore can do little to change the overall direction of a growth-driven economy. For that, we'll need additional tools like HEIRLOOM CURRENCIES, DEBT FORGIVENESS, and COORDINATED NONCOMPLIANCE.

APPLYING THE PATTERN

Where are the currency flows through your community? What is already being done to redirect the flows back into the community? How can you or your organization help to redirect these flows? What other forms of capital can you convert financial capital into? How can those forms benefit your community long-term?

61. DEBT FORGIVENESS

Interest-bearing loans are a powerful economic catalyst—and, nearly as frequently, a brutal tool of oppression. A periodic clearing of the accounts keeps debt's darker sides in check.

Neither a borrower nor a lender be;
For loan oft loses both itself and friend,
And borrowing dulls the edge of husbandry.
This above all: to thine ownself be true,
And it must follow, as the night the day,
Thou canst not then be false to any man.

—*Polonius (Shakespeare,* Hamlet)

At the foundation of nearly every economy is a dynamic of ongoing mutual obligation. From raising a child to investing in a business, social cooperation frequently entails someone sharing his or her resources without expecting an immediate return from the recipient. In many small-scale communities—including most present-day families—these obligations have long been settled through THE GIFT, in a manner that strengthens interconnective relationships. But as communities grew in size and complexity, necessitating economies greater than the zone of recognition (see RELATIONSHIP ZONES), these mutual obligations began to be quantified through the innovations of currency and debt. By putting a price tag on our dues, we could separate them from our personal relationships, making them easily transferable and increasingly abstract. This innovation made economies much more efficient—while at the same time separating it from the human compassion and accountability embedded in a gift economy.

As economic historian David Graeber lays out in his aptly titled *Debt: The First Five Thousand Years,* the development of indebtedness led equally quickly to exploitation. Within decades of the first recorded instances of debt, societies began to condone behavior that no culture of reciprocal relationships would ever deem allowable: repossession of property, debt slavery, rape, and worse. Yet even these draconian punishments were insufficient to ensure a stable debt system. In fact, they often backfired, as debt slaves attempted to flee the fields they labored in. This meant fallow fields, a threatened grain supply, and fewer soldiers available to conquer more fertile soil to plant in. As a way of keeping debtors around, rulers began pushing the reset button, freeing the debtors of their obligations and allowing them back to their homes.[101]

Eventually these "debt jubilees" became standardized, and by the Biblical era, both debt and debt forgiveness were a central part of agricultural economies. According to the Old Testament, farmers were to cancel all debts of non-foreigners and let their fields lie fallow every seven years, while every forty-nine years, they were to return property to its original owner and free any slaves. At around the same time, Solon was advocating debt relief in Athens, and debt relief laws were codified in India several centuries later under the Laws of Manu.

While these cycles of indebtedness and debt forgiveness were commonplace for centuries, the charging of *interest* on debt was often strictly prohibited. Recognizing that interest-bearing loans inevitably tended to magnify the concentration of wealth, laws and moral codes throughout the ancient world warned against the sin of usury. From the Hindu Vedas of second millennium BCE, through the Old and New Testament, the Qur'an, and medieval Catholic scriptures, there was consensus among the great religions that interest was immoral.

With the rise of mercantilism and early antimarkets, however, this moral code began to loosen. Throughout much of Western Europe, the definition of *usury* began to shift from charging any interest at all to charging an unfairly high interest rate. As early legal structures like joint-stock companies evolved into contemporary corporations, interest-bearing loans became a fundamental mechanism for securing start-up funding. Eventually, though decades of incremental policy choices, our entire global financial system grew to become dependent on interest and debt for its very well-being.

Needless to say, the concept of debt forgiveness has long since bit the dust in mainstream economic discourse. The growth of debt is now closely linked to the growth of our economy as a whole, which, in turn, is seen as the ultimate indicator of our society's health. And yet the fundamental challenges of debt and interest—namely, the dehumanization of exchange and the concentration of wealth—have only grown more pronounced.

Today, of course, wealth inequality has emerged as one of the primary grievances of our age. The interest on trillions of dollars of loans accumulate at the apex of the financial pyramid, while the rest of us struggle to stay afloat amid a rising tide of mortgages, student loans, and credit card payments. The dynamics of debt and interest, if they were ever stable to begin with, have conclusively become unhinged.

Never has there been a time more ripe for a jubilee: a grand clearing of the books and a rebalancing of the scales. While our approach toward charity and welfare are increasingly narrow and targeted, a growing body of evidence is emerging that simply giving people money is among the most effective means for eradicating poverty. Cancelling debt does just that: by eliminating the downward spiral of ever-increasing interest payments, former debtors are free to stretch their limited resources much farther in meeting their actual needs.

As Graeber's comprehensive history points out, most class conflicts throughout history were in some way related to debt forgiveness and a reallocation of resources. Today, we may be primed for another round of such conflict. With our addiction to debt growing like an increasingly wobbly Tower of Babel, a coordinated response has begun to take hold, waging a form of NONVIOLENT STRUGGLE against the antimarkets. The Rolling Jubilee, an offshoot of Occupy Wall Street, managed to forgive over $30 million in debts owed by strangers by purchasing debt from lenders for pennies on the dollar and simply refusing to collect. Another organization called the Debt Collective, is organizing debt strikes, in which mass numbers of students are refusing to pay back their exorbitant loans. As THE EDGE OF CHANGE widens, we can begin to take on not just student debt but also payday loans, credit cards, and even mortgages. With enough momentum, such actions can usher in a greater transformation of the financial system, one built around ethics of SUBSIDIARITY and COMMONING and that restores the economy to its proper place in society.

FURTHER LEARNING

Graeber, David. *Debt: The First Five Thousand Years.* Brooklyn, NY: Melville House, 2011.

Strike Debt. *The Debt Resistors' Operations Manual.* Available at http://strikedebt.org/drom.

APPLYING THE PATTERN

What is your relationship with debt? Your organization's relationship? How has debt affected your community? What effect would DEBT FORGIVENESS have there? Are there opportunities to advocate for DEBT FORGIVENESS in your community?

62. HOUSEHOLD ECONOMIES

In most ecologically literate societies, many of the community's essential needs are met at the family scale, within the home. These household services create value that we should recognize and encourage.

In British architect Azby Brown's quaint tome *Just Enough: Lessons in Living Green from Traditional Japan,* the reader is given a tour through the fictional (but historically accurate) household of a rural peasant named Shinichi. While he doesn't have many material goods, Shinichi lives a surprisingly comfortable life, with an elegant wood farmhouse, his own well, and plenty of field and forest in which to cultivate a variety of crops. Perhaps the most striking facet of Shinichi's life, though, is the extent to which his world is self-contained.

> Shinichi's household, like all the others, is nearly self-sufficient in food, producing enough rice for itself and for government levy and enough vegetables. Each household has at least a few fruit trees, can gather its share of forest foodstuffs, and can fish in the rivers. They press their own oil and ferment miso from soybeans. Unavoidably, temporary surpluses and deficits occur for each family, but more often than not, these can be remedied by the informal exchange that characterizes social interaction: one may receive a bushel of persimmons from a relative and reciprocate with a basket of fish.[102]

Later, Brown goes on to detail how Shinichi's home is similarly self-sufficient in its energy and water needs and how he is assiduous about recycling everything from human waste and broken pots to ash from the fireplace. While Brown's portrayal may be especially vivid, it's hardly unique. In rural households from ancient Cascadia to medieval France to nineteenth-century Illinois, humble homemakers did justice to the original meaning of the word *economics*—"study of the home." For these people, the house wasn't merely a space to eat, sleep, and relax; it was also a site of the most basic forms of production.

Most of today's households fail to qualify as such sites of production. In fact, twenty-first-century homes are almost exclusively dependent on outside sources for their needs. Urbanization and its attendant explosion of consumer goods has shifted many activities that used to take place at home into the market economy. Preparing food, looking after children, entertaining each other—each of these needs has slowly been usurped by commercial interests. The more we shift from production to transaction, the more we lose valuable know-how and the more we become enmeshed in the global antimarket. Mundane as it may seem, the process of making households productive again is critical to patterns like DETHRONING THE ANTIMARKETS, COMMONING, and REDUCE THE NEED TO EARN.

That process starts with valuing the STEWARDSHIP that is currently done at home. Every household requires an array of simple, routine tasks to run smoothly, from playing with our kids to cleaning the shower. Most of us don't have the means (or desire) to pay for others to do these tasks, so they're not counted as part of the formal economy—yet their importance to our society is tremendous. Just how important are they? In her 2000 book *The Price of Motherhood*, journalist Ann Crittenden cites studies estimating that the everyday acts of motherhood contribute between $100,000 and $500,000 in value to society every year.[103] With numbers like these, it's seems obvious that we should be including the household economy as part of our economic modeling. Fortunately, Dr. Riane Eisler and her colleagues at the Center for Partnership Studies have begun doing just that, developing a set of "social wealth economic indicators" to help bolster arguments for policies like tax credits for caregivers and paid family leave. If included in our formal economy, Eisler claims, home-care work would add another 30 percent to 50 percent to our country's GDP.[104]

Of course, we don't have to wait for that day to start acknowledging the value of the household economy. Even if it's never given its due in dollars, HEIRLOOM CURRENCIES like time banks and credit-clearing exchanges can fill the gap, providing user-generated platforms for swapping chores, garden harvests, tools, services, and more. These platforms not only restore value to the home economics already in action but also serve as catalysts for "household economic development," encouraging us to increase the productive capacity to our homes. In this regard, society's marginalized have much to teach the rest of us—by necessity, many rural communities in the Global South (and their immigrant relatives throughout the Global North) still treat their homes in much the same way as Shinichi did his centuries ago. Here in the overdeveloped world, contemporary members of the maker, crafting, and urban homesteading movements are rediscovering and adding to this cultural capital, seeking to make the home a site of self-sufficiency even in our urban areas.

With the right design, skill, and time, even a small urban lot can be responsible for many of its basic needs. Fruit, vegetables, medicinal herbs, eggs, and meat can all be raised and preserved. Water can be stored in cisterns and carefully reused multiple times. Well-crafted homes can be heated with sunshine and biomass grown on-site. The garage can be a workshop for all kinds of cottage industries or converted into an apartment for an in-law or for another helping hand or two.

It's worth inserting a dose of realism here—creating and running a truly closed-loop household represents a significant investment of time and work, on top of the already-undervalued work of the contemporary home economy. And even the most successful household economy is unlikely to generate enough to replace the income from a full-time job. Is it possible, then, to truly have a household economy like Shinichi's in the contemporary world? Certainly—but it might require a shift in how we operate at home. Bit by bit, the productive tasks of the household economy help REDUCE THE NEED TO EARN. Smaller houses reduce the need to clean. And restoring our traditional living arrangements to a more historically typical level can increase the number of helping hands or income-earners in a household.

These changes might not be easy or practical to implement right away. They may never make sense for many of us. But if we're serious about bringing our world back to a sane level of resource use, many of our living spaces are going to have to increase their productive capacity. By growing our HOUSEHOLD ECONOMY, we become more integrated with the breath of the rest of life, providing us with an embodied understanding of sustainable systems that no amount of theory can replace. A more perfect world starts, quite literally, at home.

FURTHER LEARNING

Bane, Peter. *The Permaculture Handbook: Garden Farming for Town and Country.* Gabriola Island, BC: New Society, 2012.

Brown, Azby. *Just Enough: Lessons in Living Green from Traditional Japan.* North Clarendon, VT: Tuttle, 2012.

Emery, Carla. *The Encyclopedia of Country Living.* Seattle, WA: Sasquatch Books, 2012.

APPLYING THE PATTERN

What skills do you and the members of your household have that can be used to become less dependent on the market economy? What skills would you like to acquire? Does your organization or workplace value household economies? What can be done within them to make more room for household economies? How can you and your community share resources among households? How would you design or redesign the physical and invisible structures of your home to be more self-sufficient?

63. SMALL BUSINESS

Entrepreneurship is a primary indicator of a thriving local economy. Small businesses are more flexible and adaptive to change than large ones, and they are more accountable to the communities of which they are a part.

As in many domains of our society, our economic systems are operating far from THE RIGHT SIZE for optimal prosperity. To be sure, today's antimarket economy provides communities with cheap and abundant goods and—as long as the conditions are right—some jobs, too. But inevitably, the very design of antimarkets as investment vehicles leads them to draw knowledge and materials out of the local community and into the hands of the privileged few.

Clearly, an economics of the commons demands something closer to the human scale. What scale is best? Small networks of HOUSEHOLD ECONOMIES have the ability to provide many of our most basic needs, while collective acts of COMMONING can develop bottom-up institutions to sustainably manage nearby natural resources. Even so, thriving communities are likely to require more than just what we can produce in our own homes or harvest from nearby ecosystems. This economic niche is best filled by the small business, an institution well scaled to drive community prosperity.

How big is the small business? Large enough, at the lower end, to support a division of labor among specialists. While some people are able to thrive as solo entrepreneurs, HUMAN POLYCULTURES of employees—each one focusing on a specific role like accounting, manufacturing, or sales—dramatically increase an organization's efficiency and the quality of its product. The limiting factor on the high end, meanwhile, is accountability. How many employees can an enterprise have and remain a CONSENSUAL HIERARCHY? How much economic energy can it wield before it is no longer beholden to the community that birthed it? The federal government's official definition of a small business is one with no more than five hundred employees, but the upper limit is likely much closer to 150—the number that evolutionary psychologist Robin Dunbar determined was the maximum number for consensual hierarchy.

What are the advantages of small business for the regenerative economy? For one thing, they tend to be significant drivers of local economic activity. They hire locally, purchase supplies locally, and recirculate currency in their community rather than sending it to banks or distant corporate headquarters. A 2013 study by Civic Economics in British Columbia quantified these impacts by concluding that independent retail stores created about 2.6 times more local jobs than chain stores[105]. And while small businesses are modest in size, they are substantial in number. In 2012, more than a third of employed Americans worked for companies with fewer than one hundred employees. Finally, small businesses are bellwethers of innovation and resilience. In the aftermath of the 2008 financial crash, gross job gains of small business outpaced those of large businesses by as much as three to one.

For all these economic benefits, however, the real promise of the small business is bigger than money. Besides creating financial capital, the best small businesses act as generators of social, cultural, and even spiritual capital, as well, acting as hubs of education, community building, and social change. One of the crucial distinctions between small businesses and antimarket institutions like corporations is their ability to engage with their customers as *individuals* rather than as *data points*. Mission-driven organizations are responsive to the communities in which they are embedded and often see themselves as part of a business guild, collaborating with other small businesses to save resources and reduce waste.

Unfortunately, starting a small business, especially one with a social impact, is not easy. According to *Invisible Capital* author Chris Rabb, it's statistically easier to get into an Ivy League college than it is to start a business that generates more than $25,000 for three years. But with enough social capital, patience, and flexibility, the small business owner can succeed in not only earning a RIGHT LIVELIHOOD but also nourishing the soil of healthy community.

APPLYING THE PATTERN

What small businesses do you patronize in your community? What do you like about them? Are there others you can direct your financial capital toward? If you're starting a small business, how can you balance big ideas with small scale? How can you integrate the needs of the community into your business plan? Is there a place for social capital? Can your business practice XERIC ENTERPRISE? If you have an established business, what other small businesses can you nurture with your experiences?

64. IMPORT SUBSTITUTION

Cooperation is a vital feature of healthy economies. Organizations that focus on replacing external inputs with more local ones stand to enrich their neighbors while reducing costs.

Over the last couple decades, an entire subgenre of journalism has emerged that documents the far-flung processes that come together to manufacture everyday consumer items—a T-shirt, say, or a Big Mac. Typically, these stories strike a tone that's equal parts amazement and consternation, marveling at the impersonal efficiency of global supply chains while fretting over their environmental and social consequences: unsafe working conditions, carbon emissions, rock-bottom wages, and toxic pollution. With their window into the inner workings of the antimarket machine, these stories are often illuminating. But most of them miss the opportunity to analyze our global economy against the first and most enduring economy—that of natural systems.

Just like our human market of commodities and tariffs, ecosystems are constantly engaged in the exchange of materials and information. And like the human market, each ecosystem has honed those dynamics of exchange for optimal efficiency. But whereas today's high-energy, high-tech economy searches around the globe for the cheapest resources, productive ecosystems keep things local, cycling materials many times within a small area. A molecule of water, for instance, may stick within the same hundred-mile radius for years, finding its way into the stomata of a leaf, the underground hyphae of a fungus, the saliva of a squirrel, and the blood of an owl before making its way into the watershed and out to sea. Molecules of carbon and nitrogen follow similarly circuitous routes through natural systems, often sticking around for centuries.

What's the lesson for the human economy? Briefly, that the antimarket economy is one spread disturbingly thin. Our era of cheap fuel has obscured the fact that a tight cycling of inputs and outputs is critical for any economy to support its members in the long term. To be sure, a healthy amount of interregional trade can provide welcome luxuries, new technologies, and a vital exchange of knowledge, but a community that relies on imports to meet its basic needs is dangerously fragile, susceptible to the whims of economic disruption, transit attack, climate change, and more.

While the past fifty years have been a time of profound centralization, there have been plenty of times in history when communities valued self-reliance over interconnectedness, creating wealth through the replacement of faraway goods and services with local ones generated by SMALL BUSINESSES. This process, called *import substitution* by economists, was integral to the industrialization of England and the United States in the nineteenth century and of developing countries in the twentieth. In each case, local economies bootstrapped their way to prosperity by replacing one import at a time with a local source, until they had a diverse mix of small businesses providing stable and well-paying jobs.

Revered urbanist Jane Jacobs frequently sang the praises of import substitution as a critical part of the development of healthy cities. Discussing the evolution of the feudal-era European trade centers, for instance, Jacobs wrote that "the key to the strengthening, diversification, and ramification of their own and the others' economies was the fact that the cities repeatedly replaced, with their own production, imports from one another."[106] More recently, Local First economists like Michael Shuman have revived the discussion of import substitution, using contemporary economic analysis to show that money spent locally has a "multiplier effect" on the entire region. "The more you can produce locally through locally owned businesses," Shuman explains, "then the more you can minimize your vulnerability to nasty surprises, the more you can maximize your economic multiplier, and the more you can maximize tax proceeds to the public sector and the many good things that come from it."[107]

In practice, import substitution can happen in a couple different ways. A business might make an explicit choice to become more of a closed system, making more efficient use of its own materials and information. Alternatively, a group of new or existing businesses might choose to work together to share resources and reduce imports.

From 2010 to 2015, I was fortunate enough to participate in the development of the GrowHaus, a food justice organization based in a half-acre greenhouse in Denver. From the beginning, our team had envisioned the organization as a collection of mini-enterprises, each one exchanging materials, people, and profits with others for the benefit of the organization as a whole. As the plan unfolded, we settled on a commercial lettuce farm, a small retail market, and an educational space as our core operations. The farm covered its costs by selling lettuce to restaurants and grocery stores, as well as by providing some for the retail market to sell to locals. The market purchased other staples from local farmers and sent any food that was spoiled to an educational farm for composting. Through our educational programs, meanwhile, we built relationships with youths and adults from the community, many of whom eventually joined us as apprentice farmers, market clerks, and teachers and who helped spread the word to other neighbors. The cumulative effect of these and many more linkages meant that the GrowHaus was able to leverage our scarce resources much more effectively, garnering momentum quickly while earning the trust of foundations and community members alike.

Just as individual organizations can create *operational polycultures* that reduce costs by cycling materials, groups of organizations can create *business polycultures,* sharing everything from insurance to customer information to waste products and feedstocks. The GrowHaus would hardly have been able to accomplish as much as it has without participating in this kind of external polyculture of organizations, each one dedicated to regenerative community in

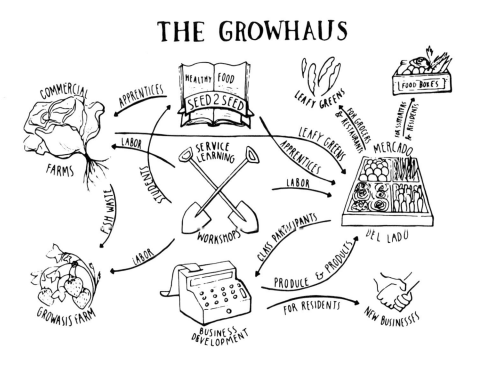

THE GROWHAUS

Denver. As part of this network, the GrowHaus benefits in all kinds of ways—the cross-promotion of events, the bulk purchase of seeds and compost, and a closer pulse on community needs, to name a few.

Other places take this business polyculture to a regional scale. Denmark's Kalundborg is an oft-cited example of an eco-industrial park, where complementary industrial operations are built together in one complex with the express purpose of facilitating resource cycling (an arrangement often called *colocation*). In Kalundborg's case, an enzyme manufacturer sends its waste to another business to become agricultural fertilizer, while next door, the world's largest producer of insulin sends its leftover yeast slurry to a biogas plant that provides heat and energy for the entire complex. Meanwhile, northern Europe's largest water treatment plant recycles the water coming from each of the businesses, saving nearly eight hundred million gallons per year. Similarly, in the Emilia-Romagna region of Italy, a network of EMPLOYEE OWNERSHIP businesses generates a full 30 percent of the region's GDP while employing 10 percent of the population. In *Throwing Rocks at the Google Bus,* Douglas Rushkoff writes that these businesses "source from one another instead of seeking the lowest bidder or attempting to expand into an additional horizontal." The firms also CONVERGE AND DISPERSE, forming partnerships on specific projects and separating when the work is done.[108]

As GrowHaus, Kalundborg, and Emilia-Romagna demonstrate, an intentional mindset of import substitution can profoundly reshape the operations of a small business, moving it away from the ruthlessly competitive mindset of the antimarket economy and toward an orientation of COMMONING. But one needn't be located in an eco-industrial park or work in food justice to take advantage of these dynamics. Over the last decade, new businesses of all kinds have embraced an ethos of mutual collaboration as a means to collective prosperity. The coworking movement, for instance, allows smaller desk-based businesses to lower their overhead by sharing rent, utilities, and office equipment while at the same time tapping into the network effect of colocation. Similarly, makerspaces are giving small-scale manufacturers a vital edge by pairing access to the latest 3D printing and laser cutters with workshops and community-building events to encourage collaboration. Regardless of the sector or scale, the logic of IMPORT SUBSTITUTION offers a vital alternative to the cutthroat mindset of business as usual, offering our economies a model rooted in the logic of ecology.

FURTHER LEARNING

McDonough, William, and Michael Braungart. *Cradle to Cradle: Remaking the Way We Make Things.* New York: North Point Press, 2002.

APPLYING THE PATTERN

What inputs of businesses and organizations in your community are being sourced locally? How can products and services be tweaked to rely more on local inputs? What businesses and organizations might be able to incorporate the waste from local producers? Which ones might complement each other? How would you make those connections? Could HEIRLOOM CURRENCIES help nurture this exchange?

65. REGENERATIVE ENTERPRISE

Generating income and making a positive social impact and need not be mutually exclusive; many of the most robust and resilient organizations are ones that manage to do both.

Our current economic arrangement sorts institutions into two categories: those that make money and those that make the world a better place. It's assumed that the institutions that make the world a better place *don't* make money and must subsist off things like grants and donations. Unfortunately, most of these mission-driven organizations find it awfully hard to raise the kind of funding needed to accomplish their goals. In fact, for many of them, it's necessary to devote a hefty chunk of their resources just to fundraising—resources which then can't go toward doing the actual work of making the world a better place. And when funding does arrive, it often does so with all kinds of strings attached.

In systems-thinking terminology, anything that falls apart without a constant infusion of outside energy is called a *degenerative structure*. We are surrounded by degenerative structures—our cars need new parts on a regular basis and our homes need to be cleaned regularly and repainted every once in a while to stay in top shape. Similarly, with their continuous treadmill of fundraising, most save-the-world institutions can be considered degenerative structures—spend too much energy focusing on the actual mission instead of running on the treadmill, and the whole thing falls apart.

Look outside of human society, however, and a different sort of logic prevails. Most natural systems, from individual cells to entire ecosystems, work as *regenerative structures:* they not only support their own needs but also reproduce themselves. Nobody needs to trim the trees in a forest. Nobody needs to find replacement parts for injured rodents or construct new insects when the old ones die. As long as stable inputs like sunlight, water, and healthy soil remain in ample supply, ecosystems can keep going indefinitely.

For-profit businesses—the successful ones, at least—also work like regenerative structures. Money spent on inventory, personnel, and marketing is more than made back in revenue. The surplus revenue is reinvested in making the business bigger and better. Indeed, this ability to reproduce is one of the main reasons why businesses have come to play such a central role in our society. They take over.

What would happen if our save-the-world organizations rejected the degenerative beg-for-pennies model and worked more like regenerative businesses and forests? That's the premise behind a broad and rapidly growing movement that's variously referred to as *triple-bottom-line, social enterprise,* or *regenerative enterprise.* The exact aims and methods of it practitioners vary, but what they share is a commitment to making the world a better place through sound business principles.

Regenerative enterprise is hardly easy. Starting any SMALL BUSINESS is always a risky endeavor, and doing so while trying to restore social, natural, or cultural capital makes it even riskier. Nevertheless, the promise of regenerative enterprise is too alluring to ignore, and more and more mission-driven organizations are adopting it to ensure ongoing success. As the field has evolved, a number of successful patterns have emerged for regenerative enterprises to generate their own income:

- *Fee for service.* Many charitable organizations assume that they are obliged to provide their goods and services for free—and it's true that many people have been so battered by antimarkets that they have little left to pay for goods and services. But besides depriving organizations of a potential income source, giveaways can also be disempowering, creating unhealthy dynamics of shame or dependence. Recognizing these drawbacks, some regenerative enterprises choose to charge the populations that need it. In an example of COMMUNITY-SUPPORTED ENTERPRISE, the members of Denver Permaculture Guild each pay a membership fee to support staff and programming.

- *Employment and skills training.* Many regenerative enterprises help hard-to-employ individuals gain the skills they need to succeed in the workplace. Baltimore's Details Deconstruction, for instance, has created dozens of jobs for inner-city residents by taking apart abandoned homes piece by piece and reselling the salvaged bricks and timber on the burgeoning reclaimed materials market. By training employees to sell a product or service to the general public, companies like Details, Goodwill Industries, and the Women's Bean Project leverage the power of the consumer to create economic opportunity for those that the antimarkets have forgotten.

- *Cross-compensation.* Cross-compensation is a form of DYNAMIC PRICING that involves selling a product or service at full price to one set of customers as a way of subsidizing products and services for a target population. The GrowHaus operates according to this model, providing education and fresh food to Coloradans with disposable income while offering similar food and programming at much cheaper rates to its core community of immigrant Latino Americans.

- *Independent support.* Some organizations use their income from one source to fund an unrelated product or service. The community arts organization AS220, based in Providence, Rhode Island, generates millions each year by leasing prime storefront space in a downtown building it's owned since 1992. AS220 uses that revenue to subsidize cheap studio space for emerging artists and provide an array of programs that would take countless hours to fund from grants or donations.

- *Market connectors.* Some regenerative enterprises' sole purpose is providing other enterprises with access to a market. By taking a cut of revenue or charging fees, fair trade programs, farmers markets, and craft fairs are able to sustain themselves financially while nurturing local networks of cottage industries and SMALL BUSINESSES.

- *Co-ops.* Finally, cooperative business models leverage the collective purchasing power of a well-organized group to provide products or services to members of that group at a low cost. Co-ops themselves can be organized in a number of ways, depending on their missions or memberships. For example, food co-ops are often run by the consumers, while agricultural co-ops are run by the producers. And worker co-ops use the model of EMPLOYEE OWNERSHIP.

What all these models show is that there are many ways to think about regenerative enterprise. Models can be combined with one another or with the traditional model of grants and donations. Even if self-generated revenue is only a fraction of your total income, that diversity of income streams makes you more flexible and resilient.

FURTHER LEARNING

Larsen, Rolfe. *Venture Forth! The Essential Guide to Starting a Moneymaking Business in Your Nonprofit Organization.* Saint Paul, MN: Amherst H. Wilder Foundation, 2002.

Lynch, Kevin, and Julius Walls. *Mission, Inc.: The Practitioner's Guide to Social Enterprise.* San Francisco: Berrett-Koehler, 2009.

APPLYING THE PATTERN

Think about your or your organization's goals for social change. What kinds of products or services are related to those goals? What opportunities exist for you to market them? Which revenue models above would fit well? Do you have the expertise to engage in regenerative enterprise on the terms of the market? If you don't, who else in your community does?

66. XERIC ENTERPRISE

Keeping overhead costs low reduces a business's exposure to changing market forces, allowing it to survive the lean times while thriving during good ones.

Desert ecosystems are among the most challenging places for life to thrive. With their scorching days, chilly nights, rocky soil, and lack of precipitation, it's a wonder that anything exists in them at all. But over thousands of generations, plants have developed a number of ingenious adaptations to withstand the challenges of arid living. Thick, fleshy leaves can store water for months, while their waxy coatings keep the sun from drying them out. Deep taproots reach down to groundwater even in the most severe of droughts, and spines and poisonous leaves deter thirsty predators. But perhaps the most remarkable thing about desert plants is what happens when it finally does rain. Right after a downpour, the desert comes to life—bright flowers blossom and soon produce seedpods, and plants use the precious water to grow another inch or two. Adaptations like these characterize plants that botanists call *xeric,* able to survive in times of drought and thrive in times of plenty.

If you're an entrepreneur, you can probably relate to the struggles of xeric plants. Trying to find the money to start and maintain a REGENERATIVE ENTERPRISE can feel like trying to find water in the Sahara. Grants and investment opportunities are as fleeting as clouds in the desert sky, and few ever seem to drop rain in the right place at the right time. The gap between starting up and turning a profit can feel interminable, and in the meantime, there's payroll to make, inventory to purchase, and rent to pay.

As it turns out, sustainable businesses have a lot to learn from desert plants. In an economy where access to capital is increasingly unstable—and any efforts at COMMONING are often at a financial disadvantage—it's imperative to be able to hang on in tough times while simultaneously remaining prepared to grow when a windfall occurs. Like desert plants, a XERIC ENTERPRISE can reduce the energy it needs to operate when times are tough.

- *Eliminate waste.* An approach to streamlining a business evolved in Japan's industrial boom of the 1970s and 1980s that has been called *lean thinking*. It is focused on ruthlessly identifying any kind of waste in an effort to stay competitive and has since been applied to many kinds of businesses. Its methods include cutting utility costs by investing in good heating and cooling systems and choosing workplaces that have abundant natural light; sharing office space with like-minded businesses to cut down on rent; and developing policies to streamline the production process and eliminate idle inventory. (See sidebar at the end of the pattern.)

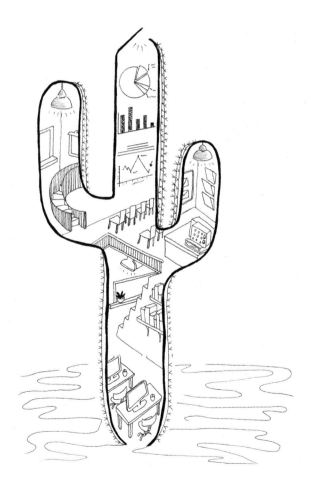

- *Share resources.* Business polycultures mimic natural systems by creating closed-loop processes and pooling resources. Whether it's converting manure into fertilizer or using someone else's office during nontraditional hours, think creatively about how your business can meet its needs by taking advantage of the wasted resources of others.

- *Make use of mutual credit systems.* As described in HEIRLOOM CURRENCIES, mutual credit systems allow self-contained networks of businesses to eliminate the need for cash by tracking the debits and credits of each business in a public ledger. If your business isn't part of such a network, look for opportunities to begin building one by establishing individual barter relationships with like-minded businesses.

- *Adopt a subscription payment model.* If it fits your product or service, experiment with shifting from an à la carte payment system to one that charges customers a fixed rate every month. While you may lose some cash by offering a payment plan at a discount, this loss is often outweighed by the security and stability provided by a consistent revenue source.

- *Flexible schedules.* For most businesses, paying employees is far and away the largest expense, and for good reason—the people on your team deserve to be compensated well. But it doesn't do your business any good to pay for talent unless you're making the most of it. Depending on the nature of your business activities, the traditional business schedule may not make sense for every employee position. Instead, talk with each employee about his or her specific goals for balancing work and other commitments, and come up with plans that meet the needs of both of you.

- *Cut your own salary.* One of your reasons for starting your business was making a living, but to make your business sustainable, it can help if you REDUCE THE NEED TO EARN. You can always give yourself a raise if conditions improve.

- *Have a flood plan in place.* For xeric plants, making the most of the rare downpour is just as important as conserving water. Likewise, a xeric enterprise ought to have a plan in place for when the capital does start to flow. Whether it's positive media attention, a big contract from a new customer, or just changing economic conditions, there are many reasons why a SMALL BUSINESS might want to scale up rather quickly. Thinking through the procedures, materials, and people necessary to do so long in advance will make a big difference in the smoothness of the transition.

SEVEN FORMS OF WASTE IN THE TOYOTA PRODUCTION SYSTEM

by Taiichi Ohno

- *Overproduction.* Making more products than is necessary.
- *Waiting.* When employees or products are idle, time, energy, and resources are wasted.
- *Transportation.* Moving materials from place to place is expensive and can erode the quality of the final product.
- *Inappropriate processing.* Any part of a product or service that doesn't directly add value to the customer is waste of time and materials. Trim any ornamentation, ingredients, or activities that don't increase customer satisfaction.
- *Excessive inventory.* Every product not sold is one that has incurred expenses without generating income.
- *Unnecessary motion.* The physical layout of a workplace should be designed to minimize unnecessary walking or physical strain.
- *Defects.* Resources spent repairing or remanufacturing can't be used on new products.

FURTHER LEARNING

Ries, Eric. *The Lean Startup: How Today's Entrepreneurs Use Continuous Innovation to Create Radically Successful Businesses.* New York: Crown, 2011.

APPLYING THE PATTERN

If you have a business or work in one—how resilient is it to changes in the economy? Are there wastes you can reduce, resources you can recycle, and ways you can store resources for the lean times? Can you reduce the need to earn for your business as well as yourself?

67. COMMUNITY-SUPPORTED ENTERPRISE

The best way to ensure that a business or organization is meeting a real need—and keeping itself accountable to its community—is to have the customers become the investors.

While running a business or organization as a XERIC ENTERPRISE may be ideal for minimizing risk, it's not always practical to be entirely debt-free. Some businesses require a substantial up-front investment in equipment, space, or skilled staff members. And it might be necessary to seek outside funding for the founders' own salaries until the income starts flowing in.

Unfortunately, many of the typical means of raising capital are a poor fit with ideals like SUBSIDIARITY and DETHRONING THE ANTIMARKETS. As a rule, loans from institutions require repayment with interest, which only increases the flow of cash to antimarket actors like banks and wealthy individuals. While the field of "impact investments" continues to grow, the fact remains that most lenders are looking for a financial return first and a social impact second—if at all. There is also equity investment, in which an investor forgoes immediate repayment in exchange for a perpetual cut of the organization's profit. Depending on the size and terms of the investment, equity investors can wield formal decision-making power in the organization, compelling the business grow toward short-term profit and away from long-term impact.

At its core, the challenge is one of misalignment. In both debt and equity arrangements, the folks putting up the money usually are not—and have nothing in common with—the people that the organization is intended to benefit. As a result, investors have no compulsion to care about the ultimate fate of the customers, as long as they reap their financial reward. More ethically minded investors in your business can be found by realigning those two groups, making the up-front customer and initial investor one and the same—or, as media theorist Douglas Rushkoff puts it, "making your customers rich." *Community-supported enterprise* is a broad term for a number of strategies that attempt just that.

Since the turn of the millennium, several forms of COMMUNITY-SUPPORTED investment have entered the mainstream as new ways companies get their start-up money. COMMUNITY-SUPPORTED agriculture programs (CSAs) ask customers to subscribe in the winter or early spring and pay up front for a season's worth of produce. This model has grown exponentially since 2000, with over six thousand CSAs active in 2015. The amount raised on crowdfunding platforms such as Kickstarter and Indiegogo, meanwhile, has been doubling every year; it was $34 billion in 2015. While the money raised is technically donations, most organizations seeking crowdfunding provide perks to those who donate, and the most successful crowdfunding campaigns make the donations, in effect, up-front payments for eventual product. Finally, consumer or member cooperatives have continued to grow in popularity since their inception in the 1960s. Essentially a retail store owned by its own customers, these cooperatives pool their collective

PATTERNS FOR SUCCESS IN
COMMUNITY-SUPPORTED ENTERPRISE

- *Prove yourself first.* Take time to build a name and a trustworthy reputation among your potential customers before asking them to invest in you.

- *Deliver what you promise.* Regardless of the platform, engaging in community-supported enterprise is not easy money, and it's not an excuse to avoid developing a solid business plan. Failing to deliver on your promises will erase any trust or goodwill you've built for your business—and it will erode the credibility of community-supported investment as a whole.

- *Engage with your customers.* Once customers are invested financially in an organization, it's not hard for them to become invested in other ways, as well. Build social capital with your community by asking for their input and setting up opportunities for them to connect with you and each other. Increase intellectual capital by sharing information and relevant events.

buying power to get discounts on goods. Food co-ops are the most familiar example, but co-ops can be focused on any kind of product and be quite successful in their own right: the national outdoors retailer REI and the hardware chain Ace both function with variations on the cooperative model.

Less familiar in the overdeveloped world, but increasingly popular in cash-strapped communities in the Global South, are lending circles. Also called *huis* and *su-sus* (and there are other names as well), these semiformal groups are comprised of neighbors—frequently women—who meet regularly to pool their resources and invest in each other's businesses.

As technology and social innovation evolves, each of these forms of community-supported enterprise is sure to evolve as well. Some may become obsolete, while new forms may arise to take their place. But regardless of how it manifests, the underlying strategy of aligning customers with investors remains a sound approach to REGENERATIVE ENTERPRISE.

APPLYING THE PATTERN

Who are the target customers for your enterprise? How supportive are they of your business? What kinds of capital (financial or otherwise) can they contribute to making your enterprise a success? How can you direct your capital and purchases toward community-supported enterprises? Can you identify any niches for community-supported start-ups in your community?

68. EMPLOYEE OWNERSHIP

Imbuing a company's employees with the power of collective ownership often leads to higher wages, better business decision making, and many other benefits.

Most businesses today are owned either by a small group of founders or by a large group of distant shareholders. While there are significant differences between these two models, both share a lack of accountability to the two groups of stakeholders that businesses are ostensibly there to serve: employees and customers. Decisions about what to sell, how much to charge, where to source parts and labor, and other important issues are made behind closed doors, with workers and consumers alike expected to trust that they've been made wisely. For the occasional compassionate and visionary organization, that's indeed the case. But most of us have long ago surrendered the illusion that businesses exist to make our lives better, instead eyeing the relationship between a company and its employees and customers with a healthy dose of cynicism and suspicion.

Among the first and most important tasks of a post-antimarket economics is restoring this trust by designing businesses to serve communities rather than dominate them. COMMUNITY-SUPPORTED ENTERPRISE is one way of putting more control in the hands of customers. Putting ownership in the hands of the company's employees, meanwhile, is a way to balance networked and hierarchical structures inside the organization. Like community-supported enterprise, employee ownership can take many forms. Here in the United States, the two most common are the employee stock ownership plan (ESOP) and the worker-owned cooperative.

In ESOPs, employees are granted shares in a corporation's stock via a trust, which are bought back when the employee retires or leaves the company.[109] According to the National Center for Employee Ownership, nearly fourteen million Americans participate in ESOPs, owning shares totaling $1.2 trillion.[110] In addition to granting employees equity in the organization, many ESOPs engage their employees in key decisions of the organization. New Belgium Brewing, for instance, provides each of its 570 worker-owners access to company financials as well as participation its annual retreat.

Still, it's important to distinguish between ownership of a company's stock and management over its day-to-day operations. While New Belgium's democratic culture is far from unique, it's not an intrinsic part of an ESOP. In fact, most ESOPs are managed similarly to any other corporation, with a classical hierarchical decision-making process. Employees within an ESOP may share in the rewards of their company, but they have no say in how those rewards are gained.

Worker-owned cooperatives, on the other hand, democratize both ownership and management. Every member of a worker co-op is granted an equal share in the organization—and if the organization is profitable, every member receives a share of the profits in the form of an annual dividend. Meanwhile, worker-owners are also given decision-making authority over every aspect of the organization, from the bylaws to day-to-day operations. This doesn't mean that every worker-owner is involved in every decision—or even the major ones. As we've seen in THE RIGHT WAY TO DECIDE, leaving a decision to a large group is a recipe for inefficiency. Rather, many worker co-ops—particularly larger ones— tend to create CONSENSUAL HIERARCHIES, delegating decision-making power to managers, executives, or elected boards.

Without any one default set of rules, each worker co-op has the responsibility of determining guidelines for doing business that fit its own internal values. This flexibility means that forming a co-op requires a much greater time commitment than, say, starting an LLC. But for worker-owners with a balanced, trusting team, SKILLED FACILITATION and plenty of patience, the payoffs are worth it. Members of worker cooperatives consistently describe their experience as going far beyond the typical company-employee relationship, instead speaking of their company as a true INTERDEPENDENT COMMUNITY, rooted in trust and affection. Gustavo Salas, a forty-year member of the Cecosesola network of cooperatives in Venezuela, shares this anecdote of the vendors selling the cooperative farms' produce:

> At some point, the idea came up to start using cash registers at the markets. Cash registers are the norm everywhere, but we don't use them. The cooperativistas at the markets take the money to the office in the envelopes. That's it. So at some point, this idea to use cash registers came up

to make it easier to monitor the transactions. We discussed it in countless assemblies for almost three years. And then we finally realized that these cash registers serve one function above all: to monitor the cooperativistas at the markets. That would amount to withdrawing trust. And we didn't want to do that. So we continue as before, without cash registers, and using envelopes. We saved the money for the investment. And we gained trust.[111]

With stories like this, it's not hard to argue that EMPLOYEE OWNERSHIP represents a more equitable way of doing business. But in the cutthroat environment of our global economy, doing the right thing is often seen as a luxury that businesses can't afford. It may be surprising to learn, then, that one thing that worker cooperatives and ESOPs share is a track record of financially outperforming conventional businesses. In one recent study, for instance, Rutgers researchers Douglas Kruse and Joseph Blasi found that ESOPs had annual sales growth figures 2.4 percent higher than non-ESOPs, and in 2013, the Democracy at Work Institute found that worker cooperatives had profit margins 0.5 percent higher than other businesses.[112]

FURTHER LEARNING

Abrams, John. *Companies We Keep: Employee Ownership and the Business of Community and Place.* White River Junction, VT: Chelsea Green, 2008.

Nadeau, E. G. *The Cooperative Solution: How the United States Can Tame Recessions, Reduce Inequality, and Protect the Environment.* Madison, WI: E. G. Nadeau, 2012.

APPLYING THE PATTERN

If you're thinking about starting a SMALL BUSINESS, have you considered employee-owned models? Would any of the models work with your plans? Who would your partners be? What employee-owned businesses in your community could you direct your financial capital toward?

69. DYNAMIC PRICING

The relative affordability of basic goods and services differs drastically depending on an individual's financial means. Flexible pricing systems avoid pricing out the underserved by setting higher prices for those who can afford to pay them.

In a time of rampant income inequality, larger and larger numbers of people are finding it hard to afford even the most basic goods and services. According to the National Low Income Housing Coalition, over seven million households—nearly one in five renters in the country—spend over half their income on rent.[113] An annual census conducted by the Department of Housing and Urban Development found that there were 422,619 homeless households in the United States on a given night in January 2015.[114] And according to the World Food Programme, almost 800 million people worldwide lack the calories to lead a normal, active life—in many cases because they simply can't afford it.[115]

To make matters worse, the most affordable goods are usually produced by cutting all sorts of ethical corners, eroding natural and social capital and externalizing the true cost. As a result, ethically and sustainably sourced goods are even further out of reach to the most vulnerable populations.

One of the most important ways out of this conundrum is rejecting the idea that goods should have a single fixed price. Indeed, the single-price assumption is a relatively recent addition to our economic landscape. For most of the past several thousand years, currency transactions in general played a much smaller role in meeting our needs. But when we did exchange goods for currency, prices were usually assumed to be a matter of negotiation. Strangers were generally charged the most, while relatives, friends, and those we owed favors to would get the biggest discounts. The lines between barter, gift, and currency were blurred. As late as the mid-nineteenth century, most Americans purchased their basic necessities this way, and throughout much of Asia, the Middle East, and Latin America, haggling is still the default for procuring everyday goods.

Over the last several generations, however, our understanding of price in the West has been inverted. As antimarkets have consolidated their hold on economies, the value of personal relationship was supplanted by that of standardization and efficiency, and retailers began using a fixed-price system as a means of touting their fairness and modernity. Today, most of us in the overdeveloped world have come to expect that there is one clear price for every item, and that that price doesn't go up or down based on the whim of the seller.

And yet variable prices remain a fixture of our day-to-day transactions—they've just become more obscured from view. All along, retailers have understood that one-size-fits-all is a poor strategy for maximizing profit. Think of senior Tuesdays at the thrift store, buy-one-get-one sales, happy-hour specials, and matinee versus evening prices for movies. In each of these cases, the "fixed" price is temporarily cut to attract more customers and sell more product.

As it turns out, one-size-fits-all also happens to be a poor strategy for maximizing equity. Just as dynamic pricing can be used to liquidate old inventory or increase revenue during times of high demand, it can also used as a tool for lowering the price of goods for populations who otherwise couldn't afford them.

Vegan chef and author Bryant Terry has gained international influence and acclaim for his blend of traditional African and African American cuisine and his use of fresh, vegan ingredients. And while he's happy to spread the message to anyone who will listen, his heart remains in improving health outcomes for the African American community. When he accepts paid speaking engagements and cooking demonstrations across the country, he looks for opportunities to give similar talks in the low-income parts of town—a philosophy he calls "one for the money, two for the hood."

Even for those of us who aren't rock-star chefs, the principle of charging more for those who can afford it in order to subsidize those who can't is a powerful strategy. Here are a few specific models for adjusting pricing for inclusivity.

- *Installment pricing.* In this model, the business eases the financial burden for the customer by spreading the cost over a period of time. This might require the business to front some of the costs in advance, but it receives a consistent, predictable stream of revenue in return. Installment pricing is one of the most common ways for businesses to reach customers that would ordinarily be priced out from their offerings. It's the principle behind mortgages and student loans, and it is employed to sell consumer goods throughout the Global South. But in nearly all of these cases, the installment pricing carries interest, often resulting in much higher total costs for the consumer. Meanwhile, there's always the danger of customers defaulting on their loans, which can put a business or an entire sector of the economy underwater.

- *Sliding scale.* Perhaps the most obvious strategy for DYNAMIC PRICING is also the most radical—asking the customer to choose his or her own price. Within an INTERDEPENDENT COMMUNITY, in which people are bound by more than just economic ties, pay-what-you-can models can help those with limited economic means access valuable goods and services. Over the last decade, for example, a movement of nonprofit pay-what-you-can restaurants has begun providing good meals and the experience of dining out to everyone. Restaurants like One World Cafe in Salt Lake City, SAME Cafe in Denver, and FoCo Cafe in Fort Collins, Colorado, have served tens of thousands of meals. These establishments keep costs down by accepting donations of food, keeping the menu to a few dishes per meal, and relying on volunteers to help with dishes and prep work. The inherent risk of pay-what-you-can models can be mitigated by setting a minimum price, as well as simply by being transparent with the customer about the cost of providing the goods. Even so, pay-what-you-can is hardly the best fit for every situation. Communities that lack the necessary social capital may suffer from customers cheating the system, paying less than they can truly afford. Customers used to a single-price system, meanwhile, can be confused by the pay-what-you-can model. And as with any system of variable pricing, there needs to be enough people in the market willing to pay a higher price to offset the potential losses from those paying a low price.

- *Conditional scale.* This arrangement uses a model that changes pricing based on predefined customer categories. Many businesses, for example, offer discounts to students, seniors, or veterans, while service-oriented nonprofits may have income- or location-based qualifiers for reduced-price or free services. Conditional scales are able to match the price with the ability to pay much more precisely than a pay-what-you-can system. But this requires a method for verifying those conditions. Pricing based on income is the most obvious system, but it's also one of the most challenging (and sensitive) to gather. Age and location are sometimes used as proxies, since they require only a driver's license or other form of identification, but they are far less accurate.

- *Scholarship pricing.* This is a good way for events or courses to achieve a balanced diversity of incomes. By setting the regular price of tickets at the high end of what the market will bear, event organizers can use the resulting profits to cover losses on scholarship recipients. By following this pricing model, the Denver Permaculture Design Course has been able to cover the costs of dozens of changemakers from low-income backgrounds, giving them valuable skills to take back to their communities and making for a more diverse student body. Successful scholarship programs require clear and transparent scholarship criteria, as well as ample organizational capacity to follow up with all the scholarship applicants.

APPLYING THE PATTERN

Does your business or organization sell products or services? If so, how do you price them? How could you rework your pricing model to be more dynamic and to provide more access to those in diverse economic situations? If you are a consumer with greater financial capital, how could your purchases support or subsidize members of your community with less? If you have less, how can you stretch your resources through dynamic price purchases?

70. DESIGN TOOL: CAPITAL ANALYSIS

Each community and institution has a unique set of strengths and resources available to it. Capital analysis helps the designer systematically inventory a group's areas of wealth and impoverishment.

In a healthy, INTERDEPENDENT COMMUNITY, members are engaged in complex webs of relationships with one another and their surrounding ecosystems. It's the strength of these relationships—from local trading networks to forest management—that allow communities to prosper independently of global conditions. Sadly, however, this web has been badly damaged in many of our communities. Population pressures, antimarket enclosures, government policies, resource depletion, climate change, and any number of other factors have eroded the multifaceted forms of wealth present in healthy communities. Creating vibrant communities means repairing these webs of interrelationship—and that, in turn, requires examining what forms of wealth are present and absent.

This is the premise behind CAPITAL ANALYSIS, a design tool for assessing a community's forms of wealth. Systematic inventories of community resources and opportunities are already common in many contexts. Practitioners of Asset-Based Community Development, for instance, commonly use "asset maps" to document the skills, resources, and institutions of value in a community. Meanwhile, SWOT Analysis is employed by corporate executives and grassroots organizers alike to document the strengths, weaknesses, opportunities, and threats surrounding their work.

CAPITAL ANALYSIS takes a similar approach as these tools but also integrate other concepts from the social permaculture framework. It's designed to be relevant for communities of all sizes, from small collaborative groups to entire neighborhoods and cities. Either way, performing a CAPITAL ANALYSIS consists of four steps, each tracking a different stage in THE CREATIVE PROCESS:

1. *Create a vision.* The first step, representing the goal-setting stage of the creative process, is about articulating a vision for what a thriving group or community would look like. In it, participants systematically review each form of capital and share their hopes, dreams, and ideas for how each one would be represented. (See COMMONING for a chart of eight forms of capital.)

2. *Document the existing assets.* Next comes analysis and assessment. Examine how each form of capital is already present in the group or community. Be sure to include specific people and places, as well as broad themes and patterns. It might be helpful to make a map or diagram charting how the forms of capital are connected.

3. *Identify areas of depleted capital.* Now, compare your vision from step 1 with your list of existing assets from step 2. What's missing? What forms of capital are eroded or depleted? Can you identify any specific trends or factors that have resulted in a lack of capital? Try to think of patterns as well as details.

4. *Develop a set of solutions and roadmap.* The final stage of capital analysis moves from assessment to design, finding specific solutions to the problems you have identified and determining the steps needed to create a wealthy community. This is where the patterns of the book come into play, as well as some of the other design tools like NETWORK ANALYSIS and POWER ANALYSIS. During this phase, it's important to think about leverage points, dependencies, and setting up cascades of beneficial actions.

FURTHER LEARNING

Roland, Ethan, and Gregory Landua. *Regenerative Enterprise: Optimizing for Multi-Capital Abundance.* N.p.: Lulu, 2015.

71. DESIGN TOOL: BUSINESS MODEL CANVAS

Just like landscape designs, businesses can benefit from conceptual "basemaps." The Business Model Canvas provides a flexible backdrop for quickly prototyping entrepreneurial ideas.

Ecologically attuned landscape design starts with a basemap: a scale drawing of the property, noting permanent features like property lines, topography, structures, and infrastructure. Without this document in hand, the landscape designer would be hard-pressed to come up with realistic design concepts or understand how design elements might fit together into a cohesive whole.

As it turns out, basemaps can be just as valuable for entrepreneurs. While a basemap for a landscape features physical structures, the equivalent document for a SMALL BUSINESS or REGENERATIVE ENTERPRISE makes note of the invisible structures: the concepts and ideas that underlie a successful organization. There are many ways to demarcate these structures, from pro formas to mind maps. But one of the most helpful frameworks comes from consultants Alexander Osterwalder and Yves Pigneur in the form of a template called the Business Model Canvas. Crowdsourced over several years from nearly five hundred entrepreneurs, the template provides a visual diagram of key elements necessary for a successful business and how each one is connected to the others.

As opposed to a business plan, which provides pages and pages of detailed speculation, a business model is intended to be something much more nimble: a living document that can be revised and improved as the business evolves. Like a landscape basemap, it serves as a sketchpad upon which a business designer can quickly and effectively play around with business ideas. Osterwalder and Pigneur wisely released the Business Model Canvas as an open-source model, encouraging revision and adaptation. In the ensuing years, dozens of variations have been developed, each one focusing on a niche like tech start-ups, nonprofits, or internal communications.

In the same vein, I've developed my own twist on Osterwalder and Pigneur's original, this one aimed at the unique challenges and opportunities of REGEN-ERATIVE ENTERPRISE. It contains twelve sections, arranged in roughly the same order as original.

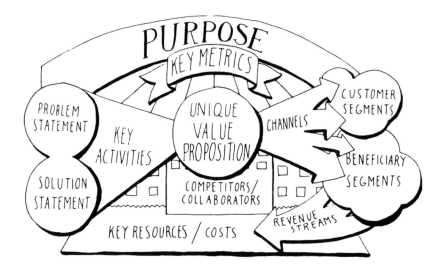

PURPOSE

What is the impact you are trying to make?

Most businesses primarily exist to provide a living for their founders or profit for their shareholders. They might produce interesting products and employ many people along the way—but at the end of the day, a conventional business is in it for the money. But for the REGENERATIVE ENTERPRISE, money is simply a vehicle that allows the organization to achieve a greater purpose of social or ecological change. This forms the core around which all the other aspects of the business revolve. If your business has a mission statement, vision statement, or set of fundamental values, this is the section where they are placed. Everything else about the model might shift—the customers, the revenue streams, even the legal structure—but your purpose ought to stay relatively stable.

PROBLEM STATEMENT

What is the one-sentence summary of the problem your business is attempting to solve?

Every solution starts with a problem. And while most communities have problems that are varied and complex, it's critical for regenerative entrepreneurs to start their efforts by focusing on a clear and simple solution. Is your organization trying to fix a degraded natural habitat or a lack of biodiversity? Is your work attempting to address access to affordable housing or the availability of living-wage jobs?

The overall purpose of an organization is based on values and therefore tends to remain pretty stable, but the problem statement is responsive to the context you're working in, which can change over time. And in many cases, what we originally identify as the problem is later revealed to be a mere symptom of a larger problem. As a result, problem statements are likely to evolve as you learn more information or as the outside context changes.

SOLUTION STATEMENT

What is the one-sentence summary of how this business model will address the problem?

If the problem statement is what's going wrong in a nutshell, the solution statement is a similarly concise articulation of how you're going to fix it while staying profitable. As such, it serves as your executive summary of the whole business model. And if the regenerative entrepreneur's definition of the problem may shift occasionally, the intended solution is likely to be even more variable. The whole point of the canvas, in fact, is to test multiple solutions—so the more you can think of, the better.

BENEFICIARY SEGMENTS

Who will benefit from the impact of your venture?

It's hard to know if you're successful at solving your challenge if you can't clearly explain who—or what—you're trying to benefit. Successful regenerative enterprises target their impact toward a specific group of people or organisms: residents of the Elmwood neighborhood, immigrants in Maine, or forests in the local watershed. Clearly identifying your beneficiaries becomes even more important as you identify your key metrics and begin MEASURING SUCCESS.

CUSTOMER SEGMENTS

What segments of the population will be buying your product or service? Be as specific as possible.

Successful regenerative enterprises have sustainable streams of income—streams that might or might not be directly related to the solution. Whether that income arrives in the form of donations, the sale of products and services, or monthly membership fees, it's got to come from *somewhere*. And in order to keep it coming, it's important to get inside the heads of the people and organizations who are providing it. Where do they live? What are their demographic characteristics? What do they value? Try coming up with a fictional character who embodies all the characteristics of your ideal customer—or better yet, talk with people that you think might have good customer potential to see what they would value.

It's also worth pointing out that many successful models for regenerative enterprises have multiple customer groups. You might find yourself selling one product to affluent parents of young kids and another to college students, with other funding coming from foundations. Know and understand each of these customer groups, and don't assume that they'll respond to the same messaging.

UNIQUE VALUE PROPOSITION

Why would a customer buy from you instead of from any of your competitors? What is the advantage you have that nobody else can copy?

The unique value proposition (UVP) is a simple explanation of what sets you apart from the competition and makes your products or services valuable to the customers and beneficiaries whom you're trying to reach. UVPs could represent quantitative value, such as being cheaper than anything else on the market, or qualitative value, like being more friendly and accessible. Either way, it should be something that can't be copied by anyone else, something that's unique to your organization. Here are a couple example UVPs:

"We're the only edible landscaping company in the region to offer a free cooking class teaching you how to prepare your new crops."

"We are the only organization with both the grassroots base and political connections to successfully pull off this campaign."

The UVP is placed dead center in the BUSINESS MODEL CANVAS for a reason: it serves as the vehicle for connecting your organization to its customers and beneficiaries. That's why coming up with a compelling and accurate UVP requires a deep understanding of each customer and beneficiary, as well as the solutions you offer for the problem you are addressing.

CUSTOMER AND BENEFICIARY CHANNELS

How will people find out about your organization? How will the product or service be delivered?

Flyers. Flash mobs. Hashtags. Mysterious street-art campaigns. These days, there seems to be an unlimited number of ways for organizations to creatively get their message to the customers and beneficiaries they want to reach. While marketing tends to be scorned as a tool of the antimarket elites, the techniques used to hawk disposable consumer goods can be subverted to rally communities around ideas like COMMONING and DECOLONIZATION.

Think about how your audience captures new ideas. What sources do they use? What spokespeople do they trust? Are there ways you can engage cultural translators to authentically make use of the channels they frequent?

COMPETITORS AND COLLABORATORS

Who else is meeting the same customer needs? Do they do this directly or indirectly? Are there ways to partner with them instead of compete?

Every business, even one with the most novel idea, has competitors. *Direct* competitors provide similar programs and services to the same customers. Just as important to consider are *indirect* competitors, who meet the same underlying needs, but through a different means. Two concert venues are direct competitors; a venue and a movie theater are indirect competitors.

Just as every regenerative enterprise has some form of competition, it's also bound to have collaborators. It takes a network of dedicated partners—clients, funders, partner organizations, and more—to make a sustained impact in a community. The earlier you can map out that network, the better luck you'll have leveraging relationships with competitors into cooperative relationships, or at least "coopetition."

KEY ACTIVITIES

What are the day-to-day processes and procedures that would take up most of the organization's time?

Even the most visionary organizations spend a good deal of their energy on mundane tasks like managing inventory, entering data, or processing invoices. As much as we may want to focus on the exciting stuff, the truth is that we also need to plan and budget for these details. Try developing a process map of all the day-to-day tasks necessary to deliver your core product or service. If you're feeling stuck, interview experienced professionals at similar organizations—as they're all likely to admit, 90 percent of their time is probably spent getting everything in place for the 10 percent that counts. Learning how others organize their efforts may help you improve your own.

KEY METRICS

How will you measure your social impact and your financial performance?

It's a lot harder learn from your mistakes and improve if you aren't tracking your impact. As discussed in MEASURING SUCCESS, developing the right set of metrics is critical to understanding your organization's social, environmental, and financial health. Try to develop a mix of qualitative and quantitative measures, and think through how you'll track and report on them regularly.

KEY RESOURCES AND COSTS

What upfront investment will this business require to succeed? What ongoing costs will it require? What kinds of skills and talent do you need on your team?

Launching a new enterprise requires working personal connections, using unique skills and talents, leveraging the right tools and infrastructure, and spending money—in other words, it takes capital, in all its many forms. Use CAPITAL ANALYSIS to estimate the various forms of capital your venture will need to get off the ground. Does your success rely on specialized expertise? The right facilities? Community buy-in? Once you've tracked which forms of capital you currently possess and what you're lacking, you'll be in a great place to figure out how to get to where you need to be.

REVENUE STREAMS

How will this business generate income? What is your pricing model? What kinds of start-up capital do you need, and how will you go about sourcing it?

Many regenerative enterprises have a polyculture of income streams, relying on some combination of products, services, subscriptions, donations, and grants. What's an appropriate and realistic mix for your project? Will you employ some form of DYNAMIC PRICING to balance revenue with equity? Will you earn income as a COMMUNITY-SUPPORTED ENTERPRISE and allow your community to hold you accountable? Sketch out multiple budget scenarios until you arrive at one that you feel confident about.

FURTHER LEARNING

Osterwalder, Alexander, and Yves Pigneur. *Business Model Generation: A Handbook for Visionaries, Game Changers, and Challengers.* Hoboken, NJ: Wiley, 2010.

PART 5

Training the Sacred Warrior

For all the social struggles being lost and won on picket lines, courtrooms, and dining room tables, some of the most insidious barriers to social change lie in our own heads and hearts. Internalized narratives of shame, guilt, or apathy can cripple our plans before they even hatch. The food we choose to nourish our bodies—and the media we choose to nourish our minds—can dull our senses and raise our blood pressure. And even our most well-intentioned actions can end up recycling age-old patterns of domination, keeping ourselves and others locked into spirals of social erosion.

In short, we can't heal the systems around us if we don't heal ourselves first. For those dedicated to social change, self-care frequently means going beyond the trite (but true) reminders about good diet, exercise, and sufficient sleep to encompass an entire mindset and lifestyle. The work of building a better society isn't suspended in the evening or on the weekend—it just takes a different form. As feminist poet Audre Lorde once put it, self-care is an "act of political warfare."

What self-care strategies are most effective for warriors of peace and justice like Lorde? They're myriad and diffuse, but many of them boil down to one thing: self-knowledge. If we're to be effective stewards of social and environmental change, it's our responsibility to understand who we are as individuals, where we came from, and where we want to go. We all need to develop our capacities for self-awareness and self-improvement and to learn to read our internal compass on an ongoing basis. We've got to know our strengths, acknowledge our weaknesses, and serve our communities with dedication and joy. Each one of those tasks could easily entail years of study and practice. But in order for those journeys to even begin, we've got to carve out the time for them to take place at all. Whether it's through journaling, meditation, yoga, dancing, or prayer, many of the most successful changemakers cultivate a practice that helps them connect with their deepest selves.

As we each engage with our own processes of self-awareness, we inevitably uncover some warts and scars that are difficult to face. Even when we have the courage to acknowledge these challenges, our default response is to keep them out of our interactions with others and project a confident, seamless facade. Yet, as noted social scientist Brené Brown has found, this kind of cover-up only serves to further erode our connections with our peers. "When leaders choose self-protection over transparency," explains Brown, "when money and metrics are more valued than relationships and values, and when our self-worth is attached to what we produce, learning and work becomes dehumanized.... The equation is simple: Invulnerability in leadership breeds disengagement in culture." The corollary, proven by brave leaders again and again, is that being honest with peers about our challenges and fears engenders respect and trust, bringing groups closer together. Vulnerability—counterintuitively—is strength.

The patterns and design tools of this final section are an attempt to provide signposts for our personal journeys of self-awareness, grounding, and vulnerability. The first pattern, SACRED ACTIVISM, explores how our work can be catalyzed by a connection to forces beyond our control. RIGHT LIVELIHOOD examines how that work can intersect with our need to pay the bills, while SPIRALS OF ABUNDANCE describes how to apply design thinking to our own good and bad habits. Thoughtful observation of the social landscape is an equally critical part of successful change—a process described by KNOW YOUR COMMUNITY. Finally, ACTIONS, NOT INTENTIONS focuses on integrity and accountability, reminding us that our values are of little practical value without a corresponding change our behavior.

The final four patterns concern strategies for staying grounded amid the mania of daily life. First, iSites illuminates what CONNECTION TO NATURE looks like on an individual level, providing examples and tools for observing the landscape around us. UNPLUGGING reminds us to periodically disconnect from digital flights of fancy, and COMMITMENT PRUNING demonstrates the importance of being honest about our personal capacity. REDUCE THE NEED TO EARN positions thrift as a political act, one that keeps us free from the snares of the antimarket. Finally, PERSONAL MYTHOLOGY invites us to find deeper meaning in our own histories, personalities, and priorities by connecting them to age-old archetypes. As with the previous four sections, Training the Sacred Warrior concludes with a design tool, PERSONAL VISION, which invites us all to develop our own vision statements for the world we want to create, closing the loop with the very first patterns of the book.

72. SACRED ACTIVISM

We are each called to play a part in transforming our society. It's our job to figure out what is being asked of us and to develop the skills to do it well.

A mysticism that is only private and self-absorbed leaves the evils of the world intact and does little to halt the suicidal juggernaut of history; an activism that is not purified by a profound spiritual vision ... will only perpetuate the problem it is trying to solve, whatever its righteous intentions.

—Andrew Harvey

Pushing THE EDGE OF CHANGE is exhausting. The bold endeavor of envisioning and building a different world while living in the present one can quickly drain even the most resolute soul. We can face criticism and scorn from many around us, as well as from ourselves. The acts of COMMONING that we're able to eke out face the constant threat of enclosure from antimarket forces, and many fail under the pressure. Meanwhile, the convenience-oriented world we live in tempts us to forego the necessary work of THE LONG GAME and succumb to the easy pleasures of short-term comfort. All told, it can be hard to find the motivation to keep going for the years it takes to restore our social, cultural, and natural capital.

How do the most successful and dedicated activists keep up their work under such trying conditions? Joanna Macy, a well-known scholar of Buddhism, systems thinking, and deep ecology, has struggled with these dilemmas throughout her half-century of activism. In her essay "Three Dimensions of the Great Turning," Macy offers her model of sustainable activism as a sort of three-legged stool. The first (and often most visible) leg is made up of the forms of NONVIOLENT STRUGGLE we use to halt destruction and oppression: legislation, COORDINATED NONCOMPLIANCE, DISROBING THE EMPEROR and others. The second leg is the work of building ZONES OF AUTONOMY, or what Macy calls "green shoots pushing up through the rubble":[116] off-the-grid households, antiracist institutions, REGENERATIVE ENTERPRISES, HEIRLOOM CURRENCIES, and count-less other expressions of the world we know is possible.

But according to Macy, neither of these two forms of activism can be sustained without the third leg: sacred activism, a personal, deeply rooted worldview that aligns with our work and sustains us with inspiration and hope. This worldview might be informed by scientific research or ancient texts. It might be expressed through intellectual discourse or RITUAL AND CEREMONY. Regardless of its nature, it's this steadfast way of seeing the world that keeps us rooted in our intentions amid the swirling currents of twenty-first-century life. Macy's third leg, in other words, is about using the power of faith to make our activism a *sacred* activism.

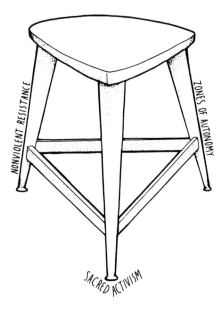

In today's secular society, the concept of faith is often disregarded as a quaint anachronism or vilified as a dangerous scourge used to justify oppression. Yet these narratives overlook the powerful role faith has played in the ages-old story of social change, giving dissidents from Arjuna to Jesus to Martin Luther King Jr. the strength to challenge hegemony and speak truth to power. For these individuals (and countless others, including many whose names have been lost to history), a practice of channeling something larger than themselves was an integral part of their role as servant leaders.

Beyond providing us with a source of inner strength, spiritual practices can be powerful tools for weaving INTERDEPENDENT COMMUNITIES. In *Liberating*

Voices: A Pattern Language for Communication Revolution, Evergreen State College professor Douglas Schuler highlights several ways that faith can bring people together in the struggle for social change: "Singing together, marching together, or sitting quietly in Quaker meeting together can strengthen the sense of community. Charitable giving, cooking for the poor, and visiting prisoners can feel like religious practices when inspired by a spiritually grounded activism. Priests, imams and other religious leaders offering blessings over an action can ease the qualms and concerns of their followers. In all of these ways, organizational resilience gains support from adherence to a spiritual or religious path."[117]

Granted, Schuler's examples aren't for everyone. Many activists have little interest in traditions of faith, especially ones with a history of violence. But while the phrase *sacred activism* carries undeniable spiritual overtones, connecting one's work to larger narratives has relevance for even the staunchest atheist. Whether it's a secularly derived moral compass, a science-based call to action,

ANDREW HARVEY'S SEVEN LAWS OF SACRED ACTIVISM

Andrew Harvey is the founder and director of the Institute of Sacred Activism. His 2009 book *The Hope: A Guide to Sacred Activism* is an in-depth examination of seven laws that guide the sacred activist in his or her practice.

- *Law of Sacred Practice.* Committing to a daily spiritual discipline.
- *Law of Surrendering the Fruits of Action to the Divine.* Performing our actions selflessly, on behalf of all life.
- *Law of Recognizing Evil.* Acknowledging the destructive powers within ourselves and the world at large.
- *The Law of the Alchemy of Anger.* Channeling our anger at injustice and destruction into productive action.
- *The Law of Constant, Humble Shadow Work.* Acknowledging the destructive potential of our own shadows.
- *The Law of Joy.* Ensuring that we're capable of finding joy, even in the most trying circumstances.
- *The Law of Networks of Grace.* Creating communities of like-minded individuals who can strengthen and support one another.

a passionate belief in a political agenda, or simply a commitment to build a livable future for our children, we all have faith in *something*. Sacred activism invites us to honor that faith and use it to nourish our work for a better world.

FURTHER LEARNING

Harvey, Andrew. *The Hope: A Guide to Sacred Activism*. New York: Hay House, 2009.

APPLYING THE PATTERN

Seek motivation and inspiration by grounding your efforts in narratives of meaning that span space and time. Seek connection to forces larger than yourself. What worldviews do you hold in a sacred space? How do they inform your work and your activism? Do they conflict with your work or with the work of others? How does your practice fit into Andrew Harvey's seven laws of SACRED ACTIVISM? Are there areas where you feel a lack of sacred engagement?

73. RIGHT LIVELIHOOD

Paying the bills while maintaining your ethical integrity can be challenging, but finding the balance between the two is both possible and rewarding.

You have to find a way to earn your living without transgressing your ideals of love and compassion. The way you support yourself can be an expression of your deepest self, or it can be a source of suffering for you and others.

—Thich Nhat Hanh

How shall I spend my time? What is my highest and best calling? For most of history, questions like these were idle speculation that only the wealthiest could afford to contemplate. As historian Yuval Noah Harari puts it, what we tend to think of as "history" consists of "something that very few people have been doing while everyone else was ploughing fields and carrying water buckets."[118] For most humans, their greater contributions to the world were less a matter of choice and more about staying fed and keeping warm. Even the slow and steady rise of skilled trades created livelihoods that were not chosen, but handed down from generation to generation.

Today, for the first time in history, many of us are given the opportunity to choose what we want to become. But like many choices in consumer society, the options we're given are suspiciously proscribed. If we're interested in maintaining a stable, middle-class lifestyle, our choices are limited to those opportunities that generate sufficient financial capital to support that life. And these alternatives seem to be getting ever narrower, funneling us into industries or tasks that we have no taste for.

Meanwhile, the work that desperately needs doing never seems to pay enough to sustain us, no matter how talented we are at doing it. This is not a coincidence: as long as we remain tied to growth-based currencies like dollars, most of the profitable careers will be ones that maximize returns of that currency at the expense of other forms of capital. The rules of the game intentionally dis-incentivize acts of COMMONING, which redirect capital away from antimarkets and central banks and back toward the local communities that need it.

And so the SACRED ACTIVIST must negotiate the paradox of finding the right livelihood in a wrong world. For the time being, we're compelled to walk a seemingly impossible line, with one foot planted in the present exploitative reality and another in the regenerative future. But while there are few perfect solutions to this paradox, plenty of committed and thoughtful changemakers have found clever strategies of handling it. Through her series of interviews with "regene-preneurs," permaculture teacher and designer Karryn Olson-Ramanujan has profiled a series of SACRED ACTIVISTS who have managed to develop a path of right livelihood amid the crosscurrents of capitalism. While their stories are unique and varied, there's a thread that connects them all: each one has found his or her calling by seeking opportunities at the intersection of what's fulfilling, what's necessary, and what's lucrative.

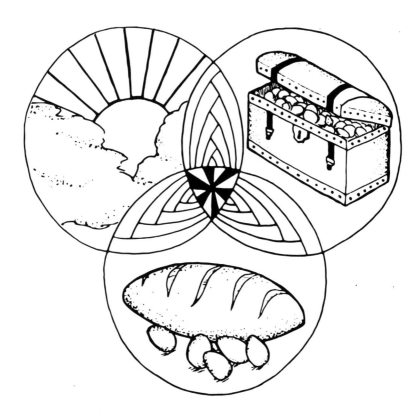

RIGHT LIVELIHOODS ARE FULFILLING

None of us wants to spend eight hours a day engaging in work that's not aligned with our personal values. Not only is it erosive to our sense of self, but our indifference leads to mediocrity—a losing proposition for employee and employer alike. But unless we're able to articulate exactly the kind of work we *want* to perform, we'll be stuck choosing among the less-than-perfect options offered to us. Many of us, conditioned our whole  lives to think inside the career box, have hardly even dared ask the question of what we'd most like to be doing. But by exploring what makes us happy, we can begin to develop a more three-dimensional story of who we are and who we want to become, guiding us toward moments of professional fulfillment that we didn't even know were possible.

What causes do you feel most passionate about? What classes, jobs, or volunteer opportunities have you been most excited to participate in? How would you spend your time if earning money wasn't an issue? Through answering questions like these, as well as design tools like the PERSONAL VISION, you can start to hone in on what kind of work feels most fulfilling to you.

RIGHT LIVELIHOODS ARE NEEDED

There are plenty of activities that make us happy that hardly qualify as a RIGHT LIVELIHOOD. While we might choose to pass our free time watching the sunset or playing video games, we also have to consider what our community needs. In the same way that every species has a niche in its ecosystem, each one of us must find  our niche in our community's path toward independence and abundance. Some of us are healers, born with a nurturing impulse that can be honed to solve physical, emotional, spiritual, or interpersonal ailments. Some of us are creators, pouring our love into manufacturing useful and beautiful objects. And still others are communicators and translators, inspiring others with the gift of the spoken and written word.

Sometimes it takes time to figure out exactly what your community needs from you. Bonita Ford, a successful permaculture designer, organizer, and author based in Ontario—and one of Olson-Ramanujan's regenepreneurs—admits that finding her niche was as much her community's decision as her own. "This whole process," she explains, "has been about also being willing to be curious, to be flexible, to really work with and be receptive to what people were interested in, what services people were interested in, what people were willing to pay for, what opportunities existed within our community and what needs there were."[119]

RIGHT LIVELIHOODS ARE LUCRATIVE

As rewarding as it may be to find a match between our passions and our community's needs, it's not sustainable if it can't meet our financial obligations. Monetizing our work for a better world requires persistence, creativity, and sometimes painful compromises—but it's entirely possible. For one thing, it's important to REDUCE THE NEED TO EARN: the less money you need to meet your needs, the more flexible you'll be to take on opportunities that are meaningful and necessary. A farmer, for instance, might offer to take care of a property in exchange for room and board, while a chiropractor could accept payment in an HEIRLOOM CURRENCY.

But strategies like these will only go so far—especially if you have student loan payments to make, children to support, or a mortgage to pay. That's why it's just as important to practice increasing our monetary yield for our work. One key component of maximizing our yield is diversification: cultivating a set of interrelated skills that can be put to use at different times, depending on what's most necessary and profitable. The permaculture practitioners profiled by Olson-Ramanujan, for instance, often rely on a polyculture of teaching, designing, and gardening to make ends meet, while healers might offer a combination of acupuncture services, homemade tinctures, and educational workshops.

Regardless of which skills we're using in our polyculture, we ought to make sure we're getting the payment we deserve. Many of us have a hard time negotiating payment on our own behalf—especially women, people of color, and others who have been told they're less valuable by society. While you may have to undercharge or even perform your services for free while you're getting started, there's no shame in asking for a living wage as you begin to perfect your expertise. Becoming familiar with marketing and self-promotion are also critical, as are basic bookkeeping skills, for when the money does start flowing.

—

All told, these factors point toward a conception of RIGHT LIVELIHOOD that looks quite different than the steady career that remains the default goal for most Americans. For starters, it demands a much more self-directed path. It might be possible for some to find a full-time, salaried position at an existing organization that checks the boxes of *fulfilling, needed,* and *lucrative.* But more often than not, following the path of RIGHT LIVELIHOOD takes the courage to step outside existing institutional structures. Ultimately, RIGHT LIVELIHOOD is less a destination than a journey. The livelihood path of Bonita Ford and others wasn't something they arrived at and stuck with, but instead a constantly shifting balance. By developing a polyculture of related skills that can wax and wane as the situation demands, the regenerpreneurs profiled by Olson-Ramanujan were able to embrace change and uncertainty with less fear.

FURTHER LEARNING

Olson-Ramanujan, Karryn. *Regenepreneurs.* http://regenepreneurs.com.

APPLYING THE PATTERN

What are your marketable skills? What is your niche? What do you love doing? Can you make a living doing it eventually? Can you do something else in the meantime? What are the gaps you see in the capital in your community and your niche? How can you gain the necessary skills?

74. SPIRALS OF ABUNDANCE

Identify the behaviors that lead to unhealthy feedback loops in your own lifestyle, and work to shift them to create cycles of positive behavior.

Eating junk food. Binge-watching reality TV. Saying something nasty to our significant other. We all do things we know we shouldn't—and then do them again and again, until they became habits. Whether it's because of the seduction of consumerism, family pressure, irrational fears, or sheer laziness, we all fall into patterns that don't serve us well in the long run. Sometimes these patterns result in no more than a bigger belly or a tired day. But sometimes they can add up and severely limit our potential or harm others in our community.

In her book *People and Permaculture*, Looby Macnamara labels these self-undercutting behaviors as spirals of erosion:

> Erosion is usually associated with natural resources such as soil, but it is the gradual destruction, reduction or weakening of anything. It describes something that has been useful becoming less useful....

> Problems interact with each other the way systems do. To make effective change we need to know the cause of the problems. This is a far more complex issue and sometimes we may be looking at the symptoms rather than the causes. Some factors initiate the erosion and others just perpetuate it; the effect is cyclical. These are known as spirals or erosion or vicious cycles.[12]

Macnamara goes on to detail several examples of these spirals of erosion:

- Poor education, leading to poor teachers.
- Family dynamics of addiction and abuse.
- Not getting enough sleep, not having enough energy the next day, not getting things done, and lying awake in bed worrying about what didn't get done.

Using the same approach, she then explains how getting to the root of the problem and implementing a different design solution leads to a mirror image of this vicious cycle, which she terms a spiral of abundance.

Since reading *People and Permaculture*, Macnamara's spirals of erosion and abundance have become helpful design tools for my own life. By carefully observing my daily moods and habits, I've found all kinds of harmful spirals of erosion—and made an effort to cultivate spirals of abundance in their place. For instance, when I use my computer in bed before going to sleep, I'm often sucked down an internet vortex watching biochar lectures or learning about Peter Gabriel's discography. Before I know it, it's two in the morning—and when I finally do turn off the screen, I don't sleep well, because my brain's still racing. The next morning, I need to sleep late to compensate, meaning I don't give myself enough time to establish a healthy circadian rhythm before going to work.

After observing the behavior that starts this spiral of erosion—using my computer in bed—it was easier to make a choice that leads to a spiral of abundance.

Now I try to unplug from my computer after dinner and try not to use it in bed at all. With these simple rules in place, I'm much more likely to get to bed at a reasonable hour, sleep well, and get an early start to my day.

FURTHER LEARNING

Macnamara, Looby. *People and Permaculture: Caring and Designing for Our-selves, Each Other, and the Planet.* East Meon, England: Permanent, 2012.

APPLYING THE PATTERN

Think of times when you're not at your best. Can you follow your choices back to the starting point of a spiral of erosion? How could you transform it into a spiral of abundance? What is one choice you could make differently that would have the most effect on the direction of your behavior?

75. KNOW YOUR COMMUNITY

Successful solutions emerge from a deep and thoughtful engagement with the people involved in the system.

Deep in the heart of the Rocky Mountains, Jerome Osentowski has been practicing permaculture on the same rocky hillside for nearly forty years. At first, the place didn't have much going for it beyond a sunny aspect and a constant trickle of water. The high-altitude climate left precious few months without frost, while the site's dry red soil offered little in the way of nutrients for a garden. As he slowly pieced together a passive-solar home with materials hauled up from the scrap yard, Jerome tried growing vegetables on the land, with little success. Year after year, his crops wilted, froze, or failed to sell at the market.

But slowly Jerome began to notice patterns. Certain contours of the land had a milder microclimate. A few rare varieties of fruit trees survived the chilly winters and bore fruit. He figured out how to keep tender plants lasting well into the cool season by blowing warm daytime air through tubes underneath the greenhouse soil, and a careful combination of timed watering and rabbit manure began to increase the land's fertility. After a decade, Jerome began converting his acre of annual salad greens to a perennial food forest. After another two decades, he'd perfected pruning, grafting, and greenhouse management. And after thirty years on the land, people were traveling thousands of miles to learn from the wise old man on the mountain.

Jerome's persistence and eventual payoff vividly illustrates the virtue of patience when engaging with ecosystems. Any environment is a complex system, filled with dynamic and subtle patterns that may take years to become clear. In order to properly perceive these patterns—let alone use them for the good of the whole system—countless hours of observation and engagement are often necessary. As it happens, communities are systems too, and they're every bit as complicated as the ecologies in which they're embedded. The broad patterns of what makes a community thrive are nearly universal, but the specifics vary widely. What works in one neighborhood might be a total flop in the next one over. What worked five years ago might be irrelevant today. Simple, one-size-fits-all solutions might grab the headlines and capture our imaginations, but they can often backfire if they aren't applied with a deep understanding of the individual community you're working with.

Backfiring is particularly common in the realms of social change, where individuals and organizations are often expected to develop solutions for communities that aren't their own. Picture a development agency tasked with reducing the debilitating health and environmental effects of wood cookstoves in the Global South. As a solution, they turn to solar ovens, spending months prototyping models out of local materials. Eventually, they engineer a high-performing design and take a year to teach the locals how to make and repair the ovens themselves. With their mission accomplished, the development workers head home—only to find, years later, that the solar ovens have barely been used. As it turns out, they'd overlooked the small but crucial fact that the smoky flavor of foods cooked over wood was an integral part of the local cuisine. The solar ovens may have been cleaner and healthier, but the food they made was considered too bland to eat.

This situation is far from hypothetical: a 2014 study found similar comments from locals in Kenya, Nepal, and Peru.[121] In each case, the development agencies involved likely had the best of intentions, and they likely thought they were doing a good job understanding the community's needs. But their oversights in place after place underscore the fact that knowing a community inside and out takes time. By the time outsiders really understand everything they need to know to do their job, they probably wouldn't be considered outsiders anymore.

All of which means we must be judicious about which communities we choose to know. For many SACRED ACTIVISTS, knowing a community is intertwined with GOING HOME, as we slowly develop a relationship with a single community over the course of years and decades. And whether we're in our native habitat or working in another one, our aim should be oriented toward cultivating LEADERSHIP FROM WITHIN, for which a deep knowledge of community is essential. In the same way that a skilled landscape designer takes his or her time noting the cycles of the seasons, the textures of the soil, and the migration patterns of elk, the social designer aims to leave no stone unturned in his or her understanding of a community.

What is the process by which the social designer can develop this deep understanding? First, it's best to start small. While the term *community* is often used to encapsulate an entire city or ethnic group, it's unlikely that one person can capture all the nuances of groups like these in a few short years. Instead, try starting with communities within the RELATIONSHIP ZONE of recognition, like a neighborhood or a high school. Within that group, meanwhile, be sure to explore as many sides of the community as possible—particularly the ones that seem to be lurking in the background.

There is no cookie-cutter checklist of what it takes to get to know a community, but it's always a good idea to start by exploring the history. Try to uncover the indigenous history of the area as well as the stories of the first modern inhabitants. Ask locals to help you learn about the histories of everyday people who aren't captured in official records. Learn about the choices that shaped the present land use: What were the first structures in the area? Why are streets and landmarks named the way they are? What natural features helped determine the layout of the community?

Meanwhile, several of the design tools presented in this book can be particularly helpful in assessing the community's present-day dynamics. TEAM ANALYSIS can be applied at the community scale to identify a community's elders, griots, radicals, and network weavers (see HUMAN POLYCULTURES for more on these roles). It can also uncover the fault lines of the community and the underlying divisions they represent. Finally, it can help highlight the community's CAUCUSES and how they communicate, both internally and externally.

CAPITAL ANALYSIS, meanwhile, illuminates what forms of wealth are intact and what forms are lacking. Does the community have access to parks and natural areas, or is it a superfund site? Do people acknowledge and celebrate their cultural heritage, or are they too stressed just getting by? Do people know their neighbors?

Finally, POWER ANALYSIS is a critical tool for exploring pathways to change. Who helps make the big decisions that guide the community's fate? Government agencies? Businesses? Established nonprofits? What forms of power do they have, and where are they oriented in relation to the values of the community's citizens? Is there a culture of SUBSIDIARITY or domination? Antimarkets or COMMONING?

Regardless of which of these questions you end up asking, consider answering them through a variety of methods. Value personal stories as well as statistics. Conduct archival research as well as one-on-one conversations and focus groups. Attend local events and make conversation with the people you see there. The more perspectives you use, the deeper your understanding of the community becomes—and the more well informed your design solutions will be.

APPLYING THE PATTERN

Answer the questions under the design tools of TEAM ANALYSIS, CAPITAL ANALYSIS, and POWER ANALYSIS for the community in which you live or work. Where are the gaps in your knowledge? What do you need to learn? What people or organizations from the community might be willing to engage with you, to teach you?

76. ACTIONS, NOT INTENTIONS

Good intentions are a dime a dozen, but they do little to actually change the oppressive systems that surround us.

Those who profess to favor freedom, and yet depreciate agitation, are people who want crops without plowing up the ground. They want rain without thunder and lightning. They want the ocean without the awful roar of its many waters. This struggle may be a moral one; or it may be a physical one; or it may be both moral and physical. But it must be a struggle. Power concedes nothing without a demand. It never did and it never will.

—Frederick Douglass

The night of July 5, 2016, African American CD vendor Alton Sterling was gunned down by police officers in front of a convenience store in Baton Rouge, Louisiana. And the next night, at a routine traffic stop, cops in a St. Paul suburb killed Philando Castile, with his girlfriend and her four-year-old daughter as shocked witnesses. They were two more in what had become of string of widely publicized killings of black men at the hands of police. With the shootings and their aftermath captured on cell phone video and shared to millions on social media, they became a flashpoint of national stature in a summer of growing racial tension.

On a personal level, the killing of Sterling and Castile was a wake-up call for me. I'd long been sympathetic to the issue of racism in policing, but deaths like these had become publicized so frequently that my outrage was beginning to wear off, making me more and more numb to each new story. This time around, though, things were different for me, and it wasn't just because of the videos. Earlier that week—the night of July 4—someone had broken into my house while nobody was home, throwing a rock through the glass door to the backyard. The thief rifled through our possessions, stole some jewelry that was of little financial but great sentimental value, and left.

Fortunately, the material losses were minimal, and nobody was hurt. Even so, the robbery shattered something invisible within me: the glass door of comfort that surrounded my lifestyle of relative ease. With that door gone, I was forced to acknowledge the violence that had been occurring all around me, every day. For days afterward, I felt violated, exposed, stressed, and wary of strangers. For a brief few days, in other words, I felt the way our society's most vulnerable are forced to feel their whole lives.

As the cofounder of a nonprofit dedicated to social justice, I'd been thinking about these issues for years. I'd researched oppression, intersectionality, microaggressions, and all the other stifling structures of supremacy, talked with my peers about them—even led workshops on how to dismantle them. But for all the times I'd thought and spoken about injustice, rarely had I allowed myself to feel it. I'd avoided the toughest conversations, stayed on the sidelines of the action, refrained from offering acquaintances the emotional support they needed. At the time, I convinced myself that I was too busy, that I was doing meaningful work in other ways. I absolved myself of responsibility.

The plain truth, however, was that I was scared. Scared of facing the visceral reality of violence, unfiltered by the hashtags and intellectualization. Scared of allowing pain into my soul. After all, who wants to voluntarily experience pain? But what I began to realize after that week in July was that ignoring pain wasn't making me happy. It was making me numb. By averting my gaze, I was putting up imaginary walls between myself and all those around me who were in pain.

And it wasn't just me. Despite our best intentions, despite whatever sympathies we may have for the disenfranchised, we are all complicit in choosing to ignore the pain of others in our society. By averting our collective gaze, by removing ourselves emotionally from struggle, we've allowed the violence happening at a safe distance to escalate. As we fret from afar, the mass shootings and the drone bombs and the slaughter of kids and queers and young black men have become normal.

If we're to be of service to our community, if we're to leave the world better than we found it—if we truly believe that our own liberation is bound up with that of those around us—then we have no choice but to open ourselves up to the pain of others and to our own shadow pain. We have no choice but to feel hurt too. Acting in allyship and SOLIDARITY means making sure we never allow ourselves to become numb. It means offering more than just our thoughts to those on the front lines; we must offer our hugs, our time, and our home-cooked meals, and, sometimes, we must put our bodies on the front lines as well.

Often, it won't be enough. Things will sometimes get worse before they get better. Despite our best efforts, many more hearts will be broken, arrests will be made, blood will be shed. Our own actions will, most of the time, feel insignificant. Yet by allowing our own hearts to be broken, too, we will feel little more human. By sharing in the pain of others, we'll all be made a little more whole. And the world we're all struggling so hard to birth will be that much closer to reality.

APPLYING THE PATTERN

Where are you starting from with your intentions? What causes do you value? What injustices do you wish were righted? How are those intentions manifesting themselves? Are you willing and able to feel them deeply? Are you acting on them? If not, what are some ways you can? Pick one and do it—how did it make you feel? How did it change your perspective on your initial intentions?

77. iSITES

Natural systems are best understood by observing how they change over time. Pick a convenient, quiet location that's relatively undisturbed by human activity, and return to it on a regular basis for solace and inspiration.

As adults, we need to put down our books about nature and actually get into a rainstorm, be startled by the deer we startle, climb a tree like a chameleon. It's good for the soul to go where humans do not have a great say about what happens.

—Janine Benyus, *Biomimicry: Innovation Inspired by Nature*

I believe in God, only I spell it Nature.

—Frank Lloyd Wright

Georgia O'Keeffe had an obsession. The famous twentieth-century painter was smitten not with a person, a flower, or a brand of paint, but with a specific place in nature. Dozens of times between 1936 and 1977, O'Keeffe returned to the same spot to paint—a remote rock formation in New Mexico known as the "Black Place." She compared the spot to "a mile of elephants with gray hills and white sand at their feet," and it served as inspiration for some of her best-known works.

While O'Keeffe's talent with a brush may have been exceptional, her fascination wasn't. For most people growing up in the twentieth century and earlier, there were specific spots in nature that held a special emotional resonance and added to their PERSONAL MYTHOLOGY. Whether it was a special tree in the backyard, a suburban creek down the street, or a magical spot in the remote wilderness, it was a place that we visited again and again as children—and even adults. But as more humans move into cities and as our rural landscapes have become reshaped by the homogenizing hands of the antimarket, these experiences of unique natural places have become more rare. And when we do spend time outdoors, it's often treated as a scenic backdrop for relaxation, adventure, or socializing.

But when we lose our reflective experience of natural systems, something disappears in our psyches as well. Nature is constantly changing, and if we don't observe it long enough to bear witness to that change, we fail to grasp its lessons in full. The cultures that have managed to demonstrate sustainability over many centuries are ones that, by definition, have a sophisticated understanding of nature's complexities. And they were able to develop that understanding only through many years of observing and engaging with one ecosystem—in many cases, over many generations.

Biomimicry, an ecological engineering movement, has recognized the value of this sort of sustained reflection by encoding it into their training program.

SUSIE'S ISITE

By Susie Lewis, changemaker

468. By my rough calculations, this is the number of times I biked to the same location over the course of three years. Three bike rides a week along the Gainesville-Hawthorne State Trail to a lookout point in Paynes Prairie State Park. It was a time of real growth in my life. I was at my first "real" job after college, working hard to prove myself in an environment that wasn't always welcoming of my presence.

My regular trips to the prairie lookout quickly became highly invaluable, for they served as a source of inspiration, a physical release, and an escape from my human-made office surroundings. Sitting and watching the sunset over the prairie, I would observe the gradual entrance of nighttime and, over the long term, the changes of the prairie itself.

In many ways, this patience and calm I learned from the natural environment allowed me to honor the incremental change I was making in my professional life in the world of twenty-first-century capitalism, despite how slow it sometimes felt. Equally important, this hour or two would allow the ideas and work of the day to sink in. Had I gone straight home, I might have easily become distracted with other tasks. Returning to the same place each time signaled that I was back to my spot, and my brain would automatically relax, release, and reflect.

The *Biomimicry Resource Handbook* uses the term *iSite* to denote the practice of visiting a special place in nature for at least thirty minutes on a regular basis to simply observe and reflect. Through a series of exercises, aspiring biomimics are trained to look at nature through a different set of eyes. "Where I once saw leaves, gravel, grasses and rock," writes ecological designer Alëna Konyk of the iSite process, "I learned to see a masterfully orchestrated mosaic of shapes, textures, and tone. I also learned that every creature, no matter how small and seemingly ordinary, and every natural setting, even the most barren, possesses a unique beauty and purpose of its own."[122]

Even for those of us without engineering degrees, iSites can provide invaluable sources of inspiration, becoming more than just places of observation, but of sanctuary as well. As we engage a practice of repetitive observation, we learn to observe which plant species are moving in and which are on the wane, which birds are migrating through the area and how the whole system is being altered by a changing climate. In so doing, we internalize a rich understanding of complex systems that can be applied to many facets of the rest of our lives.

EIGHT ISITE EXERCISES

Used with permission from The Biomimicry Resource Handbook.

Test your skills of observation

Sit in front of an organism or natural object. Draw a quick sketch of the object (don't worry if you "can't draw"). Now, draw the organism or artifact again, but this time look only at the object and not at your paper while you draw. Try following the outline of the object with your eyes and make your pen follow the path that your eyes take. Compare your drawings. Did you really observe the first time?

Make a sound map

With your journal or paper in front of you, mark yourself on the page with an X. Then close your eyes and listen. Create a symbol on your page to represent each sound that you hear (keeping your eyes closed). Using these symbols, make a map of the sounds you hear all around you, in all directions, whether human-caused or not. Are the sounds related or responsive to each other? Open your eyes and write down other observations.

Look for patterns in nature

Look for and record, using words and sketches, patterns that you can see, hear, or feel. Patterns might include structural angles, edges, distribution systems, or gradients. Guess the function that each pattern might serve.

Track change over time

Visit the same spot in as many different conditions, times of day and seasons as possible. Record your observations each time, noting differences and changes in both the site and your perception of it.

Translate what you see

Create a technical drawing of one system in the environment you see around you. For example, draw the system of energy flows. Use arrows, symbols, and notes like those you would find in an engineering drawing.

Imagine being one of the organisms that you observe

Imagine how you perform each of the functions that you and your species need to survive. What are you made of? What and who do you depend on to survive? Who depends on you to survive? What roles do you play in your ecosystem throughout your life? What is your special niche? What are your special adaptations that make you fit best in your niche?

Discover interactions among the organisms at your iSite

Try to find many different types of interactions, thinking about different scales of time and size. Describe and sketch the interactions

Look for multifunctional design

Study an organism and guess the primary function of something you observe (for example, ears designed for hearing). Then try to think about other functions that the forms, processes, or systems associated with that design might serve. Why else is that ear shaped that way? What else might it do for the organism or for the system?

APPLYING THE PATTERN

Pick a place in an intact ecosystem that speaks to you and that you can easily access, and visit it regularly. What do you hear and see there? What other life forms (plants, animals) are there with you? How does it change with the seasons? What do you feel when you are there?

78. UNPLUGGING

In a world where connection and meaning are increasingly mediated by motors and touchscreens, we must make a conscious effort to remove ourselves from these influences on a regular basis to stay fully human.

More so than any other species, *Homo sapiens* is a prolific toolmaker. The tools that we shape have, in turn, shaped us. Our ability to manipulate fire reconfigured everything from our habitat to our internal microbiology. The development of language transformed our perception of the world from a fabric of sensations into a set of discrete objects and events. And the emergence of agriculture didn't just change our diets; it also wrought massive changes in our systems of social organization.

None of these changes were clear at the time. It takes generations to fully understand the implications that new tools have on our bodies, habitats, and psyches—if we ever understand them fully at all. Since the Industrial Revolution, the pace of technological change has grown exponentially, far outstripping our ability to track it in real time. As a result, many of today's most daunting problems—suburban sprawl, diabetes, and climate change, to name a few—are a direct result of yesterday's "solutions."

Meanwhile, powerful new technologies are coming at us more quickly than ever. Just since the turn of the millennium, we've developed the capacity to follow the day-to-day events of our friends in other countries, broadcast our homemade videos to millions, and virtually browse roads thousands of miles away—all with a few swipes of a handheld screen. Scratch beneath the surface of all the techno-utopian proselytizing, and the side effects of this latest wave of innovation are already beginning to become clear. Our late-night screen viewing is disrupting our circadian rhythms. The constant multitasking of an always-on mentality is wearing down our brains. Our reliance on virtual mapping software is causing our brain's own spatial processing abilities to atrophy. And those are just the physiological repercussions; a quick examination of the ecological, social, and economic side effects of these same advances yields equally troubling information.

The solution to these dilemmas, for most of us, is not as simple as forswearing new technologies altogether. For one thing, most of them *do* have a real value that it would be foolish to deny. Even for SACRED ACTIVISTS, these technologies have had profoundly positive implications—amplifying our voice, simplifying tedious tasks, connecting us with like-minded changemakers, and allowing us to accomplish more work with less money. Given these benefits, an all-out rejection of new technology would make us comparatively less efficient and increasingly disconnected from our peers.

Instead, we can take a more nuanced approach, one grounded in knowledge of self. By carefully observing how a given tool affects us, we can consciously design our engagement with it to maximize the positive benefits while minimizing side effects. That process begins with the understanding that the ability to use a certain technology doesn't equal the necessity to do so. Just because we can doesn't mean we have to. Instead, it's up to us to think critically about how to use technology on our own terms. We can install apps that distract us with idle consumption or ones that empower us as creators. We can leave our phones at home—or at least in the next room. We can choose to value a deep, restful sleep over the lure of late-night screen time. We can prioritize the time to experience the world around us with "no filter," unmediated by lenses, earbuds, hashtags, or even internal combustion engines.

I've practiced each of the above choices at various times as part of my own efforts toward UNPLUGGING. For many years, I stubbornly chose to take all my notes by hand. I resisted getting a smartphone for many years, and when I finally caved, I was judicious about which apps I chose to install. I've recontextualized the Jewish tradition of Shabbat I was raised with, striving to set aside one day a week to not make any plans and limit my engagement with motors and screens.

That said, there's no single right way to unplug. Each of us needs to make our own choices about how to engage with technology. But the important thing is that we make the choice. Because if we don't, the choice will be made for us.

FURHTER LEARNING

Carr, Nicholas. *The Shallows: What the Internet Is Doing to Our Brains.* New York: W. W. Norton, 2011.

APPLYING THE PATTERN

Track how much time each day you use your tools, and whether you're using them productively or distractedly. Which tools are you overusing? Are there times during the day when you can unplug? Try going a day without using them—how are your behaviors different? How are your patterns of thinking affected?

79. COMMITMENT PRUNING

Take time to reflect on the projects and people that you're invested in, and don't be afraid to cut back those commitments that are no longer serving you.

In ecology, an organism is said to be under stress when it faces a challenge to its well-being. Often, a stress response is produced when an organism reaches a limit with regard to the system it's a part of—a tree dying due to a lack of water, for instance, or a predator going hungry when it has overhunted its prey. From an ecological perspective, our species as a whole certainly seems to fit that description—with a mushrooming population and exponential curve of resource use, we're beginning to hit the limits of what our environment can provide.

If our entire species is under increasing stress, it's no wonder that we each feel stress in our daily lives. Food costs are rising. The cost of living is spiraling upward. Stable employment is harder to come by, and the salaried work that's available has fewer and fewer benefits. Real wages have been on a long and bumpy decline for the last forty years, forcing us to work longer and longer hours just to make ends meet. Pair that with the deluge of messages and requests we receive from advertisers, social media, and the like, and it's no wonder that the routine question "How are you?" is just as likely to be answered with an emphatic "I'm busy!" as it is with "I'm well."

There's no doubt about it—being overextended has become the new normal. And for anybody trying to make the world a better place, the situation is even harder. The work that pays seems inane, and the work that's actually necessary to heal our ecosystems and communities generally has little to no economic value—meaning we're forced into compromising our ethics for a paycheck, learning to live with less, or pursuing our true passions outside of work.

How are we possibly expected to juggle the responsibilities of making ends meet and raising a family while actively helping society move toward a better place? To begin with, it's important to acknowledge that our highest-quality work never happens under prolonged stress. Study after study has confirmed what we all know intuitively: being overextended depresses our mood, makes us less able to think clearly, saps our productivity, and taxes our immune system.

It's clear that reducing our stress should be a primary objective in living a fulfilling life. But if we knew how to reduce our stress, wouldn't we have done it already? Not necessarily. Managing overcommitment takes intention and a certain amount of dedication—dedication that pays off pretty quickly once its benefits accrue.

Consider fruit trees in a neglected orchard. The natural tendency of a fruit tree is to send branches out every which way, each covered with fruit, to maximize the tree's chance of reproductive success. But all those branches are competing for light, which puts stress on each one. Meanwhile, the fruit on those branches have to share a finite supply of nutrients and water drawn up from the roots, with the result that none of them will end up particularly large or tasty. In contrast, the trees in a well-managed orchard are pruned regularly to let in more light and send all the available water and nutrients to the remaining fruit. The result is a crop that's larger, tastier, and healthier than it otherwise would have been.

Similarly, engaging in regular acts of pruning our commitments frees up more time and energy to be spent on the commitments that remain. Using those clippers might feel scary at first, but if they're applied skillfully, the fruits of our labor will be that much more satisfying.

But what is the proper pruning technique? How shall we decide what to keep and what to cut? THE CREATIVE PROCESS can be a helpful starting point. According to that process, the first step is *setting goals:* what, exactly, are we trying to accomplish in all those frenzied hours of waking life? The chances are that the answers are manifold—earning a decent living, raising well-adjusted children, maximizing our positive impact on the world, and so forth. List as many as you can. Which ones can be combined into larger goals? Which ones are most important, and which ones are less so?

Once your goals are listed and prioritized, you can shift to the *analysis and assessment* phase of the process. In this case, this means observing how you actually spend your time and how each activity makes you feel. Start with a big-picture list of all your various commitments and approximately how much time each one consumes. Then, verify those approximations by tracking how you spend your time on a day-to-day basis. You can use the schedule of activities already noted in your day planner or digital calendar as a guide, but be sure to pay attention to the activities not written down as well.

Once you've observed your daily schedule closely, you'll probably notice patterns about how your commitments line up with your goals. How many hours per week are you engaged in volunteer commitments that feel meaningful but don't seem to be going anywhere? How frequently are you hanging out with friends who don't support your personal growth? And how long does that commute actually take, anyhow?

At this point, you're ready to make some tough choices about what to prune. Of course, cutting back a commitment is usually a process that unfolds over months or even years. More often than not, doing so successfully requires some planning as well as clear, honest communication with all parties involved.

APPLYING THE PATTERN

Make a list or a map of your commitments. What needs of yours do they meet? What needs of your community do they meet? How much time do they take up? How do they support or distract from your PERSONAL VISION? Which two or three commitments are most central to your ideals and goals? How can you prune those commitments that are not central in a healthy way?

80. REDUCE THE NEED TO EARN

To the extent that it's realistic in your life, make choices that keep you debt-free and with minimal monthly expenses.

According to the experts, today's economy is pretty good—and for some of us, it actually feels that way. For people in the right place with the right set of skills and privileges, growth industries like fracking, real estate, and tech have provided an engine out of the Great Recession and into a new time of prosperity. But for the rest of us, a deep anxiety continues to permeate our sense of economic security. While the cost of our rent, health care, and education spirals out of control, our paychecks have flatlined or even started to fall—and that's if we're lucky enough to have a steady job. Tens of millions of others are participants in the gig economy, scraping by with whatever combination of short-term jobs they can cobble together.

For more and more Americans, the American dream is slipping away. A 2014 *USA Today* analysis found that a family of four would need to make over $130,000 a year—twice the actual median income—to afford the trappings of a "normal" middle-class life: homeownership, two cars, a college education for their kids, annual vacations, and a cushion for retirement.[123] And while it's possible that sustained investments in vocational training, infrastructure upgrades, or renewable energy might turn things around, it seems just as likely that we've entered a new normal, one in which the intertwined effects of political dysfunction, resource depletion, and climate chaos will make the late twentieth century seem like a Golden Age.

If we can't get what we used to expect, we might need to start expecting something different. Fortunately, even as the old American dream is vanishing, a new one is coming into focus. Rather than accumulating dollars, euros, or yen—and the material comforts they provide—this dream explicitly rejects antimarket currencies in favor of COMMONING: restoring our reserves of the forms of capital that the current economy has worn down. Under this approach, the goal isn't to buy our way to prosperity—it's to create it ourselves, place by place, by building soil and strong community and by restoring a sense of purpose and meaning to our lives. After all, if dollars are at the root of so many of our challenges, why keep ourselves addicted?

To be sure, pursuing this new dream requires a shift in attitude and life-styles—and it won't come easy to many. But for those who embrace the idea of leaving the dollar economy in the dust, all kinds of new opportunities emerge to pursue a life that's much richer in meaning. And for those who already lack the good health, education, or job security that the antimarkets have failed to provide, there's little left to lose.

Reducing the need to earn is a necessarily personal process, and depending on our interests, personalities, responsibilities, and stage in life, it can take any number of forms. It might entail a set of strict goals and budgets, or an informal process of incremental observation and change over time. Even so, those who choose to pursue it are likely to draw from a number of common strategies:

- *Multifamily living.* For most of us, the rent or mortgage represents our largest single expense. Our choices about where and how we live, there-fore, can be one of our biggest leverage points to shift our need to earn. One way to reduce the cost of living is to live with more people. For a cul-ture accustomed to the nuclear family lifestyle, this might seem imma-ture, stressful, or otherwise unpleasant. But thousands of years of history show that it's entirely possible and—when developed with intention—quite desirable. For the millions of people living in collective houses, housing cooperatives, homeshares, cohousing, and intentional commu-nities, living together is much more than just a way of saving money; it's also a way of building INTERDEPENDENT COMMUNITY and flourishing HOUSEHOLD ECONOMIES.

- *Live somewhere cheaper.* While cities offer pleasure and economic opportunity, they also add to our stress, not the least due to the skyrock-eting cost of living in them. Meanwhile, there are thousands of smaller towns and rural communities desperately in need of revitalization. After decades of gentrification in our metropolitan cores, THE EDGE OF CHANGE may be shifting back toward less dense and more affordable set-tlements—and if the past ten millennia are any guide, most of us ought to be living in much smaller communities anyway.

- *Value creation over consumption.* For the last several generations, we've defined ourselves by what we consume—the car we drive, the designer clothes we wear, the food we eat. But a rejection of antimarket economics brings with it an inversion in emphasis from consumption to production. When we reduce the need to earn, we begin to define ourselves by the goods we produce, the commons that we create, and the change we make.

- *Reject new.* There are currently 261.8 million cars, 145 million refrigerators, and 327 million cell phones in the United States—far more than our population needs to get around, store food, and communicate. With the global economy producing more products than we could ever need, there are plenty of perfectly good items floating around in thrift stores, flea markets, garage sales, and online. Living a secondhand lifestyle is both financially efficient and ethically sound.

- *Join or create mutual aid networks.* Among the many roles social societies like the Masons and Kiwanis played in the nineteenth and twentieth centuries was assistance with big expenses. Members' annual dues acted like a self-contained insurance pool, supporting medical bills, funeral costs, and business loans. Today, lending circles in the developing world act similarly, especially by giving women in poverty a critical boost. In tightly knit communities, these kinds of institutions can play the same role for us, relying on the fortune and good will of the community to help each of us weather our individual ups and downs.

- *Purchase in bulk.* Economies of scale aren't just for businesses. Individuals and families can also save substantial amounts by cutting out intermediary retailers and purchasing large quantities of essential items from wholesalers. This is a natural fit for multifamily living situations, where enough of a micro-market exists to justify frequent bulk purchases. But even conventional nuclear families can participate in this cost-saving strategy by joining or forming buying clubs that source produce, dry goods, toiletries, and other household items directly from distributors.

- *Fewer products, more services.* Many of the consumer goods we're led to believe that we each require actually sit idle 99 percent of the time. Instead of every home paying to own its own sewing machine, lawnmower, or car, groups of households can pool their resources to purchase these products collectively and pay a much smaller fee to rent them exactly when they need them. We already do this with books in the form of public libraries—why not extend the idea to other items? These sorts of "dematerialization" schemes have been kicking around in sustainability circles for over a decade, but the increasing availability and flexibility of peer-to-peer platforms are making them easier to implement than ever. Tool libraries have emerged in dozens of cities across the country, allowing members to save the hundreds of dollars it would take to buy tools by paying an annual fee to have access to a full array of them. Thanks to antimarket investment capital, car sharing is already becoming mainstream, although many peer-to-peer solutions exist for it, too.

- *Forage.* For most of our species' history, we managed to meet our needs quite well through hunting and gathering. You might say that we have the foraging instinct in our bones. And while we don't have the skills, intact ecosystems, or population densities to support hunting and gathering in the wild anymore, there's plenty to be found by foraging in our human-made environments. Most cities have hundreds of fruit trees in public rights-of-way, while the wasteful flow of our current urban ecosystems result in torrents of completely usable construction materials, furniture, and organic matter ready for the taking in alleyways and dumpsters across the country. Once we get over our culturally inherited revulsion of "waste" and learn to see these items as resources ready to forage, whole new realms of opportunity open up for creative reuse.

- *Practice preventative health care.* Even for those fully able to partake in the twentieth-century American dream, our present-day health care system is a mess of escalating prices and byzantine regulations. The more we take our physical and mental health into our own hands, the less we need to rely on hospitals and emergency rooms. Whether it's studying herbalism, bartering with massage therapists, or simply eating fewer processed foods, we all have opportunities to save thousands by investing in our own good health.

- *Exchange differently.* For all the ways we can reduce the amounts and costs of our transactions, there will always be a need for economic exchange. But even many these transactions can escape the dollar system through the use of bartering, GIFTING, lending circles, cryptocurrencies, time banks, and other HEIRLOOM CURRENCIES—most of which have the added benefit of restoring social capital at the same time.

- *Travel differently.* More often than not, today's vacations involve plane flights, hotel stays, and fancy restaurants—expenses that quickly accumulate into the thousands. But there are many ways to explore the world on a much cheaper budget. We can avoid the financial and ecological costs of air travel and instead traverse the ground on trains, buses, and bicycles. We can forego exotic locales, instead choosing to acquaint ourselves with the subtle wonders in our own vicinity. We can leverage our social capital and online tools to find like-minded folks to stay with for free. Not only do these choices save us our hard-earned money, but they also give us a more grounded and authentic perspective of place.

APPLYING THE PATTERN

Observe or develop a budget of your financial capital flows. Where are the outflows? Which outflows can be reduced now, and which can you reduce with a long-term plan? Which of the strategies above can you use to reduce your outflows?

81. PERSONAL MYTHOLOGY

Use the motifs of your own heritage and life path to create meaning from the present and direction for your future.

The work of the SACRED ACTIVIST can be lonely and confusing. We forego opportunities for companionship and material wealth for what can seem like impossible dreams. Our hopes for a better world can feel eroded by endless hours of mundane tasks. And no matter how hard we work toward a vision of a different world, society at large often seems to be getting worse and worse. Amid these choppy waters, TELLING THE STORY can act as an anchor, giving us meaning and reminding us of our greater purpose as healers. And as it turns out, the narratives we create about ourselves—our own private stories—are just as important as those stories about the world that we share with the people around us. By placing the twists and turns of our own lives into a timeless narrative arc and character archetypes, we center ourselves within the larger patterns of the world around us.

It's no surprise, then, that personal mythologies have been a common feature of many cultures for millennia. Most early empires of the Middle East and Mediterranean shared a belief in invisible spirits that followed individuals around; Greeks called them *daemonia,* Romans *genii,* and Arabs *djinn.* The Hindu pantheon of thousands of deities, meanwhile, represents a spectrum of the supernatural, with omnipotent gods like Shiva and Vishnu complemented by hyper-local spirits worshipped by individual clans or towns. And indigenous cultures from Australia to West Africa to the Pacific Northwest are enlivened by sacred places, objects, or spirits that anthropologists call *totems.*

Today, the continuity of blood descent that defined many of these systems has eroded. And for many, the idea of real-life daemons or totems acting as guardian spirits sounds superstitious or silly. But removed from its animistic context, the idea of applying myth and legend to an individual story nevertheless remains potent. We don't need to believe in the supernatural to understand that our own life story fits into well-worn tropes, or that the ups and downs of our fortunes can be tied to larger narratives of meaning. Here are five ways of bringing the idea of a PERSONAL MYTHOLOGY into your own life:

- *Name your own patterns.* Use journaling, dialogue with people in your zone of intimacy, meditation, or other grounding rituals to identify patterns that are unique to your own personality and life path. Once those patterns have been identified, give them names that resonate with meaning.

- *Cultivate sacred objects.* Find physical objects to represent key attitudes, places, or people that you hold dear, and keep them in a special place in your home. Return to those objects in moments of reflection, confusion, or inspiration.

- *Develop a creation myth.* Write or draw a narrative of your life up to this point. What have been the key moments that have made you who you are? What are the events, locales, and ideas that have shaped your path?

- *See yourself in nature.* Choose an ISITE to go to on a regular basis, and use the time spent there to reflect on your own changing relationship with natural systems.

- *Best and worst selves.* Take a few minutes to consider a few times when you've been your very best self. What were the qualities and attitudes you possessed? What practices did you participate in? What people were supporting you? Now think about times when you've been at your worst. How did you interact with yourself and the world around you? Turn these best and worst selves into characters. Flesh them out by drawing them, making masks of their faces, or acting them out.

APPLYING THE PATTERN

Where do you come from? Who are your ancestors, and what did they believe? How did you come to believe what you do? What point in the narrative are you in currently? If you could choose, how would you write the ending?

82. DESIGN TOOL: PERSONAL VISION

Each one of us must cultivate his or her own vision of a more perfect world in order to bring that vision about.

Nearly every organization that aims to make the world a better place has a vision of the world they seek—a mission statement summarizing the change they are trying to accomplish. This can be a short phrase or an entire paragraph. It can be modest in scope or—more frequently—it can be wildly implausible. But practicality isn't the point. Instead, the value of the mission statement lies in acting as a compass point, keeping the organization moving in the right direction. It provides a simple way for everyone to understand and focus on the organization's purpose, from the organization's leaders to the people it serves and the people contributing financially to make it a success.

If mission statements are such an effective tool for organizations, why shouldn't people have them too? Crafting a personal vision can help us clarify our strengths and goals and recognize our potential allies as we each find our niche in making a better world. Amid the myriad distractions, stressors, and countervailing forces in our lives, visions can help keep us grounded and focused on our long-term goals.

Given its personal nature, the way a vision sounds—and the way it's created—should fit your personality like a glove. Below are three different processes (one reflective, one artistic, and one embodied) for developing a personal vision. You can explore these processes privately—in a journal or quiet contemplation, or you can discuss them with a dialogue partner or small group. And remember that these processes are just a starting point. Look them over and then create your own recipe for making a vision statement based on what you see!

Reflective:

> What is the world you want to leave for to the next generation?
>
> What values, if any, are you willing to die for?

What things about our current world do you treasure and want to preserve?

What things about our current world do you want to work to dismantle?

What people, places, cultures, and historical eras are you most inspired by? What about them inspires you?

Artistic:

Make a drawing, collage, or Pinterest board of the world you want to leave for the next generation.

Place the finished product in a place that you'll see regularly. Use it as part of your grounding ritual.

Embodied:

Think back to times in your life when you've felt the most inspired. Who were you with? What did it feel like?

be like a tree: mighty but patient, generous to all, graceful in calamity

Once you've written your vision statement, consider ways to integrate it into your RITUAL AND CEREMONY. Perhaps you could look it over at the start of each week or at the beginning of a new project. Maybe you can memorize all or part of it and recite it in the shower. Keep in mind, also, that visions are always evolving. Take the time to return to your vision once or twice a year and see which parts of it need revising.

NOTES

1   Thomas Jefferson, "Letter to John Jay, Paris, August 23, 1785," the Avalon Project, Yale Law School, http://avalon.law.yale.edu/18th_century/let32.asp.

2   Omid Kardan, Peter Gozdyra, Bratislav Misic, Faisal Moola, Lyle J. Palmer, Tomas Paus, and Marc G. Berman, "Neighborhood Greenspace and Health in a Large Urban Center," *Scientific Reports* 5 (2015).

3   Jill Suttie, "We Know Nature Makes Us Happier. Now Science Says It Makes Us Kinder Too," *Yes! Magazine*, March 12, 2016, www.yesmagazine .org/planet/we-know-nature-makes-us-happier-now-science-says-it-makes -us-kinder-too-20160312.

4   Patricia Taylor, Burke D. Grandjean, and James H. Gramann, *National Park Service Comprehensive Survey of the American Public 2008–2009: Racial and Ethnic Diversity of National Park System Visitors and Non-Visitors* (Laramie: Wyoming Survey and Analysis Center, University of Wyoming).

5   David Bollier and Silke Helfrich, ed., *Patterns of Commoning* (Amherst, MA: Commons Strategy Group, 2015), 272.

6   Ibid., 36.

7   Ibid., 52.

8   W.-X. Zhou, D. Sornette, R. A. Hill, and R. I. Dunbar, "Discrete Hierarchical Organization of Social Group Sizes," *Proceedings of the Royal Society of Biology* 272 (2005): 439–44.

9   Robin Dunbar, *Grooming, Gossip, and the Evolution of Language* (Cambridge, MA: Harvard University Press, 1998), 76.

10 Christopher Alexander, *A Pattern Language* (New York: Oxford University Press, 1977), 71.

11 Stephen Schneck, "What Is Subsidiarity?" *The Catholic University of America*, June 2, 2011, ipr.cua.edu/blogs/post.cfm/what-is-subsidiarity.

12 Manuel De Landa, "Markets, Antimarkets, and Network Economics," www.cddc.vt.edu/host/delanda/pages/markets.htm.

13 Hakim Bey, *T.A.Z.: The Temporary Autonomous Zone, Ontological Anarchy, Poetic Terrorism* (Brooklyn: Autonomedia, 2003).

14 Moyna Baker, "1,500 Scientists Lift the Lid on Reproducibility," *Nature* 533 (2016): 452–54, http://www.nature.com/news/1-500-scientists-lift-the -lid-on-reproducibility-1.19970.

15 "Sam Cooke: Portrait of a Legend," *NPR's Morning Edition,* July 30, 2003, www.npr.org/templates/story/story.php?storyId=1369740.

16 Nancy C. Andreason, "Secrets of the Creative Brain," *Atlantic,* July-August 2014, www.theatlantic.com/magazine/archive/2014/07/secrets-of-the -creative-brain/372299.

17 Douglas Schuler, *Liberating Voices: A Pattern Language for Communication Revolution* (Cambridge, MA: MIT Press, 2008), 146.

18 Donella Meadows, "Leverage Points: Places to Intervene in a System," *The Sustainability Institute,* 1999.

19 Kevin Carrico, "Ritual," *Cultural Anthropology.*

20 Starhawk, *The Spiral Dance* (New York: HarperOne, 1979), 141

21 L. Vinsel, and A. Russell, "Hail the Maintainers," *Aeon,* April 2016, https: //aeon.co/essays/innovation-is-overvalued-maintenance-often-matters-more.

22 A. Aron, T. McLaughlin-Volpe, Stephen C. Wright, and Stacy A. Ropp, "The Extended Contact Effect: Knowledge of Cross-Group Friendships and Prejudice," *Journal of Personality and Social Psychology* 73, no. 1 (1997): 73-90; R. Mendoza-Denton and E. Page-Gould, "With a Little Help From My Cross-Group Friend: Reducing Anxiety in Intergroup Contexts Through Cross-Group Friendship," *Journal of Personality and Social Psychology* 95, no. 5 (2008): 1080–94, http://liz.nfshost.com/documents/Page-Gould _Mendoza Denton_Tropp_2008.pdf.

23 Krista Tippett, "James Doty—The Magic Shop Of The Brain," *On Being* (podcast), www.onbeing.org/program/james-doty-the-magic-shop-of-the -brain/transcript/8418.

24 Jonathan Matthew Smucker, "Principle: Seek Common Ground," *Beautiful Trouble,* http://beautifultrouble.org/principle/seek-common-ground.

25 Santa Fe Institute, "Cities, Scaling, and Sustainability," www.santafe.edu /research/cities-scaling-and-sustainability.

26 Robert D. Putnam, *Bowling Alone: The Collapse and Revival of American Community* (New York: Simon and Schuster, 2000), 206.

27 Elizabeth Pinnington, Josh Lerner, and Daniel Schugurensky, "Participatory Budgeting in North America: The Case of Guelph, Canada," *Journal of Public Budgeting, Accounting, and Financial Management* 21, no. 3 (2009).

28 Andrea J. Nightingale, "Commons and Alternative Rationalities: Subjectivity, Emotion and the (Non)rational Commons," in *Patterns of Commoning*, edited by David Bollier and Silke Helfrich (Amherst, MA: Commons Strategy Group and Off the Common Press, 2015).

29 Friends of the MST, "What Is the MST?" http://www.mstbrazil.org/content /what-mst.

30 David Bollier, "Co-operative Place Making Through Community Land Trusts," *bollier.org* (blog), December 5, 2013, http://bollier.org/blog /co-operative-place-making-through-community-land-trusts-0.

31 Lao Tzu, *Tao Te Ching*, trans. by Stephen Mitchell (London: Frances Lincoln, 2009), poem 74.

32 Maria J. Stephan and Erica Chenoweth, "Why Civil Resistance Works," *International Security* (2008): 8.

33 Srdja Popovic, *Blueprint for Revolution: How to Use Rice Pudding, Lego Men, and Other Nonviolent Techniques to Galvanize Communities, Overthrow Dictators, or Simply Change the World* (New York: Spiegel and Grau, 2015), 175.

34 Jamie Washington and Nancy J. Evans, "Becoming an Ally," *Readings for Diversity and Social Justice: An Anthology on Racism, Antisemitism, Sexism, Heterosexism, Ableism, and Classism*, ed. by Maurianne Adams, Warren J. Blumenfeld, Rosie Castañeda, Heather W. Hackman, Madeline L. Peters, and Ximena Zúñiga (New York: Routledge, 2000), 312–18.

35 Chris Dixon, "Ten Things to Remember: Anti-Racist Strategies for White Student Radicals," SOA Watch, http://soaw.org/index.php?option =com_content&view=article&id=491.

36 JLove Calderón and Marcella Runell Hall, *Love, Race and Liberation: 'Til the White Day is Done* (New York: Love-N-Liberation Press, 2010), 67.

37 Popovic, *Blueprint for Revolution,* 110.

38 Stephen Duncombe, "Theory: Ethical Spectacle," *Beautiful Trouble,* http://beautifultrouble.org/theory/ethical-spectacle.

39 Braden G. King, "The Tactical Disruptiveness of Social Movements: Sources of Market and Mediated Disruption in Corporate Boycotts." *Social Problems* 58, No. 4 (November 2011): 491–517.

40 Philippe Delacote, "Are Consumer Boycotts Effective?" presented at THEMA Research Seminar, Universite de Cerge, France, March 2006.

41 Shane Burley, "Historic Justice for Janitors Campaign Inspires a New Generation of Janitorial Organizing," *Waging Nonviolence,* June 22, 2016, http://wagingnonviolence.org/feature/justice-for-janitors-seiu-raise-america.

42 Steve Early, "Strike Lessons from the Past 25 Years: Walking Out and Winning," *Against the Current* 124, September-October 2006, www.solidarity-us.org/node/113.

43 Emily Wilson, "What Made the Chicago Teachers' Strike a Success? Their Commitment to the Community." *AlterNet,* April 16, 2014, www.alternet.org/education/what-made-chicago-teachers-strike-success-their-commitment-community. An interview with Micah Uetricht, author of *Strike for America: Chicago Teachers Against Austerity.*

44 Krista Tippett, "Rachel Yehuda: How Trauma And Resilience Cross Generations," *On Being* (podcast), 2015, www.onbeing.org/program/rachel-yehuda-how-trauma-and-resilience-cross-generations/transcript/7791.

45 Douglas Shuler, *Liberating Voices: A Pattern Language for Communication Revolution* (Cambridge, MA: MIT Press, 2008), 259.

46 Yessina Funes, "Finally, the US Steps Closer to Racial Healing with a National Truth and Reconciliation Commission," *Yes! Magazine,* April 13, 2016, www.yesmagazine.org/peace-justice/finally-the-us-steps-closer-to-racial-healing-with-a-national-truth-and-reconciliation-commission-20160413.

47 Alice P. Julier, *Eating Together: Food, Friendship, and Inequality* (Urbana: University of Illinois Press, 2013).

48 *U.S. Grocery Shopper Trends 2015.* Food Marketing Institute.

49 Lynn Wu, Benjamin N. Waber, Sinan Aral, Erik Brynjolfsson, and Alex
    Pentland, "Mining Face-to-Face Interaction Networks Using Sociometric
    Badges: Predicting Productivity in an IT Configuration Task," May 7, 2008,
    http://ssrn.com/abstract=1130251.

50 Rieva Lesonsky, "Not Socializing at Work Could Be Hazardous to Your
    Health: Survey Says," *Huffington Post,* October 3, 2011, www.huffingtonpost
    .com/2011/10/03/socializing-at-work_n_958716.html.

51 Scott Lawson and Lloyd Martin, "Risk Taking and Rites of Passage,"
    Reclaiming Children and Youth (2012): 38.

52 David G. Blumenkrantz and Marc B. Goldstein, "Seeing College as a Rite
    of Passage: What Might Be Possible," *New Directions for Higher Education*
    (2014): 88.

53 Lawson and Martin, "Risk Taking and Rites of Passage," 39.

54 Rebecca Solnit, *A Paradise Built in Hell* (New York: Penguin, 2009), 2.

55 Solnit, *A Paradise Built in Hell,* 7.

56 Michael I. Norton and Francesca Gino, "Rituals Alleviate Grieving for
    Loved Ones, Lovers, and Lotteries," *Journal of Experimental Psychology*
    143, no. 1 (2014): 266–72.

57 Nicole Vosper, "Overcoming Burnout, Part 7—Composting Grief," *Empty
    Cages Design* (blog), April 25, 2016, www.emptycagesdesign.org
    /overcoming-burnout-part-7-composting-grief.

58 Srdja Popovic and Matthew Miller, *Blueprint for Revolution* (New York:
    Speigel and Grau, 2015), 52.

59 Jo Freeman, "The Tyranny of Structurelessness," *The Second Wave* 2, no. 1
    (1972): 20.

60 Amy B., Brunell, William A. Gentry, W. Keith Campbell, Brian J. Hoffman,
    Karl W. Kuhnert, and Kenneth G. DeMarree, "Leader Emergence: The Case
    of the Narcissistic Leader," *Personality and Social Psychology Bulletin* 34,
    no. 12 (2008): 1663–76.

61 Iain D. Couzin and Albert B. Kao, "Decision Accuracy in Complex Environ-
    ments Is Often Maximized by Small Group Sizes," *Proceedings of the Royal
    Academy B.* 281, no. 1784 (2014), http://rspb.royalsocietypublishing.org
    /content/281/1784/20133305.full.

62 D. H. Gruenfeld and L. Z. Tiedens, "Organizational Preferences and Their Consequences," in *Handbook of Social Psychology,* edited by S. T. Fiske, D. T. Gilbert, and G. Lindsay (New York: Wiley, 2010).

63 Marcia W. Blenko, Michael C. Mankins, and Paul Rogers, *Decide and Deliver: Five Steps to Breakthrough Performance in Your Organization* (Boston: Bain, 2010).

64 Rachel Gillett, "Productivity Hack of the Week: The Two-Pizza Approach to Productive Teamwork," *Fast Company,* October 24, 2014, www .fastcompany.com/3037542/productivity-hack-of-the-week-the-two-pizza -approach-to-productive-teamwork.

65 Warren D. Smith, "Range Voting," November 28, 2000, http://citeseerx .ist.psu.edu/viewdoc/download;jsessionid=B4BFE045907B6A9AD0A1D- 9C50A55C21C?doi=10.1.1.32.9150&rep=rep1&type=pdf.

66 Lottie L. Joiner, "Black May Not Crack, But We're Aging Faster Inside," *The Root,* November 20, 2013, www.theroot.com/articles/culture/2013/11 /black_women_and_health_extreme_stress_causes_accelerated_ biological_aging.html.

67 Transition United States teleseminar, November 4, 2015, www.transitionus .org/sites/default/files/Just_Transition_transcript_1.26.pdf.

68 Transition United States teleseminar.

69 "Jemez Principles for Democratic Organizing," adopted at the Working Group Meeting for Globalization and Trade, Jemez, New Mexico, December 6–8, 1996.

70 Glenn R. Carroll, "Dynamics of Publisher Succession in Newspaper Organizations," *Administrative Science Quarterly,* 29 (1984): 93–113.

71 D. R. Dalton, "CEO Tenure, Boards of Directors, and Acquisition Performance," *Journal of Business Research* 60 (2006): 331–38, quoted in Donald DePamphilis, *Mergers and Acquisitions Basics: All You Need to Know* (Academic Press, 2010), 217.

72 Susan K. Stevens, *Nonprofit Lifecycles—Stage-Based Wisdom for Nonprofit Capacity* (Wayzata, MN: Stagewise Enterprises), 2001.

73 "Magic of the Facilitator," the Canadian Institute of Cultural Affairs, 2009, https://icausa.memberclicks.net/assets/docs/whitepaper%20-%20 magic%20of%20the%20facilitator.pdf.

74   Brian Stanfield, "Magic of the Facilitator," International Association of Facilitators, http://growpartnerships.com/pages/resource-library /articles-of-interest.php.

75   Jack Zimmerman and Virginia Coyle, *The Way of Council* (Bramble Books, 2009), 4.

76   The Center for Contemplative Mind in Society. "Council Circle." Web. May 23, 2016.

77   Damon Centola, "The Social Origins of Networks and Diffusion," *American Journal of Sociology* 120, no. 5 (2015): 1295–338.

78   J. L. Bell, "Colonial Boston Vocabulary: 'caucus' part 2," *Boston 1775* (blog), January 7, 2008, http://boston1775.blogspot.com/2008/01/colonial -boston-vocabulary-caucus-part.html.

79   William Harris, "The Caucus: History and Etymology," *Middlebury College,* http://community.middlebury.edu/~harris/caucus.html.

80   Karryn Olson-Ramanujan, "Best Practices to Support Women in Permaculture" *Permaculture Design* No. 98, Winter 2015: 42–47.

81   Ngọc Loan Trần, "Calling IN: A Less Disposable Way Of Holding Each Other Accountable," *Black Girl Dangerous,* December 18, 2013, www .blackgirldangerous.org/2013/12/calling-less-disposable-way-holding -accountable.

82   Tochluk, Shelly. *Witnessing Whiteness: The Need To Talk about Race and How to Do It,* 2nd ed. (Plymouteh: Rowman and Littlefield, 2010), 219.

83   Michelle Alexander, *The New Jim Crow: Mass Incarceration in the Age of Colorblindness* (New York: New Press, 2012).

84   A. Goldstein, *Restorative Practices in Israel: The State of the Field,* paper presented at the Eighth International Conference on Conferencing, Circles and other Restorative Practices, Bethlehem, PA, October 2006.

85   Brock-Utne, Birgit, *Indigenous Conflict Resolution in Africa,* paper presented at Seminar on Indigenous Conflict Resolution, University of Oslo, February 2001.

86   Roujanavong, W., "Restorative Justice: Family and Community Group Conferencing (FCGC) in Thailand," paper presented at the Seventh International Conference Defining Restorative Conferencing, Circles and other Restorative Practices, Manchester, UK, November 2005.

87 J. Metoui, "Returning to the Circle: The Reemergence of Traditional Dispute Resolution in Native American Communities," *Journal of Dispute Resolution* 2, no. 6 (2007).

88 N. Rodriguez, "Restorative Justice at Work: Examining the Impact of Restorative Justice Resolutions on Juvenile Recidivism," *Crime and Delinquency* 53 (July 2007): 355–79.

89 E. Richmond, "When Restorative Justice in Schools Works," *Atlantic,* December 29, 2015.

90 W. C. Kim and R. Mauborgne. "Fair Process: Managing in the Knowledge Economy," *Harvard Business Review,* January 2003.

91 Ted Wachtel, "Defining Restorative." International Institute for Restorative Practices, www.iirp.edu/what-we-do/what-is-restorative-practices /defining-restorativ

92 C. A. Gregory, *Gifts and Commodities* (London: Academic Press, 1982).

93 Douglas Rushkoff, *Throwing Rocks at the Google Bus* (New York: Portfolio/ Penguin, 2016), 131.

94 Katie Gilbert, "Why Local Currencies Could Be On The Rise In The U.S.— And Why It Matters," *Forbes,* September 22, 2014, www.forbes.com/sites /katiegilbert/2014/09/22/why-local-currencies-could-be-on-the-rise -in-the-u-s-and-why-it-matters.

95 Bernard Lietaer, "The Story of Curitiba in Brazil," *Currency Solutions for a Wiser World,* September 8, 2010, www.lietaer.com/2010/09 /the-story-of-curitiba-in-brazil.

96 Community Currencies in Action, *People Powered Money: Designing, Developing, and Delivering Community Currencies* (London: New Economics Foundation, 2015).

97 Greco, Thomas, *Money: Understanding and Creating Alternatives to Legal Tender* (White River Junction, VT: Chelsea Green Publishing Company, 2001).

98 Schneider, Nathan, "After the Bitcoin Gold Rush," *New Republic,* February 24, 2015, https://newrepublic.com/article/121089/how-small-bitcoin -miners-lose-crypto-currency-boom-bust-cycle.

99 Diana Ngo, "Deloitte Report: 'State-Sponsored Cryptocurrencies' Will Become Reality in 5 Years Time," *CoinJournal,* March 7, 2016,

http://coinjournal.net/deloitte-report-state-sponsored-cryptocurrencies
-will-become-reality-in-5-years-time.

[100] The Giving Institute, "Giving USA 2015 press release." June 16, 2015,
www.givinginstitute.org/?page=GUSA2015Release.

[101] Jason J. Kilborn, "The 5000-Year Circle of Debt Clemency: From Sumer
and Babylon to America and Europe" *Nederlands Tijdschrift voor Burgerlijk
Recht,* 2013, http://ssrn.com/abstract=2165581,

[102] A. Brown, *Just Enough: Lessons in Living Green from Rural Japan* (New
York, Kodansha International, 2011).

[103] Ann Crittenden, *The Price of Motherhood: Why the Most Important Job In
the World Is Still the Last Valued* (New York: Henry Holt, 2001).

[104] Indradeep Ghosh, "Social Wealth Economic Indicators," Center for Partnership Studies, November 2014, http://caringeconomy.org/wp-content
/uploads/2015/03/Social-Wealth-Economic-Indicators-Full-Report-20152.pdf.

[105] "Independent BC: Small Business and the British Columbia Economy," Civic
Economics, 2013, http://nebula.wsimg.com/31f003d5633c543438ef0a
5ca8e8289f?AccessKeyId=8E410A17553441C49302&disposition
=0&alloworigin=1.

[106] Jane Jacobs, *Cities and the Wealth of Nations* (New York: Random House,
1984), 143.

[107] Michael Shuman, "Going Local: New Opportunities for Community
Economics," speech at the Community Land Trust of the Southern Berk-
shires Annual Meeting, Great Barrington, MA, January 2002, www
.centerforneweconomics.org/publications/lectures/shuman/michael
/going-local.

[108] Rushkoff, *Throwing Rocks at the Google Bus,* 219–20.

[109] Cooperative Development Institute, "Ask Co-op Cathy: What's the
Difference Between a Worker Co-op and an ESOP?" October 29, 2014,
http://cdi.coop/coop-cathy-worker-coops-esops-difference.

[110] National Center for Employee Ownership, "A Brief Overview of Employee
Ownership in the U.S.," 2014.

[111] Silke Helfrich, "Venezuela: 'We Are One Big Conversation,'" *The Green
Political Foundation,* January 21, 2016, www.boell.de/en/2016/01/21
/venezuela-we-are-one-big-conversation.

112 "U.S. Worker Cooperatives: A State of the Sector." The Democracy at Work Institute, March 9, 2016, http://institute.coop/news/us-worker-cooperatives-state-sector.

113 National Low Income Housing Coalition, *The Gap: The Affordable Housing Gap Analysis 2016* (Washington, DC: The National Low Income Housing Coalition, 2016), 3.

114 Aurand, *The Gap*, 4.

115 World Food Programme, "Hunger Map 2015," www.wfp.org/content/hunger-map-2015.

116 Joanna Macy, "Three Dimensions of the Great Turning," www.joannamacy.net/thegreatturning/three-dimensions-of-the-great-turning.html.

117 Douglas Schuler, *Liberating Voices: A Pattern Language for Communication Revolution* (Cambridge, MA: MIT Press, 2008), 175.

118 Yuval Harari, *Sapiens: A Brief History of Humankind* (New York: HarperCollins, 2015).

119 Bonita Ford, "Thrivelihood Interview with Bonita Ford," by Karryn Olson-Ramanujan, http://seedsustainabilityconsulting.com/interview-bonita-members.

120 Looby Macnamara, *People and Permaculture* (East Meon, England: Permanent, 2012), 35.

121 Evelyn L. Rhodes, Robert Dreibelbis, Elizabeth Klasen, Neha Naithani, Joyce Baliddawa, Diana Menya, Subarna Khatry, Stephanie Levy, James M. Tielsch, J. Jaime Miranda, Caitlin Kennedy, and William Checkley, "Behavioral Attitudes and Preferences in Cooking Practices with Traditional Open-Fire Stoves in Peru, Nepal, and Kenya: Implications for Improved Cookstove Interventions," *International Journal of Environmental Research and Public Health* 11, no. 10 (2014): 10310–26.

122 Alëna Konyk, "iSite Basics: Everything You Always Wanted to Know About iSite* (*But Were Afraid to Ask)," *Biology to Design* (blog), August 19, 2011, https://biologytodesign.wordpress.com/2011/08/19/isite-basics-everything-you-always-wanted-to-know-about-isite-but-were-afraid-to-ask.

123 Neal Gabler, "The Secret Shame of Middle-Class Americans," *Atlantic*, May 2016, www.theatlantic.com/magazine/archive/2016/05/my-secret-shame/476415.

INDEX

A

abundance. *See* SPIRALS OF
    ABUNDANCE
Ace Hardware, 295
ACTIONS, NOT INTENTIONS,
    333–35
activism. *See* SACRED
    ACTIVISM
Adbusters magazine, 131
Ahupua'a, 15–16
Airbnb, 113
Alexander, Christopher, xxii,
    xxiii, 3, 33, 107
Alexander, Michelle, 240
Alinsky, Saul, 211, 212
allyship, 126–28, 214
Anabaptists, 5, 6
analysis
    CAPITAL ANALYSIS, 303–4,
        331
    CREATIVE PROCESS and,
        63–64, 303–4
    NETWORK ANALYSIS, 73–76
    POWER ANALYSIS, 163–66,
        331
    SECTOR AND ZONE
        ANALYSIS, 68–72
    TEAM ANALYSIS, 249–50,
        331
Andersen, Hans Christian, 133
Andreasen, Nancy, 65
Angelou, Maya, 180
Anonymous, 131
Anthony, Susan B., 183
antifragility, 117
antimarkets
    COMMONING vs., 43
    concept of, 41

DETHRONING THE
    ANTIMARKETS, 39–42,
    133
    markets vs., 40
anti-Semitism, 140
apartheid, 137, 141
apprentices, 181–82
Arab Spring, 37
Aristotle, 99–100
Arjuna, 318
ARTS OF RESISTANCE, 123,
    130–32
Assad, Bashar Al-, 135
Assange, Julian, 134, 181
assessment, 195, 209
Asset-Based Community
    Development, 303
AS220, 286
Augustine, Saint, 57
autonomous zones, 43–46,
    266

B

Bane, Peter, xxii
basemaps, 305
Beautiful Trouble, 102
Benyus, Janine, 336
Berry, Wendell, 47, 98, 121
Bey, Hakim 43, 44
Beyoncé, 130
Bezos, Jeff, 179
biomimicry, 337–38
Biomimicry Institute, 112
BIOPHILIA, 8–10
Bitcoin, 262
Black Lives Matter, xx, 130
Black Panthers, 212
Blasi, Joseph, 298

Blenko, Marcia, 179
Blumenkrantz, David, 148
Boal, Augusto, 77, 131
Bollier, David, 20, 22
Boycott, Captain Charles, 136
boycotts, 136–37, 138
Brackett, Stephen, 130
brainstorming
    location for, 225
    tributary, 208
Brand, Russell, 181
Brand, Stewart, 6
branding, 131
BREAKING BREAD, 143–44
Brown, Azby, 272
Brown, Brené, 314
Brown, Tim, 60
Brunell, Amy, 172
budgeting, participatory,
    108–9
Burning Man, 44
Burns, Ken, 184
BUSINESS MODEL CANVAS,
    305–11
business polycultures,
    281–82

C

Cahn, Edgar, 261
Calderón, JLove, 127
CALLING OUT, CALLING IN,
    236–39
Campbell, Joseph, 86
Canadian Institute of Cultural
    Affairs, 226
capital
    autonomous zones and, 45,
        46, 266

capital, *continued*
  CAPITAL ANALYSIS, 303–4,
    331
  eight forms of, 16–20, 21
  FINANCIAL RAM PUMPS and,
    265–67
  meaning of, 252
Carnaval, 44
Carrico, Kevin, 93
Carter, Jimmy, 180
Castile, Philando, 333
THE CAUCUS, 234–35
Cecosesola, 21, 297
celebrations, 145–47, 208
Center for Story-Based
  Strategy, 86, 88
Centola, Damon, 234
ceremony. *See* rituals
change
  THE EDGE OF CHANGE, 50–52
  fear and, 58
  Overton window and,
    50–52
Charm City, 114
Chatham House Rule, 222
Chavez, Cesar, 137, 143
Chenoweth, Erica, 123
Cincinnati Time store, 261
CIRCLE DIALOGUE, 229–33
cities
  paradoxes presented by,
    104–5
  SLOW CITIES, 104–6
CITIZEN GOVERNANCE, 107–11
City Repair movement, 108,
  109, 114
Clark, Dick, 63
Coalition of Immokalee
  Farmworkers, 212
Coates, Ta-Nehisi, 184
collaborative action, 199, 209
collaborators, 310
colonization, 81
comedy, 131
commitments
  COMMITMENT PRUNING,
    344–46
  common community, 222–23
commonalities, focusing on,
  102–3
COMMONING, 15–22
  antimarket forces vs., 43

INFRASTRUCTURE
  COMMONS, 112–15
community
  common commitments for,
    222–23
  COMMUNITY-SUPPORTED
    ENTERPRISE, 266,
    293–95, 296
  GOING HOME, 47–49
  INTERDEPENDENT
    COMMUNITIES, 11–14
  KNOW YOUR COMMUNITY,
    329–32
  loss of, 11
  meaning of, 11–12
  THE RIGHT SIZE, 23–26
  weak vs. strong, 13
Community Exchange
  System, 261
competitors, 309–10
conditional scale pricing,
  301–2
confidentiality, 222
conflict transformation, 185,
  198–99, 209, 240
CONSENSUAL HIERARCHIES,
  174–76
consensus, decision making
  by, 203, 205
CONVERGE AND DISPERSE,
  207–10
Cooke, Sam, 63
cooperation, zone of, 30, 34,
  209
co-ops, 286, 294–95, 297–98
COORDINATED
  NONCOMPLIANCE, 136–39
council dialogues, 230
Couzin, Iain, 174
Coyle, Virginia, 230
The Creative Commons
  licensing system, 21
CREATIVE DESTRUCTION,
  116–20, 157
CREATIVE PROCESS, 60–67,
  303–4, 345
Crittenden, Ann, 273
cross-compensation, 286
crowdfunding, 294
crowdwise process, 206
Cruz, Cesar A., 130
Cruz, Ted, 181

cryptocurrencies, 262, 263
currencies
  central, 258, 265
  crypto-, 262, 263
  dollars, 252, 258–59
  exchange, 252
  HEIRLOOM CURRENCIES,
    258–64
  local cash, 259–60, 262
  meaning of, 252
  mutual credit, 260–61, 263,
    290
  time banks, 261, 263

D

The Daily Show, 134
Dalai Lama, 187
Darwin, Charles, 117
Davis, Angela, 181
death, 159, 161
de Beauvoir, Simone, 184
Debt Collective, 270
DEBT FORGIVENESS, 268–71
decision making
  consensus process for,
    203, 205
  crowdwise process for, 206
  factors in, 204
  majority process for, 202,
    205
  by range voting, 204, 205
  THE RIGHT WAY TO DECIDE,
    201–6
  side effects of
    unaccountable, 211–12
  unilateral, 201, 205
decision thresholds, 203
DECOLONIZATION, 81–84
deep time, 6
degenerative structures, 284
Delacote, Philippe, 136–37
De Landa, Manuel, 39–41
Democracy at Work Institute,
  298
Democracy Now!, 134
Denver Permaculture Design
  Course, 302
design
  feedback on, 66–67
  implementation and, 66
  process of, 65

designer, role of, 68
design tools
    BUSINESS MODEL CANVAS,
        305–11
    CAPITAL ANALYSIS, 303–4,
        331
    CREATIVE PROCESS, 60–67
    NETWORK ANALYSIS, 73–76
    PERSONAL VISION, 354–55
    POWER ANALYSIS, 163–66,
        331
    SECTOR AND ZONE
        ANALYSIS, 68–72
    TEAM ANALYSIS, 249–50,
        331
destruction. See CREATIVE
    DESTRUCTION
Details Deconstruction,
    285
DETHRONING THE
    ANTIMARKETS, 39–42, 133
diligence, 223
DISROBING THE EMPEROR, 123,
    133–35
disturbances
    definition of, 116
    examples of, 116–17, 157
    managing, 117–18
    planning for, 118
    welcoming, 118
divestment, 137–38
Dixon, Chris, 126
DOCUMENT THE PROCESS,
    243–44
dotmocracy, 204, 205
Doty, James, 101, 102
Douglass, Frederick, 333
Dow Chemical, 135
Dreamers, 212–13
Du Bois, W. E. B., 184
Dunbar, Robin, 27–28,
    29, 30
Duncombe, Stephen, 85, 134
Dylan, Bob, 184
DYNAMIC PRICING, 266, 286,
    299–302

E

Eames, Charles, 65
ecommony, meaning of, 252
ecotones, 50

THE EDGE OF CHANGE, 50–52
editing, 197–98, 209
Einstein, Albert, 54, 55
Eisler, Riane, 273
elders, 179–80
Eliasson, Olafur, 131
emergence, 40, 174
employees
    EMPLOYEE OWNERSHIP,
        282, 286, 296–98
    flexible schedules for, 290
    as HUMAN POLYCULTURE,
        276–77
epistemology, 53
equilibrium, punctuated, 116
erosion, spirals of, 326–28
ethical spectacles, 134
exploration, 194–95, 209

F

facilitation
    archetypes of, 225–27
    frequency of, 227
    importance of, 224
    SKILLED FACILITATION,
        224–28
fair process, 241
faith, role of, 318–20
fear
    change and, 58
    FEAR BURNS BRIGHT,
        HOPE BURNS LONG,
        57–59
    fighting, with laughter, 131
feedback, 66–67
Ferguson, Rafter Sass, xvii
fight-or-flight response, 58
FINANCIAL RAM PUMPS,
    265–67
fishbowl dialogues, 232–33
The Flobots, 130
FuCu Cafe, 001
focus groups, 247
food, sharing, 143–44
foraging, 350
Ford, Bonita, 324, 325
Foucault, Michel, 240
Franklin, Benjamin, 8, 183
Freeman, Jo, 172
Freire, Paulo, 125, 212
Fuller, Buckminster, 186

G

Gabriel, Peter, 57
GADUGI, 151–55
Gandhi, Mahatma, 122
Gaskin, Stephen, 98
genius loci, 48–49
THE GIFT, 255–57
Gino, Francesca, 161
Glover, Paul, 259
goals, defining, 61, 63, 221,
    345
Gödel, Kurt, 54, 55
GOING HOME, 47–49, 330
Goldstein, Marc, 148
Gonzalez, Corky, 181
Goodwill Industries, 286
Gould, Stephen Jay, 116
graces, 182
Graeber, David, 268, 270
graffiti, 131
Gregory, Chris, 256
grief
    gates of, 159–60
    PRACTICING GRIEF, 159–62
    stages of, 82
griots, 183–84
Gross National Product, 251
groups. See also HUMAN
    POLYCULTURES
    composition of, 179
    without leaders, 172, 187
    life cycle of, 189–92
    size of, 177–79
    sub-, 234–35
    TEAM ANALYSIS and,
        249–50
groupthink, 177
The GrowHaus, 71, 76, 280–
    82, 286
guilt, 127

H

Habermann, Friederike, 22
Habitat for Humanity, 155
Hall, Marcella, 127
Halprin, Lawrence and Anna,
    60–61, 66
Harari, Yuval Noah, 321
Hardin, Garrett, 21
Harvey, Andrew, 317, 319, 320

health care, preventative, 350
HEIRLOOM CURRENCIES,
    258–64
helping hands, 185–86
hierarchies
    absence of, 172
    characteristics of, 169
    CONSENSUAL HIERARCHIES,
        174–76
    decision making in, 201
    examples of, 169
    networks vs., 167–69
    SUBSIDIARITY vs., 36
history, revisiting, 90–92,
    127–28
Holmgren, David, xvii, xviii,
    xxi, 117
Holocaust, 140, 141
hope, 57–59
Hopkins, Rob, xxi
HOUSEHOLD ECONOMIES,
    272–75
HUMANIZING THE OTHER,
    101–3
HUMAN POLYCULTURES,
    177–88
    capital and, 16–20
    of employees, 276–77
    NEMAWASHI, 189–92
    Overton windows and, 51
    roles in, 16–20, 179–87
    size of, 177–79
hyperbolic discounting,
    243–44

I

identity correction, 135
Idle No More, 212
implementation, 66
IMPORT SUBSTITUTION,
    279–83
income
    inequality, 299
    REDUCE THE NEED TO
        EARN, 324, 347–51
    RIGHT LIVELIHOOD and,
        321–25
    streams, 311
Indiegogo, 294
Indigenous Biocultural
    Heritage Area, 44

INFRASTRUCTURE COMMONS,
    112–15
innovation, addiction to,
    98–100
inspiration, sources of, 65
installment pricing, 300–301
intentions, 333–35
INTERDEPENDENT
    COMMUNITIES, 11–14
    cities and, 105, 106
    THE GIFT and, 255–57
    rituals and, 94
interest, charging of, 269
International Association for
    Public Participation (IAPP),
    109, 110
interviews, one-on-one, 248
intimacy
    INTIMACY THROUGH
        ADVERSITY, 157–58
    zone of, 28–29, 34, 209
invisible structures, xix–xx
Iroquois Confederacy, 99,
    203, 230
ISITES, 336–40, 353

J

Jacke, Dave, xxii, xxiii
Jacobs, Jane, 280
Jakubowski, Marcin, 113
Jay, John, 9
Jefferson, Thomas, 8, 9
Jemez Principles for
    Democratic Organizing,
    213
Jenkinson, Stephen, 159
Jesus, 187, 318
journalism, 134, 135
Julier, Alice, 143
justice
    punishment paradigm for,
        240
    RESTORATIVE JUSTICE,
        240–42

K

Kali, 117
Kalundborg, 282
Kao, Albert, 174
kapu, 16

Kennedy, Jackie Onassis, 182
Kennedy, Robert F., 251
Kesey, Ken, 93
keystone species, 75
Kickstarter, 294
King, Brayden, 136–37
King, Martin Luther, Jr., 318
knowledge
    KNOW YOUR COMMUNITY,
        329–32
    MULTITUDES OF KNOWING,
        53–56
    scientific, 53–54, 55
    theory of, 53
Konyk, Alëna, 338
Kozol, Jonathan, 163
Kruse, Douglas, 298
Kübler-Ross, Elisabeth, 82

L

labor
    communal, 151–55
    strikes, 136, 138–39
Lakeman, Mark, 108
Lakoff, George, 86
Lamar, Kendrick, 130, 184
Landau, Gregory, 21, 253
Landless Worker's Movement,
    113–14
Laurie, Jamie, 130
Laws of Manu, 269
Lawson, Scott, 148, 149
leaders
    groups without, 172, 187
    LEADERSHIP FROM WITHIN,
        211–15
    REGENERATIVE
        MANAGEMENT, 216–18,
        244
    transitions between,
        216–17
lean thinking, 289
lending circles, 295
Lerner, Stephen, 139
Letchworth, 114
LETSystem, 261
LETTING LOOSE, 145–47
Lewis, Susie, 337
limiting factors, 23
Lindy Effect, 120
Linton, Michael, 261

Living Building Challenge, 112
Lo, Uma, 236
local cash, 259–60, 262
Locke, John, 8
THE LONG GAME, 5–7
Long Now Foundation, 6
Lorde, Audre, 313
Louv, Richard, 8, 9
Luther, Martin, 5

M

Macnamara, Looby, xxi, 326–27
Macy, Joanna, 317–18
Madonna, 186
majority, decision making by, 202, 205
Mandela, Nelson, 187
Mankins, Michael, 179
Mardi Gras, 44
market connectors, 286
markets, 40. *See also* antimarkets
Martin, Lloyd, 148, 149
Mary Magdalene, 182
Mauss, Marcel, 256
mavens, 186
Meadows, Donella, 85
meals, sharing, 143–44
MEASURING SUCCESS, 245–48
mentors, 181–82
Mitchell, Joni, 184
Mitchell, Tracey, 145
Mollison, Bill, xix
Mondragon cooperatives, 22
Movement for a New Society, 203
Movement Generation, 212
MULTITUDES OF KNOWING, 53–56
mutual aid networks, 349
mutual credit, 260–61, 263, 290
mythology, personal, 336, 352–53

N

Nakamoto, Satoshi, 262
NAMING NORMS, 219–23

National Center for Employee Ownership, 296
National Coalition for Dialogue and Deliberation (NCDD), 193–94
National Institutes of Health, 211
National Low Income Housing Coalition, 299
National Park Service, 9–10
natural disasters, 157–58
nature
    concept of, 8
    connection to, 8–10
    deficit disorder, 9
    observing, 336–40, 353
NEMAWASHI, 189–92, 219
networks
    characteristics of, 169
    examples of, 169
    hierarchies vs., 167–69
    NETWORK ANALYSIS, 73–76
    NURTURED NETWORKS, 171–73
    spread of ideas in, 234
network weavers, 183
New Belgium Brewing, 297
New Economics Foundation, 206, 260
Nightingale, Andrea J., 110–11
No Enemies, 130
noncompliance. *See* COORDINATED NONCOMPLIANCE
NONVIOLENT STRUGGLE, 121–24
norms
    establishment of, 191
    named vs. unnamed, 219, 220, 222
    NAMING NORMS, 219–23
    violation of, 236–37
Norton, Michael I., 101
novelty, addiction to, 98–100
Nube, Mateo, 212
NURTURED NETWORKS, 171–73

O

observation, 63
Occupy movement, xx, 37, 95, 131, 171, 270

Ohno, Taiichi, 291
Ojai Foundation, 230
O'Keeffe, Georgia, 186, 336
Olson-Ramanujan, Karryn, xxii, 322, 324, 325
One World Cafe, 301
Open Source Ecology, 113
operational polycultures, 281
Oppenheimer, J. Robert, 186
optimism, 119
Osentowski, Jerome, 329
Osterwalder, Alexander, 305–6
Ostrom, Elinor, 21
other. *See* HUMANIZING THE OTHER
Otpor, 131
Overton, Joseph, 50
Overton window, 50–52

P

pair share, 208
Panama Papers, 134
Parque de la Papa, 44
participation, spectrum of, 109, 110
participatory budgeting, 108–9
past, revisiting, 90–92, 127–28
pattern languages
    concept of, xxi–xxii
    power of, xxii, xxiv
    of social permaculture, xxi–xxii
pattern literacy, xxiv
patterns. *See also individual patterns in* SMALL CAPS
    naming, xxii, 353
    rules for, xxii–xxiii
Pentland, Alex, 146
percolation, 75
permablitzes, 155
permaculture
    application of, xviii–xx
    design course, xvii
    ethics of, xvii, xx
    etymology of, xix
    flower image for, xvii–xviii
    meaning of, xvii
    principles of, xviii, xxi
    social structures and, xx–xxi

Permaculture Action Network, 146
PERSONAL MYTHOLOGY, 336, 352–53
PERSONAL VISION, 50–52, 354–55
philanthropy, 266
physiocracy, 9
Pigneur, Yves, 305–6
pillars of support, 163–66
Pollan, Michael, 184
Popovic, Srdja, 123, 131, 165, 171
potlucks, 144
POWER ANALYSIS, 163–66, 331
PRACTICING GRIEF, 159–62
pricing
    DYNAMIC PRICING, 266, 286, 299–302
    fixed, 299–300
Prince, 186
privilege
    acknowledging, 126
    CALLING OUT, CALLING IN, 236–39
progress vs. innovation, 98–99
protest songs, 130
Public Sphere Project, xxii
punctuality, 223
punctuated equilibrium, 116
Putnam, Robert, 11, 105

Q

Quaker Society of Friends, 203

R

Rabb, Chris, 277
racism, 81–82, 126, 142, 333
radicals, 180–81
Ramos, Jorge, 184
range voting, 204, 205
Reagan, Ronald, 39
reciprocity
    balanced, 256
    generalized, 256
    zone of, 30–31, 34
recognition, zone of, 31–32, 34

REDUCE THE NEED TO EARN, 324, 347–51
REGENERATIVE ENTERPRISE, 51, 284–87, 288, 306
REGENERATIVE MANAGEMENT, 216–18, 244
regenerative structures, 284
REI, 295
RELATIONSHIP ZONES, 27–34
    in cities, 105
    network analysis and, 75
    zone analysis and, 70, 72
Renaissance Community Co-op, 114
RESTORATIVE JUSTICE, 240–42
RIGHT LIVELIHOOD, 321–25
THE RIGHT SIZE, 23–26
THE RIGHT WAY TO DECIDE, 201–6
risk, minimizing, 119
rituals
    fundamental nature of, 93
    identifying, 93–94
    RITES OF PASSAGE, 148–50
    RITUAL AND CEREMONY, 93–97
Robert, Henry Martyn, 202
Robert's Rules of Order, 202
Robinson-Patman Act, 41
Rogers, Paul, 179
Roland, Ethan, 21, 253
Rolling Jubilee, 270
Rosing, Minik, 131
RSVP cycles, 61
Rubin, Rick, 183
Rushkoff, Douglas, 39, 258, 282, 294
Russell, Andrew, 99

S

SACRED ACTIVISM, 317–20
sacred objects, 353
sacred space, creating, 95
Saffo, Paul, 5
Sahlins, Marshall, 256
Salas, Gustavo, 297
Salk, Jonas, 90
SAME Cafe, 301
Sanders, Bernie, 181

SANKOFA, 90–92, 127
Santayana, George, 179
satyagraha, 122
scholarship pricing, 302
Schuler, Douglas, xxii, 85, 141, 319
Schweitzer, Albert, 187
scientific knowledge, 53–54, 55
SECTOR AND ZONE ANALYSIS, 68–72
Seder, 94
self-care, xxi, 313
self-knowledge, 313–14
servant leaders, 187, 217
Servin, Jacques, 135
sexism, 82, 126
Shakespeare, William, 268
Shiva, 117, 352
Showing Up for Racial Justice (SURJ), 128
Shuman, Michael, 280
SKILLED FACILITATION, 224–28
slavery, 81, 140
sliding scale, 301
SLOW CITIES, 104–6
SMALL BUSINESS, 276–78, 280
Smith, Adam, 41
Smith, Warren, 203–4
Smucker, Jonathan Matthew, 102
Snowden, Edward, 134
social activities, 145–47
social enterprise, 285
SOLIDARITY, 125–29, 214
Solnit, Rebecca, 157
Solon, 269
songs, 130
sound map, making, 338
SPIRALS OF ABUNDANCE, 326–28
spokescouncils, 208
Stanfield, Brian, 226
Staples, Mavis, 180
Starhawk, 95, 179
Steinbeck, John, 112
Stephan, Maria J., 123
Sterling, Alton, 333
Stevens, Susan Kenny, 216–17
STEWARDSHIP, 98–100, 273

stories
importance of, 85
TELLING THE STORY, 85–89
story circles, 231–32
Strategic Concepts in Organizing and Policy Education (SCOPE), 164
STREAMS OF ENGAGEMENT, 193–200, 207, 209
stress, reducing, 344–46
strikes, 136, 138–39
subscription payment model, 290
SUBSIDIARITY, 35–38, 126, 211
success, measuring, 245–48
sulha, 241
support clique, 29
surveys, 247
suspicion, zone of, 32–33, 34
Sustainable Food Policy Council, 163, 166
SWOT Analysis, 303
sympathy group, 29

T

Taleb, Nassim Nicholas, 116, 117
Taoism, 117
TEAM ANALYSIS, 249–50, 331
Tea Party, 37
technology, unplugging, 341–43
TELLING THE STORY, 85–89
temporary autonomous zone (TAZ), 43–44
Teresa, Mother, 187
Terry, Bryant, 300
Thackara, John, 189
Thatcher, Margaret, 39
Theatre of the Oppressed, 95, 131, 134
Thibaut, John W., 242
Thich Nhat Hanh, 321
time banks, 261, 263
Tochluk, Shelly, 238
Toensmeier, Eric, xxii, xxiii
totems, 352
Toyota, 291

Trần, Ngọc Loan, 237
translators, 184–85
travel, 351
triple-bottom-line, 285
Trump, Donald, 57
trust
as community commitment, 222
earning, 127
zone of, 29, 34, 209
TRUST South LA, 114
TRUTH AND RECONCILIATION, 140–42
Tubman, Harriet, 183
Tuckman, Bruce, 189–90

U

Uber, 113
Uetricht, Micah, 139
unique value proposition (UVP), 308–9
United Farm Workers, 137
UNPLUGGING, 341–43
usury, 269

V

vacations, 351
Vamos, Igor, 135
van Gennep, Arnold, 148
Vinsel, Lee, 99
Vishnu, 352
vision
importance of, 2
for a permanent culture, 1–4
PERSONAL VISION, 50–52, 354–55
visioning, 196–97, 209, 304
Vosper, Nicole, 161

W

Waber, Benjamin, 146
Wachtel, Ted, 242
Walker, Laurens, 242
Walker, Perry, 206
Warhol, Andy, 183
Warren, Josiah, 261

waste, eliminating, 289, 291
wealth
concept of, 15
forms of, 16–20
inequality, 270
Weller, Francis, 159
West, Geoffrey, 104
Westwood Food Co-op, 114
whistleblowing, 134, 135
Wikipedia, 21
Williams, Terry Tempest, 159
WIR (Wirtschaftsring), 158, 261
Women's Bean Project, 286
work parties, 154
World Food Programme, 299
World Trade Organization, 135
Wright, Frank Lloyd, 336

X

XERIC ENTERPRISE, 288–92

Y

Yehuda, Rachel, 141
The Yes Men, 135
Yousafzai, Malala, 184

Z

Zimmerman, Jack, 230
zones
of cooperation, 30, 34, 209
of intimacy, 28–29, 34, 209
of reciprocity, 30–31, 34
of recognition, 31–32, 34
RELATIONSHIP ZONES, 27–34
SECTOR AND ZONE ANALYSIS, 68–72
of suspicion, 32–33, 34
of trust, 29, 34, 209
ZONES OF AUTONOMY, 43–46, 266
Zuckerberg, Mark, 183

ABOUT THE AUTHOR

Adam Brock is a social-permaculture designer, facilitator, and consultant based in his hometown of Denver, Colorado. He holds a bachelor of arts degree from New York University's Gallatin School of Individualized Study and is a certified permaculture designer and graduate of the Ecosa Institute for Ecological Design. In 2009, Adam cofounded the GrowHaus, an award-winning social enterprise that transformed a historic greenhouse into a local hub for urban agriculture, education, and food justice. He is a TEDxMileHigh speaker and longtime collective house–dweller, and he was named one of Colorado's Top Thinkers by the *Denver Post* in 2013. Currently, Adam serves as a teacher for the Denver Permaculture Guild, a cochair of Denver's Sustainable Food Policy Council, and the director of social enterprise for the consulting firm Joining Vision and Action.

At home, Adam indulges in fermentation, propagating unusual edible plants, and reading postcapitalist speculative fiction. When all is said and done, Adam is just another befuddled organism trying to leave the world better than he found it.